W9-BEE-232

Researching Social and Economic Change

Household panel studies provide one of the most significant national and international resources for analysing social and economic change. In this user-friendly introduction, European and American experts in the field join forces to explain what panel studies can achieve and to illustrate some of the potential pitfalls in the construction and analysis of panel data. The authors gear their contributions to the lessons that researchers must learn and apply in their own work, assuming a basic understanding of survey methods, but not of panel studies themselves. This is an essential and accessible introduction for those contemplating the use of panel studies for the first time and will be an invaluable resource for both practising researchers and the commissioners of research.

David Rose is Professor of Sociology in the Institute for Social and Economic Research at the University of Essex. He was co-founder of the British Household Panel Study and of the European Science Foundation Scientific Network of Household Panel Studies.

Social Research Today

Edited by Martin Bulmer

The *Social Research Today* series provides concise and contemporary introductions to significant methodological topics in the social sciences. Covering both quantitative and qualitative methods, this new series features readable and accessible books from some of the leading names in the field and is aimed at students and professional researchers alike. This series also brings together for the first time the best titles from the old *Social Research Today* and *Contemporary Social Research* series edited by Martin Bulmer for UCL Press and Routledge.

Other series titles include:

Principles of Research Design in the Social Sciences
Frank Bechhofer and Lindsay Paterson

Social Impact Assessment
Henk Becker

The Turn to Biographical Methods in Social Science
Edited by Pure Chamberlayne, Joanna Bornat and Tom Wengraf

Quantity and Quality in Social Research
Alan Bryman

Research Methods and Organisational Studies
Alan Bryman

Field Research: A Sourcebook and Field Manual
Robert G. Burgess

In the Field: An Introduction to Field Research
Robert G. Burgess

Research Design second edition
Catherine Hakim

Measuring Health and Medical Outcomes
Edited by Crispin Jenkinson

Methods of Criminological Research
Victor Jupp

Information Technolgoy for the Social Scientist
Edited by Raymond M. Lee

An Introduction to the Philosophy of Social Research
Tim May and Malcolm Williams

Surveys in Social Research fourth edition
David de Vaus

Researching the Powerful in Education
Edited by Geoffrey Walford

Martin Bulmer is Professor of Sociology and co-director of the Institute of Social Research at the University of Surrey. He is also Academic Director of the Question Bank in the ESRC Centre for Applied Social Surveys, London.

Researching Social and Economic Change

The uses of household panel studies

Edited by David Rose

London and New York

H
61.26
.R48
2000

First published 2000
by Routledge
11 New Fetter Lane, London EC4P 4EE

Simultaneously published in the USA and Canada
by Routledge
29 West 35th Street, New York, NY 10001

Routledge is an imprint of the Taylor & Francis Group

© 2000 selection and editorial matter, David Rose; individual
chapters, the contributors
Typeset in Baskerville by
Prepress Projects Ltd, Perth, Scotland
Printed and bound in Great Britain by
TJ International, Padstow, Cornwall

British Library Cataloguing in Publication Data
A catalogue record for this book is available
from the British Library

Library of Congress Cataloging in Publication Data
Researching social and economic change: the uses of household
panel studies / edited by David Rose.
        p. cm. – (Social research today)
    Includes bibliographical references and index.
    1. Panel analysis, 2. Households – Statistical methods. I. Rose,
David, 1947 Feb. 17- II. Series
    H61.26.R48   2000
    302'.01'5195–dc21   00-042493

ISBN 1-857-28546-8 (hbk)
ISBN 1-857-28547-6 (pbk)

**In loving memory of
Hilary Doughty (1952–1996)**

Contents

Figures

Tables

Contributors

Karl Ashworth is currently a Research Fellow at the Centre for Research in Social Policy, Loughborough University, and was previously at the Survey Methods Centre based at Social and Community Planning Research. His interests are primarily concerned with the dynamics of poverty and welfare and with methods of management and analysis of longitudinal data.

Michael Brick is a Senior Statistician and Vice President of Westat Inc., and is a Research Associate Professor in the Joint Program in Survey Methodology at the University of Maryland. He has undertaken research in sampling and weighting methods to account for non-response in cross-sectional and longitudinal surveys.

Nicholas Buck is Professor of Sociology and Associate Director of the Institute for Social and Economic Research (ISER) [formerly Economic and Social Research Council (ESRC) Research Centre on Micro-social Change], University of Essex. He was previously at the Urban and Regional Studies Unit at the University of Kent. He has research interests in the impact of economic change on inequality, household formation and urban structure. He is author (with J. Gershuny) of a forthcoming book, *Understanding Panel Data* (2001), and was joint editor of *Changing Households* (1994).

Constance F. Citro is on the staff of the US Committee on National Statistics. She has been Study Director for a number of CNS Panels, including that for the Survey of Income and Program Participation (SIPP). Her research focuses on the usefulness and accessibility of large, complex microdata files, as well as on analysis of income measurements and demographic change. She was joint editor with Graham Kalton of *The Future of the Survey of Income and Program Participation* (1993).

Suzanne Davies Withers (PhD, UCLA) is an Assistant Professor in the Department of Geography at the University of Georgia. Her research interests include urban housing issues, spatial demography and longitudinal research methods.

Greg Duncan is Professor of Education and Social Policy and a Faculty Associate in the Center for Urban Affairs at Northwestern University. He received a PhD in Economics in 1974 from the University of Michigan. Much of his career has been spent at the University of Michigan on the Panel Study of Income Dynamics data collection project. That project has conducted annual interviews with a large and representative set of families all around the country for over 30 years. It has become a major source of information about poverty and welfare dynamics in the USA. Duncan joined the faculty at Northwestern University in 1995. His research has focused on issues of economic mobility both within and across generations. He is the author of *Years of Poverty, Years of Plenty*, a 1984 book that documented the surprising degree of economic mobility in the USA. More recently, his research has focused on how economic conditions in families and neighbourhoods affect child development.

John Ermisch is a Professor in the Institute for Social and Economic Research, University of Essex and a Fellow of the British Academy. Formerly, he was Bonar-Macfie Professor in the Department of Political Economy at the University of Glasgow (1991–4), and a Senior Research Officer at the National Institute of Economic and Social Research. His research is broadly concerned with how markets, particularly housing and labour markets, impinge on household decisions, including labour supply, housing demand, fertility and household formation and dissolution, and how decisions in the demographic and economic spheres interact, particularly their dynamics. In addition to a book, *Lone Parenthood: An Economic Analysis* (Cambridge University Press, 1991), he has published in economics journals such as *The Economic Journal, Journal of Human Resources, European Economic Review* and the *Oxford Bulletin of Economics and Statistics*, and in demographic journals such as *Population Studies* and the *European Journal of Population*. He is one of the co-editors of the *Journal of Population Economics*, and was President of the European Society of Population Economics (ESPE) in 1989.

Martha S. Hill is a Researcher at the Survey Research Center, Institute for Social Research, University of Michigan and also an Associate Research Scientist. She is an economic demographer specialising in poverty and welfare dynamics, intergenerational transmission and transfers, marital stability and household formation.

Sarah Jarvis was formerly Senior Research Officer in Economics, Institute for Social and Economic Research, University of Essex. She has published several papers on aspects of income dynamics and poverty.

Stephen P. Jenkins is Professor of Economics, Institute for Social and Economic Research, University of Essex. His research is broadly concerned with income distribution and its redistribution through taxation, social security and the labour market. He also has interests in the measurement of inequality and poverty, modelling labour supply and social security benefit spell durations. He has published widely in economics journals such as *The Economic Journal*, *Labour Economics*, *The Oxford Bulletin of Economics and Statistics* and *The Journal of Population Economics*. He was President of ESPE in 1998.

Graham Kalton is a Senior Statistician and Senior Vice President of Westat Inc., a large survey organisation located in the Washington, DC, area. He is also a Research Professor in the Joint Program in Survey Methodology at the University of Maryland. He has conducted research on methods for handling panel non-response in the US Survey of Income and Program Participation and is a sampling consultant for the British Household Panel Survey. Previously, he has held faculty appointments at the University of Michigan, the University of Southampton and the London School of Economics.

Ruud J. A. Muffels obtained his Master's Degree in 1979 in macroeconomics. From 1993 onwards, he has been part-time Professor of the Socioeconomics of Ageing. Since 1995, he has also been a Research Professor at WORC, the Work and Organisation Research Centre at the Faculty of Social and Behavioural Sciences of Tilburg University. He has published widely on income and poverty dynamics, labour market, social security and retirement and on poverty and income dynamics.

David Rose is Professor of Sociology in the Institute for Social and Economic Research, University of Essex, where he was successively Deputy Director, Acting Director and Associate Director between 1989 and 1997. Since 1994, he has been Academic Convenor of the ESRC Review of Government Social Classifications. He is author with Howard Newby *et al.* of *Property, Paternalism and Power* (1978), with Gordon Marshall *et al.* of *Social Class in Modern Britain* (1988), with Oriel Sullivan of *An Introduction to Social Science Data Analysis* (second edition 1996) and with Karen O'Reilly of *Constructing Classes* (1997) and of *The ESRC Review of Government Social Classifications* (1998). He was also joint editor of *Changing Households* (1994).

Marita A. Servais is a Researcher at the Survey Research Center, Institute for Social Research, University of Michigan, and also a Senior Systems Analyst, specialising in data management and documentation of longitudinal files.

Chris Skinner is Professor of Social Statistics at the University of Southampton, where he has been a member of the academic staff since 1978. His research is broadly concerned with the statistical methodology of sample surveys and he is Vice President of the International Association of Survey Statisticians. His work has focused especially on survey data analysis and he is co-editor of *Analysis of Complex Surveys* (1989).

Peter Solenberger is a Researcher at the Survey Research Center, Institute for Social Research, University of Michigan, and is also a Senior Systems Analyst, developing systems for complex file management.

Marcia Freed Taylor is Co-ordinator of the European Centre for Analysis in the Social Sciences (ECASS), University of Essex. She is the Editor of the *British Household Panel Study User Manual*. She was previously Director of Information and Development for the ESRC Research Centre for Micro-social Change at Essex and was for many years involved in data dissemination and other activities in the ESRC Data Archive, most recently as Deputy Director.

Robert Walker is Professor of Social Policy at the University of Nottingham. He was formerly Director of the Social Security Unit at the Centre for Research in Social Policy based at Loughborough University. Before that, he was Assistant Director of the Institute for Research in the Social Sciences at York University; he has also held posts at the Personal Social Services Research Unit, University of Kent, the Civil Service College and the Department of the Environment. He has published extensively on a wide range of issues, particularly in the fields of social security and poverty in both a national and international context.

Jeroen W. Winkels, historian and sociologist, wrote his thesis on social change in The Netherlands. He works at Statistics Netherlands in the Department of Sociocultural Household Surveys.

Acknowledgements

This book has been far longer in preparation than I could ever have imagined when it was first mooted. The main reason for its long gestation relates to the book's dedication. There are times when, for emotional reasons, a particular piece of work becomes impossible to return to, or even to contemplate. Thus, it became for this book for a period of almost 3 years following the death of my partner. What had been a joke between us on my visits to her bedside ('Is *it* finished yet?') became far from amusing all too soon. My co-authors, series editor and publisher have been more than usually patient and understanding about the time which it has taken to bring this book to completion. Every one of them has been infinitely understanding of the circumstances that eventually made this project so difficult for me. I thank them for their forbearance. Especially, I wish to acknowledge the kind support and encouragement of Graham Kalton and of the series editor, Martin Bulmer. Each has been unfailingly supportive during difficult times.

That this book was completed at all owes much to a sojourn spent as a Visiting Fellow to the Sociology Program of the Research School of the Social Sciences, Australian National University. In that connection, I wish to thank Frank Jones, Michael Bittman, Judy Wacjman and Vasa Stoyanoff for helping to make my visit so profitable.

The idea for this book originally arose from the work of the European Science Foundation's Scientific Network on Household Panel Studies. This Network operated from 1990 to 1993 and the book was initially intended to comprise some of the papers prepared for meetings organised under this initiative. However, at Martin Bulmer's suggestion, some new chapters were included and others have been reproduced from papers originally published elsewhere. In the last respect, I am grateful to Statistics Canada in relation to Chapter 2, to *Fiscal Studies* for Chapter 10 and to the *Bulletin de Methodologie Sociologique* for Chapter 11.

Finally, I wish to thank Jenifer Tucker and Janice Webb for their work on the preparation of the manuscript and other materials for the publisher, as well as for all their other great virtues as colleagues. And to the current and former staff of the Hilary Doughty Research Resources Unit, Institute for Social and Economic Research – Judi Egerton, Lesley Lingard, Terry Tostevin, Mary Gentile and Jane Rooney – my gratitude as ever. Other acknowledgements are made as appropriate in particular chapters.

David Rose
Colchester
September 2000

Part I

Introducing household panels

1 Household panel studies

An overview[1]

David Rose

Introduction

This book is intended as a primer for those interested in the purpose, design, conduct and analysis of household panel studies. Of course, in an introductory text none of these issues can be addressed in the detail necessary to allow readers to learn all the arts and sciences involved in panel studies. Rather, our intention is to make the techniques of panel studies accessible so that greater profit can be obtained from more specialist texts and especially those that deal with panel analysis. The many references in each chapter offer further avenues to explore. Equally, there will be readers, whether students, academics, policy-makers or research users and commissioners, who although not wishing to undertake panel research nevertheless do need to know what household panel studies are and what they can achieve.

This chapter provides both an introduction to the issues raised in the rest of the book and, along with the next two chapters, an overview of the world of household panel studies, a not inappropriate phrase given the increasing number of countries which have them. While this chapter is thus pitched at a general level, I will attempt to relate my comments to particular points made in the other, more focused chapters in this collection.

The first part of this chapter has two short sections addressing some general issues, one of these is about society and social change and the other is about social science and social change. This provides background to the third section, in which I discuss social surveys and social change. Here, I examine the different possible designs for surveys across time, their strengths and limitations. Following this, I look at the particular design of household panel studies. Together, these first four sections of the chapter anticipate the concerns of Chapters 2 and 3 by Kalton and Citro and by Duncan respectively. The fifth section is concerned with data quality issues in panel surveys and especially non-sampling errors.

Foremost among these is the problem of non-response in panel surveys. The chapters in Part II of the book provide more detail on quality issues. Section six deals with the analytical advantages of panel surveys and provides some simple illustrative examples of panel analysis. These anticipate the more detailed analyses provided by the chapters in Part III. The seventh section briefly sets out policy areas where panel analyses have proved useful to policy-makers. Finally, the plan of the book is discussed.

First, however, household panel studies should be placed in their scientific and policy context as tools for improving our conceptions and analyses of social and economic change. Why have the European Union, governments in Australia, in Canada, in Germany and in the USA and many national science foundations all been prepared to invest large amounts of scarce resources in household panels? To answer this question, we need to make a brief excursus into the fundamental and applied purposes of panel studies for improving our grasp of social dynamics. If the examples that I use are drawn mainly from sociology and social policy in the UK context, other chapters written by colleagues from different disciplines and from other countries will redress the balance. Notably, the perspectives of Kalton and Citro and of Duncan in Chapters 2 and 3 present a view of household panels from the perspectives of social statistics and economics in the USA respectively.

Society and social change

We are living in a time of apparently profound changes. The creation of the global, post-industrial society of the late twentieth century (or, less comfortingly, the deindustrialising society; see Rose *et al.*, 1984) has involved some major changes in both national and international social and economic structures. These *macro*-social and economic changes affect individuals, families and households, producing and interacting with change at the *micro*-level, the main substantive concern of household panel studies. Change and its correlates are daily topics in the media. At the macro-level are, for example, the so-called drivers of change: globalisation, increasing international competition and the revolution in information technology. Closer to people's everyday lives, and related to the change drivers, are economic and welfare restructuring and the transformation of work which results from a more 'flexible' labour market, as well as demographic changes such as the 'greying' of the population or the greater diversity of family and household types. In turn, individuals, families, households and communities are affected by the downsizing of organisations, plant closures, high levels of unemployment, increasing levels of poverty and greater social polarisation, the (supposed) emergence of an 'underclass', homelessness, family break-up, rising crime rates, allegedly declining moral values and a variety of other contemporary concerns. The main objective of national household panel surveys is to examine the experiences over a period of years of a representative sample of the population and, thereby, improve our scientific understanding of the incidence, pattern, duration, interrelation and impact of features of society such as those just enumerated.

Social science and social change

In the past decade, much empirical work in the social sciences has focused on the social changes induced by recent economic, political and technological change. For example, we know that there are 'work-rich' and 'work-poor' households (Pahl, 1984). The former are dual- and multi-earner households; the latter are those with little or no earned income, often located where employment prospects are bleak. The existence of work-rich households had already been greeted by some sociologists in Britain and elsewhere as the basis of symmetrical families, in part resulting from the greater financial and domestic independence of married working women (Young and Wilmott, 1975); but others see threats to the family in these developments and connect them to the rising tide of divorces and subsequent negative consequences for children (Hamnett *et al.*, 1989: 189–93). Recent British longitudinal evidence certainly points to the adverse effects of divorce on children's educational performance (see, for example, Kiernan, 1992) even if the effects of the changing role of women on rates of divorce and its association with a secular trend towards the breakdown of the family may well be questioned. The growing number of work-poor households has been connected to the idea of an 'underclass' and a concern that this group will become increasingly separated from the rest of society, a lumpenproletariat with no stake in society and no obligations towards it (Dahrendorf, 1987; cf. Smith, 1992).

Evidence of these kinds has been used to point to the increasing *polarisation* of British society over the last 20 years; yet claims such as these have often been disputed, partly because of the unsatisfactory nature of available cross-sectional evidence. For example, there is continuing dispute over the nature and extent of poverty on the basis of conflicting interpretations of data from repeated cross-sectional surveys (see *Journal of Social Policy*, 1987). Allied to the issue of the extent of poverty are questions about the composition of the poor. Who experiences poverty? Why? And for how long? Again, there is plenty of speculation but, until recently, little reference to appropriate dynamic data.

A final example of the speculative nature of much discussion of social change in the social sciences is the study of *sex*. Recent debates in sociology about the proper unit of class analysis and its ramifications and in both economics and sociology about increasing rates of female labour force participation are each vital to our appreciation of social change (cf. Dex, 1985; Marshall *et al.*, 1989: Ch. 4; and the debate initiated around the work of Hakim, 1995). Yet these debates have often generated more heat than light because of the absence of data on transitions and their correlates and of data relating women's position in the home and the labour market to that of men.

Social science is thus centrally concerned with the issue of social change, both in its macro-sense and in the more everyday sense of understanding social trends. Social scientists attempt to comprehend the impulsions behind these trends, their causes and consequences and the directions in which they are leading us. However, we need to be careful about the idea of social change. Successive generations tend to believe that it is they who are living through profound changes and that the past was a 'Golden Age' or a time of greater continuity and *stability* (see, for example, Williams, 1973; Ball *et al.*, 1989: Ch. 1). Yet there is stability in the present too, and this needs to be appreciated before we can understand the nature of change (see, for example, Abercrombie and Warde, 1992: 10). Continuity and stability form the background against which change is experienced; indeed, they are often what people most desire; their absence is what makes people feel insecure. Testimony for this may be found in the new situation for most people in the former communist countries of central and eastern Europe.

Social scientists are, of course, familiar with (although by no means exempt from) the tendency to eternalise the present (and misinterpret the past) in attempts to understand social trends. This has often led to an overemphasis on change and an insufficient appreciation of stability. As Halsey (1988: 1) has remarked, 'trends are absurdly easy to find...(but) stability may be equally significant'; nevertheless, social scientists have often had 'an extravagant preference for graphs moving upwards towards the right' (cf. Ball *et al.*, 1989: Ch. 1). Moreover, policy-makers, social commentators and social scientists often mistake *cyclical* change for *secular* change. This has alternately led to an overemphasis on social change as inevitable *progress*, leading to prosperity and *embourgeoisement* – 'we are all middle class now' – in boom times (see, for example, Bell, 1960; Kerr *et al.*, 1960), or on social change as *decline*, leading to moral and material impoverishment and social crisis – 'we are all working class now' – in the bad times (see Braverman, 1974; for an excellent debunking of both liberal and Marxist theories of social change, see Goldthorpe 1964, 1988; cf. Badham 1984). However, if we recognise that there are cycles, we should also be more aware of the repeated patterns in these cycles and, therefore, less likely to overinterpret their consequences; but, if we combine inadequate methods and data with inappropriate models and theories, the result will be a failure to appreciate the realities of change and continuity. How much better, therefore, if, instead of speculating on the basis of poor cross-sectional evidence, as is so often the case, we have relevant longitudinal micro-data with which to work.

This is the prime purpose of household panel studies: to provide both social scientists and policy-makers with prospective micro-data in order to improve our understanding of processes, causes and effects in relation to social trends and social change. These have always been among the best purposes of social science. The social sciences emerged as a response to an era of genuine and very rapid social change and the consequent need for a greater comprehension of social, economic and political processes. Ever since, the most imaginative social science has sought to connect public issues and private troubles (Mills, 1959) and thus to explore macro- and micro-interconnections. For this reason, the scientific programmes of panel studies are often aimed at the study of family, household and individual change (and stability) within theoretical frameworks which place micro-level changes in a macro-level context (as exhibited by the chapters in Part III of this volume, most especially that by Buck).

Social surveys and social change

These few remarks about the purposes of household panels need some unpacking in relation to the whole issue of appropriate survey designs for the study of social change and social trends. Why is a panel survey particularly appropriate for the purposes that I have indicated – the study of household, family and individual change?

Most social surveys are referred to as *cross-sectional* because they take a representative sample of the population which is interviewed only once, and therefore they offer us a slice through time and the various social processes with which they are concerned. In this sense, cross-sectional surveys provide us with something like a snapshot. When we analyse data from these surveys, we obtain information at the *aggregate* level or *macro*-level, e.g. the proportion of people who are in poverty or who are unemployed. What if, however, we wish to answer questions about social processes over time? One-off cross-sectional surveys are of little help if we want to know whether there is a permanent 'underclass' as opposed to a constant and steady movement of people into and out of poverty and unemployment over time, or if we want to know how changes in household composition affect the individual welfare of household members. In this volume, we are concerned with a form of survey design – a longitudinal one – which is specifically designed to deal with questions such as those we have just posed, questions about *individual change*.

Because most surveys are single snapshots, they cannot tell us much about individual change (although we can ask people *retrospective* questions about past states, such as previous occupations, or we can ask about previous events, such as the birth of children or dates of marriage). Regular or *repeated cross-sectional surveys*, in which the same questions are asked every year of a different sample of the population, are somewhat better tools for the study of change. Nevertheless, as with cross-sections using retrospective questions, they also only permit analysis of *net change* at the aggregate or macro-level, e.g. the proportion of the population below the poverty line at time t could be compared with the proportion at time $t - 1$. To study change at the *individual* or *micro*-level, however, it is necessary to use a *longitudinal* design and, therefore, a *prospective* method such as a *panel survey* in which the *same* individuals are interviewed repeatedly across time. The longitudinal data provided by a panel survey will then allow researchers not only to examine the proportion of the population at different times in states such as poverty but, because the same people are followed across time, these *micro*-data can also be used to examine flows into and out of these states, thus opening up a wider range of possibilities in terms of causal analyses and inferences. In other words, longitudinal data tell us about change at the *individual* or *micro*-level; cross-sections tell us only about *populations* at one or a series of time points. I shall expand on these points later in the chapter when discussing the analytical advantages of panel data.

Although the essence of a longitudinal survey is that it offers repeated observations of the same individuals over time, there are a number of different types of such survey, as we shall see. However, they all share one common feature. The unit of analysis is the individual and not (as in some cross-sectional surveys) the family or household. This is because there is no rigorous way of defining families or households that would allow them to be followed unambiguously across time (Duncan and Hill, 1985). Families and households change their composition and may cease to exist, while new families and new households are constantly coming into existence. Individuals are much more stable in a longitudinal context and so are easier for us to track and to follow. Of course, longitudinal surveys do tell us about the dynamics of households and families, but the data on these come from individuals who are related to their changing household and family contexts.

To expand on these points, we can refer to papers by Duncan and Kalton (1987) and Buck *et al.* (1996), as well as to Kalton and Citro's contribution to this volume in Chapter 2. I summarise their principal arguments in the rest of this section. These sources provide an overview of the various possible survey designs for dealing with the inescapable fact that survey populations change in both composition and characteristics over time. Which survey design is most suitable depends, of course, upon the objectives researchers have, i.e. the sorts of change that they wish to examine. That is to say, some survey designs are better suited for some objectives but are worse or completely useless for others. So, first, what are the basic survey designs when the general objective is to address change? Apart from the repeated cross-sectional survey, four basic designs are possible for longitudinal surveys, as Table 1.1 adapted from Buck *et al.* (1996: 2) illustrates. These are: (i) the retrospective survey; (ii) the cohort survey or panel; (iii) the indefinite life panel survey; (iv) the rotating panel survey; and (v) record linkages. Table 1.1 excludes repeated cross-sections because, although they operate across time, they are not longitudinal in design.

Table 1.2, taken from Duncan and Kalton (1987), relates repeated cross-sectional and panel designs to survey objectives. Chapter 2 discusses the issues in greater detail. I shall therefore only briefly discuss each design in turn.

As Table 1.2 indicates, repeated surveys are appropriate for survey objectives (a) and (b) in Table 1.2 because a new sample is selected for each survey. Repeated surveys can also be used to examine net change, i.e. changes at the aggregate level [objective (c) in Table 1.2].

Table 1.1 Types of longitudinal survey

Type	*Examples*
Retrospective	UK Women and Employment Survey
Cohort panel	UK National Child Development Study
Single indefinite life panel	British Household Panel Study
Multiple overlapping fixed life ('rotating')	Survey of Labour and Income Dynamics (Canada)
Record linkages	UK 1% Census Longitudinal Study

Table 1.2 Properties of alternative survey designs in relation to various objectives

Survey objective	Repeated survey	Panel survey	Rotating panel survey	Split panel survey
(a) Estimated population parameters at time points	Automatically takes population changes into account	Needs mechanism for taking population changes into account	Needs mechanism for taking population changes during life of rotation group into account	Panel component needs mechanism for taking population changes into account
(b) Estimate average values of population parameters				
(c) Estimate net changes	Estimates combined effects of changing values and changing population	Needs mechanism for taking population changes into account. Variance of change reduced by positive correlation of values between waves	Needs mechanism for taking population changes during life of panel into account. Composite estimation can be used to produce efficient estimates	Panel component needs mechanism for taking population changes into account. Variance of change in panel component reduced by positive correlation of values between waves

(d) Estimation of gross and other components of individual change	Not possible	Well suited for these purposes	Can be used for changes or aggregates over time periods shorter than the time a rotation group is in sample	Panel coponent is well suited for these purposes. Not possible for repeated survey component
(e) Aggregate data for individuals over time			Only some rotation groups can be used	
(f) Collecting data on events occurring in specified time periods	No means to detect telescoping. Probable recall error if long-term event history data are required for sample elements	Bounded recall to detect telescoping of events after first wave. Can construct long-term event history data by combining data from several waves	Bounded recall to detect telescoping of events after each rotation group	Bounded recall with panel component, but not with repeated survey component
(g) Cumulate samples over time	Excellent for static characteristics and for new events, although no means to detect telescoping of events static	Not useful for static characteristics. Useful for new events, with bounded recall to detect telescoping	Of some use for static characteristics. Useful for new events, with some bounded recall	Repeated survey component excellent. Panel survey component useful in new events but not for characteristics

Source: Duncan and Kalton (1987).

Rotating panels are so called because individual panel members are rotated into and out of the panel over a relatively short time period of anything from a few months to several years. This design therefore involves a succession of separate probability samples of the population at different time points. Thus, a panel is established, and during its life another panel is selected which overlaps in time with the first and so on. When the time limit for the end of the first panel is reached, its members are no longer followed, but the second panel continues and a third new panel begins. Thus, each panel has a fixed life, although the survey itself may be indefinite. Although longitudinal in design, the real strength of a rotating panel is for the estimation of net change. That is to say, like repeated surveys, they basically serve objective (c) in Table 1.2. Of course, as rotating panels are longitudinal, they can serve objectives (d) and (e), but only to a limited extent, as we shall see in the next chapter.

An *indefinite life (IL) panel survey* takes a probability sample of the population at the time that the panel begins, but subsequent loss of membership, or *attrition*, from the panel tends to reduce its usefulness for cross-sectional estimates. However, although an IL panel survey is thus generally less well suited to examining net change between time points, its key advantage lies in the ability to measure *gross* change and to aggregate data for individuals across time. Repeated surveys cannot do this, and rotating panels do it less effectively. Thus, IL panel surveys come into their own when we wish to meet objectives (d) and (e) in Table 1.2. *Cohort panels* are similar. They differ from the basic IL panel design in that the cohort or sample members share the same initial condition, such as being born in the same week of a particular year (a 'birth cohort' as with the UK National Child Development Survey).

One-off *retrospective surveys* are a form of longitudinal design in which respondents are interviewed once about events in their past. While this design is both simple and cheap, there is a high price to be paid in terms of measurement errors. People do not easily recall past events and circumstances, e.g. income in the past. Hence, retrospective surveys are usually limited to significant and infrequent life events such as births, marriages, divorces and job changes. Even here they have their problems, as Duncan and Ermisch demonstrate in Chapters 3 and 12 respectively.

The final longitudinal design is *record linkages*. These may link administrative records gathered by governments, as with the Australian government's Department of Family and Community Services' Longitudinal Data Set, or they may link census records, as in the case of the UK Office for National Statistics' (ONS) 1% Longitudinal Study of the Census. The principle of each is the same: linking individual information across time. Thus, the ONS Longitudinal Study took 1% of the 1971 Census records and has linked them to each subsequent census as well as to death registration and other administrative records. The advantages are obvious: the datasets which result are large and so are accurate even for small population subgroups, and they are cheap. However, analysis is limited to the data available in the records that are linked and these are generally quite limited. For example, the UK Census does not ask about incomes.

In Chapter 2, Kalton and Citro provide a fuller discussion of the principles of panel survey design. They also point to some of the problems of panel surveys, such as wave non-response, panel conditioning (or time-in-sample bias) and seam effects and the techniques available to deal with these. Some of these points are raised later in this chapter but are further examined in Part II of this volume on data quality. Finally, Chapter 2 provides a brief overview of the principal methods for analysing panel data. Examples of substantive panel analyses are the subject of Part III of this book.

To summarise the argument so far, we have seen that the key advantage of panel surveys over repeated surveys lies in the fact that they provide repeated measures over time for the same individuals. This means that panel surveys provide superior information on social processes by giving us measurements of gross change and other components of individual change; and IL panels are the best design for these purposes.

The design of household panels

There are certain basic design requirements of any household panel study if its advantages are to be maximised and its disadvantages are to be minimised. These include: an initial sample of the highest possible quality; a heavy investment in a panel maintenance programme to counter attrition; the use of feedback or feed-forward techniques as an aid to respondent recall and thus data reliability; and the collection of continuous (event history) data (see van der Pol, 1988; Rose *et al.*, 1991; Buck *et al.*, 1996). Many of these points are further developed in the next two chapters, as well as in those by Buck and Ermisch in Part III.

Because the main objective of indefinite life household panels is to advance our understanding of social and economic change at the individual and household levels, it is essential that the panel remains broadly representative of the population. However, we have noted above, and Chapter 2 develops the point, that populations are changing all the time. Hence, there must be mechanisms to take account of these changes. To achieve this goal, not only are the *same* individuals reinterviewed in successive waves but if they split off from original households to form new ones all adult members of these households are also interviewed. Similarly, children in original households are interviewed as they reach (usually) the age of 16 years (age 11 years in the British Household Panel Study from its fourth wave); and occasionally IL panels are supplemented to represent the immigrant population [as has happened with both the Panel Study of Income Dynamics (PSID) for the USA and the German Socio-economic Panel (SOEP)]. Moreover, most household panels (but not PSID) interview every member of the household, rather than only a household head. This decision, which has major cost implications, is justified by the substantive goal of exploring intrahousehold structures and processes as well as by examining individual outcomes. The importance of this design feature of household panels, pioneered by SOEP, is well illustrated by Scott (1995). Using data from the first three waves of the British Household Panel Study, Scott analyses family interdependencies and is able to show that, under certain circumstances, the unemployment experience of one family member can affect the attitudes and behaviour of other family members. This is but one way in which household panel studies can demonstrate the inextricable links between family members and thus further the investigation of 'household strategies' (see Anderson *et al.*, 1994: 1–16 and 19–67). The advantages of interviewing all household members can also be seen in various chapters in Part III.

Questionnaire design is also similar across most household panels. There is a *core* of questions that are repeated each year and form the majority of questions asked, but alongside this is a *variable* component which serves a variety of purposes. First, it allows for the insertion of new questions, reflecting changing policy and research agendas. In addition, variable components cover those questions which need to be asked less frequently than annually because the variables that they are measuring are not expected to change with great frequency, e.g. savings and assets. Finally, to establish *initial conditions* (i.e. the points arrived at in the lives of panel members at the beginning of the study), the first few variable components include one-off questions to elicit retrospective data on the life histories of panel members before the first interview. This problem of 'left censoring' of data (i.e. the absence of information for panel members before the first wave of a panel) is referred to in several of the chapters that follow. The collection of data on initial conditions also has the advantage of providing a longitudinal element to the data in the early years of a study which can be used to great effect (see, for example, Buck *et al.*, 1994).

The distinctive longitudinal research opportunities afforded by panel data guide both the content of panel questionnaires and the design of the questions in important ways. First, for example, research can be focused on change at the level of the individual or the household rather than at the population level (which is the focus of repeated cross-sectional analysis). In other words, panel data allow for the direct study of shifts at the individual level (for example changes in the preference for mothers to work), even though such shifts may cancel out when aggregated across the population. It is, therefore, important to select questions that are concerned with characteristics, behaviour or attitudes that are expected to change or that are significant factors affecting the likelihood of change.

A second, and most distinctive, feature of panel design is that it allows analysis of the interaction of different strands in individuals' lives over time. Therefore, the aim is to produce questions that will enable us to construct *continuous measures* of, for example, income, employment histories and labour market participation, household structure and residential mobility over the life cycle. This is collected much more reliably than in retrospective history surveys, but it does mean that many questions have to be concerned with events in the 12 months between interviews rather than with the current situation at the time of the interview. A further common goal is to ask about expectations of change so that these can be compared with actual subsequent changes, especially with respect to changes in occupation, economic circum-stances and mobility.

Panel data quality

Much of what has been said so far begs important questions about the quality of panel data. Groves (1991) has provided a useful framework for thinking about the quality of survey research in general. He discusses a range of possible sources of error that might affect the quality of survey estimates. As Martin (1996: 1) notes, survey research quality can be seen as 'absence of error where total error is the sum of all variable errors and all biases'. Groves divides these errors into *errors of observation* and *errors of non-observation*. Errors of observation arise from the interviewer, the respondent, the survey instrument and the interview mode. Errors of non-observation can arise from sampling, non-coverage and non-response. Martin adds a third type of error – *processing error* – arising from keying (inputting data to a computer), editing and imputation. While all of these errors can affect any kind of survey (Lyberg *et al.*, 1997), panel surveys exhibit some special problems which are considered in more detail in the chapters in Part II. My comments are similarly restricted to the particular problems of panel surveys and hence will concentrate on non-sampling errors such as *non-response* and *panel conditioning* (or *time-in-sample bias*). Kalton and Citro (Chapter 2) and Duncan (Chapter 3) make further remarks on some of these issues below.

Non-sampling errors in panel surveys

Non-response is, of course, a problem for any social survey, not only because of its effects on sample size but also because of the possible introduction of bias into the results (see Panel on Incomplete Data, 1983: vol. 1, ch. 2 and 3; cf. Bogestrom *et al.*, 1983). However, in panel surveys, non-response can be a more severe problem because some *attrition* (or loss of membership) from the sample occurs at each wave. Hence, its cumulative effect can be substantial for later waves (see Chapter 4; see also Kalton *et al.*, 1986; cf. Waterton and Lievesley, 1987).

Conventionally, a distinction is made between *unit non-response* and *item non-response*. The former refers to situations where there are no data for a sample member because of refusal or non-contact. The latter refers to missing data on some items where data should have been supplied by a respondent who has otherwise supplied responses, as when, for example, a respondent may have refused to answer a particular question or the interviewer might have skipped past a question which should have been asked. However, there is a form of non-response which is unique to panel surveys – so-called wave non-response (discussed in Chapter 5 by Kalton and Brick; see also Lepkowski, 1989; Scheuren, 1989).

Wave non-response occurs when data for a panel member are completely missing for at least one wave but present for one or more of the other waves. There is a tendency for wave non-response to increase with the age of a panel. This must, therefore, be countered in every way feasible to minimise its effects (Freedman *et al.*, 1980; Capaldi and Patterson, 1987; Farrington *et al.*, 1990; Murphy, 1990). In general, non-response can be seen as a 'more complex problem (in panel surveys) as more information about non-respondents is available for use in non-response compensation procedures' (Kalton *et al.*, 1989: 249). Each form of non-response, and the methods developed to counter it, is discussed below. Laurie *et al.* (1999) provide further details of field techniques to reduce non-response problems in panel surveys (see also *Journal of Official Statistics*, 1999).

Unit non-response can arise either from respondents refusing to become members of the panel or from a failure to contact respondents who would be prepared to co-operate. Of course, both refusals and contact failures are normal in all surveys, but special methods are required for dealing with them in panel surveys. Beyond standard survey procedures for limiting rates of refusal (see Barnes, 1980, 1991; Thomas, 1980; Rao, 1983; *Journal of Official Statistics*, 1999), panel studies mandate extra calls back to sample addresses (see Purdon *et al.*, 1999) and special efforts to gain the moral commitment of respondents while simultaneously appealing to their more material sides. Hence, it is vital to ensure that potential respondents are made aware of the importance of the study and of their participation in it. This can be achieved through such means as persuasion letters (Finch, 1981; Clarke *et al.*, 1987), leaflets and brochures (see Capaldi and Patterson, 1987) as well as by assurances of both confidentiality and anonymity. Panel members are usually also rewarded for taking part in each wave and are given an annual report on survey findings.

Of course, it is not only the moral and material commitments of respondents which need to be considered but also those of the interviewers (see, for example, Capaldi and Patterson, 1987; Barnes, 1991). Particular attention has to be given to the training of interviewers in techniques relevant to the maintenance of high response rates (Snijkers *et al.*, 1999). Since the motivation of interviewers also relates to problems of item non-response, we shall return to this point below.

Contact failures must be minimised in any panel survey, again because of the tendency for attrition to increase with the age of the panel. Tracing procedures must be devised and considerable resources need to be devoted to them (Crider *et al.*, 1971; McAllister *et al.*, 1973; Clarridge *et al.*, 1978; Thornton *et al.*, 1979, 1982; Call, 1982; Jean and McArthur, 1987; Burgess, 1989; Farrington, 1990; Laurie *et al.*, 1999). A number of such procedures are typically used, including the collection of information concerning friends and relatives of respondents who would know of address changes, the return of change of address cards (for which payment is made) and the use of administrative records such as, in the UK, National Health Service Registers and national insurance records.

Item non-response is perhaps a less severe problem unless it is either systematic and/or related to a subsequent propensity to refuse to take part in future waves. With this proviso, item non-response can be treated as a problem common to all surveys except that panel analysts need to take account of responses at other waves in order to counter its effects in analysis via the process of imputation (Little and Su, 1989). Depending on the circumstances, complete *wave non-response* may be avoidable in some cases via the collection of proxy data. However, there will always be some non-response of this type and so measures need to be devised to reduce its impact. Discussion of this problem inevitably leads to the issue of the compensatory strategies that can be used, some of which are equally relevant whatever the form of non-response.

There are three basic compensatory strategies to counter the effects of non-response. First, there are *statistical weights* based on respondent characteristics and adjusted to take account of unit and wave non-response (see Chapter 5; Oh and Scheuren, 1983). Of course, in a panel survey, there is much greater information on which to base this for those who fail to respond after the first wave. This leads to the second strategy, the intensive investigation of possible non-response bias by, for example, comparing the responses of continuing respondents with those of non-respondents for questions asked of each group in earlier waves (see Chapter 4; Hausman and Wise, 1977, 1979; Lievesley and Waterton, 1985). Finally, *imputation* of data is necessary in the case of item non-response (Ford, 1983; Herzog and Rubin, 1983; Platek and Gray, 1983; Kalton, 1986). As usual, it is easier to state the means for countering non-response than it is to achieve it in practice (cf. Rubin 1983). However, the general approach to these problems is discussed in Chapter 5 by Kalton and Brick.

Success at countering non-response, and avoiding the consequent need for too much expenditure of effort on bias checks, weighting and imputation, by no means resolves the problem of response errors in panel surveys. One of the ironies of panel studies is that they give rise to particular response problems which are the inverse of their non-response problems and a further potential source of error and bias. That is to say, respondents who are successfully contacted and interviewed from wave to wave may become atypical of the population that they represent by virtue of their panel membership and repeated exposure to its questionnaire stimuli. This is the problem of *panel conditioning*, or *time-in-sample bias*, 'the situation when repeated questioning of panel members affects their survey responses, either by changing the behavior being reported or by changing the quality of the responses given' (Kalton *et al.*, 1989: 249–50).

A number of studies have been made of panel conditioning (for example Sudman and Bradburn, 1974; Traugott and Katosh, 1979; Lievesley and Waterton, 1985; Corder and Horvitz, 1989; Silberstein and Jacobs, 1989; Waterton and Lievesley, 1989; cf. Kalton *et al.*, 1986; Bailar, 1989; Holt, 1989; O'Muircheartaigh, 1989) which provide evidence concerning the existence of the effect. As noted in Chapter 2, in principle it is possible to examine the problem through the use of rotating panel designs, but equally the practice of replicating questions from other surveys and undertaking comparisons between these and panel data can help analysts in their search for conditioning effects. However, as Duncan and Kalton (1987: 109) note, 'economic behaviour such as work effort, saving, commuting and home ownership are all unlikely to be affected by responses to occasional interviews'. Sudman and Ferber (1979) reached similar conclusions, whereas Duncan (1989; and see Chapter 3) has suggested that household panel studies can *increase* data quality.

More generally, measurement error on estimates and parameters from panel data have received some attention in the literature, although many problems remain (Groves, 1991). There have been few studies which have attempted to assess measurement error (but see Duncan and Mathiowetz, 1985; Bound *et al.*, 1990; van der Pol and Langeheine, 1997) but what evidence there is suggests that it does have some significant effects, particularly where such errors occur in explanatory variables in regression models (Rodgers and Herzog, 1989). Techniques for dealing with measurement error in panel analysis are discussed in Chapter 6 by Skinner.

Judging panel data quality

By what standards should users and funders judge household panels? In their work on the evaluation of longitudinal surveys, Boruch and Pearson (1985: 21) note that the improvement to the use and usefulness of longitudinal surveys depends on a range of requirements. These include, *inter alia*, the need for panel centres to be regarded as 'observatories' in which attention is given to the development of user communities and to the support of the calibration, validation, meaning, and uses of the data instrument. This all mandates that panel surveys be thoroughly documented, as Taylor argues in Chapter 8.

Boruch and Pearson also indicate the following standards for evaluating longitudinal surveys: the ease of data linkage between the study concerned and other data; the ease of sample modification; the extent of the resources devoted to the measurement and reporting of non-sampling as well as sampling error; and the mechanisms for minimising non-response and attrition and for adjusting for these in analyses via weighting and imputation. In other words, methodological as well as substantive research is vital to the ways in which panel studies should be judged and must, therefore, be taken very seriously. In particular, Boruch and Pearson note that assessing and improving the quality of measurement should have a high priority, that data linkage is vital to the improved usefulness of panel databases because of the need to check data quality, enlarge the data available for basic research and reduce the overall costs of research and that mechanisms should be found to document, minimise and understand non-response and attrition. This seems sensible advice which should inform all methodological work on panel studies and which is at the heart of the comparative household panel enterprise which is being developed in Europe. These and other issues concerning panel data quality (Winkels and Davies on attrition in Chapter 4 and Hill *et al.* in Chapter 7 on modelling family and household relationships) are addressed by the chapters in Part II of this book.

Analytical advantages of household panel surveys

I now turn to the analysis of panel data. We have seen that panel data are precisely concerned with the behaviour of individuals, families and households over time. For this reason, they are well suited to the statistical analysis of change and of dynamic behaviour more generally. Of course, cross-sectional surveys can introduce retrospective elements in order to study change; or we can design one-off retrospective surveys to ask about past events in respondents' lives. Nevertheless, the quality of retrospective data decreases the further back one wishes to take respondents (see, for example, Moss and Goldstein, 1979; Sudman and Bradburn, 1983; Jabine *et al.*, 1984; Bradburn *et al.*, 1987; Janson, 1990; Ornstein, 1998). Moreover, the ways in which individuals interpret their own past behaviour are coloured by subsequent events. Without retrospective elements, however, cross-sectional data produce little of help to the analyst of social change. To make inferences about dynamic behaviour requires one to make often dubious assumptions which link what indirect information can be gleaned from the cross-section to variations in the behaviour of population cohorts (Goldstein, 1979; Deaton, 1985; Heckman and Robb, 1985). What other analytical advantages do panel data have?

First, panel data make it possible to examine *transitions between states* in a way not possible when only cross-sectional data are available. In particular, because they are micro-data, panel data permit the analysis of gross change at the individual level. Thus, it is possible to make a deeper analysis of the incidence of conditions and events such as poverty and unemployment over time. In turn, such events can be examined for dynamic links with other factors.

As indicated by Duncan in Chapter 3 and by Muffels, by Jarvis and Jenkins and by Ashworth *et al.* in Part III, transitions into and out of poverty is perhaps the area in which the potentials of panel data to social science and social policy have been most clearly established. First, only panel designs can distinguish between the 'stock' and 'flow' of a condition such as poverty. By tracing variations in income over time for the same set of individuals, panel studies can identify transitions into and out of poverty and attempts can then be made to test various hypotheses regarding causal factors in this process. For example, the PSID has documented both a striking rapidity of movements into and out of poverty and a close association between such transitions and changes in household composition. PSID data have shown that in the USA the great proportion of the poor at any one time are suffering temporary rather than long-term poverty, i.e. are moving into poverty through a crisis such as divorce, redundancy or illness in the household and out again on remarriage, re-employment or the recovery of good health. These types of finding have now been reproduced for other countries. In turn, it is also possible to obtain a deeper understanding of the circumstances of persistent poverty (cf. Jarvis and Jenkins in Chapter 10; Gottschalk and Ruggles, 1994).

PSID data have also demonstrated that only a small proportion of poverty is intergenerational and so have undermined assumptions about a 'culture of poverty' and the intergenerational transmission of poverty; they also raise doubts, therefore, about the existence of an 'underclass' (see Chapter 3; Duncan *et al.*, 1993a). Beyond this, they have implications for the way in which poverty is perceived, by both analysts and policy-makers, and for the design of policies towards its alleviation. The chapters by Ashworth *et al.* and by Jarvis and Jenkins in Part III provide very good illustrations of some of these points, as does that by Muffels in Part III, not least because they demonstrate what types of poverty analysis are possible using cross-sectional, trend and panel data respectively.

A second analytical advantage of panel data [and here the European Community Household Panel (ECHP) described by Barreiros (1995) is a good example] is that they can provide observations before and after important external policy events such as the changes brought about by the Single European Market. The ECHP is designed to monitor the effects of these changes in different countries and on different social groups (see also Chapter 3; cf. Smeeding and Burkhauser, 1999).

Third, panel data have analytical advantages for the estimation of behavioural models. We have seen that household panels collect data on a continuous basis – the events in people's lives over the period between interviews. Hence, we obtain more reliable information on spells of unemployment, poverty, etc. and their duration than is possible with cross-sectional surveys and we can analyse these using appropriate event history analysis techniques (see Allison, 1984, 1994), as used in several chapters in Part III.

This advantage relates to another. Panel data allow analysts to control for certain *unobserved* determinants of behaviour on which no data have been collected, in particular those unobserved factors which vary across individuals but remain the same across time for any given individual (Galler and Poetter, 1987; Solon, 1989; Kemp, 1991). These factors are referred to as *individual specific effects* and their presence as *population heterogeneity*. For example, we know that individuals unemployed at time *t* have a higher probability of being unemployed at time *t* + 1. Is this because there is something about unemployment that increases the likelihood that the unemployed will remain in that state (for example, demoralisation)? Or is there something about the unemployed themselves which puts them and keeps them in that state? We need longitudinal data to begin to tackle such questions.

Fifth and finally, long runs of panel data also allow for the control of *period-, age- and cohort-specific effects.* Period effects are those which vary across a time period but are the same for all respondents at any particular point in time. Age-specific effects are those which vary across age but are the same for all respondents of a particular age. Finally, there are cohort effects in which effects are the same for all individuals born in a certain time period but otherwise differ across respondents. The problems (and impossibilities) of dealing with each of these effects in cross-sectional surveys are well known (see, for example, Hobcraft *et al.*, 1982; cf. Baltes, 1968; Labouvie and Nesselroade, 1985; Peters, 1988; Mayer and Huinink, 1990).[2]

Examples of simple panel analyses

We can illustrate some of the points made so far by reference to some simple examples drawn from analyses of the first two waves of the British Household Panel Study (BHPS).[3]

An unemployment example

Consider Table 1.3, which gives unemployment among adult men in the BHPS during the Septembers of 1990 and 1992. (This uses the retrospective question *'What was your employment status on September 1 last year?'* from wave 1 of the panel together with *'What was your employment status on September 1 this year?'* from wave 2 to get the 24-month spread.) We see a substantial increase in unemployment over the period, from

Table 1.3 Unemployed as a percentage of economically active men, 1990–2

	Unemployed	
	%	Number
September 1990	7.7	·225
September 1992	11.5	334

Table 1.4 Unemployed as a percentage of economically active men by education level, 1990–2

	High qualifications (A levels or above) (%)	Lower qualifications or none (%)	All (%)
September 1990	5.1	8.8	7.7
September 1992	5.8	14.2	11.5

225 (7.7% of those in the labour market) to 334 (11.5%). How does this relate to their level of education or other qualifications?

Table 1.4 suggests that in 1990 there was a relatively small but nevertheless quite clear difference in proneness to unemployment between those men with high qualifications (5.1% of whom were unemployed) and those with low qualifications or none at all (of whom 8.8% were unemployed). The 1990 cross-section on its own does not suggest a very great effect of level of qualification (although it is not inconsiderable); but, in the subsequent years, as the UK recession deepened, so the effect of possession of qualifications became larger. In 1992, the rates were respectively 5.8% and 14.2%. This indicates that the relationship between educational qualifications and unemployment became markedly stronger over the period. Apparently, education became more important as a means of avoiding unemployment through this short period of economic decline; but can we be sure that it really is education itself that has the effect?

We obtain a different view if, rather than considering the cross-sections and their change over time, we *track individuals' positions through historical time*. It is not, of course, the case that all that has happened in the panel is a simple increase in unemployment from September 1990 to September 1992. The growth in unemployment indicated in Table 1.4 represents just the net change: the eventual balance that emerges from a much more complicated set of movements or flows of people into and out of various economic statuses. (The *net change* in unemployment numbers in Table 1.4 is much smaller than the *gross movements of individuals into and out of unemployment*.)

The real strength of this sort of longitudinal evidence (and the particular reason for looking across this 24-month gap) is that we can use it to construct an altogether more powerful explanation of the incidence of unemployment. Table 1.4 was constructed just from the cross-sectional information contained in the two waves of data. It does not use any of the information about the previous circumstances of BHPS respondents in wave 2 that we can get from wave 1 data.

Table 1.5, by contrast, does use the longitudinal information about panel members. It classifies the men in 1992 by their employment status in 1990. Although the general unemployment rate for men in the panel was 11.5%, if we look just at that group of the sample who were in employment in September 1990, the 1992 unemployment rate for this subgroup was 6.3%. More remarkably, if we look just at the group who were unemployed in September 1990, their 1992 unemployment rate was 61.2%. Once we know about a man's unemployment history, we know a great deal about his current risk of unemployment.

It appeared in Table 1.4 that those with low levels of qualification in 1992 were considerably more prone to unemployment than those with high levels of qualification, but when we look at unemployment in 1992 in the light of the previous unemployment history of our respondents the picture changes. Education certainly makes a difference between the unemployment proneness of those with no unemployment record (4.3% unemployed in 1992 for those with high qualifications compared with 7.3% for those without); but Table 1.5 makes it clear that it is not education *alone* that produces proneness to unemployment.

Those with high qualifications who were *un*employed in 1990 had an unemployment rate of 25% (although there are only seven cases here so this is not a figure to be relied upon). However, of those with low qualifications who were unemployed in 1990, a remarkable 71% were unemployed in 1992. Low qualifications on their own make for a marginal increase in proneness to unemployment. Low qualifications

Table 1.5 Men's unemployment in September 1992 by educational level and employment status in September 1990 (cells with fewer than twenty cases in parentheses)

	Unemployed		
	High qualifications (%)	*Other/none (%)*	*All (%)*
All	5.8	14.2	11.5
Employed in September 1990	4.3	7.3	6.3
Unemployed in September 1990	(25.0)	71.7	61.2

together with previous history of unemployment make for a dramatically high susceptibility to it. For those with low qualifications, unemployment in 1990 increases proneness to unemployment tenfold. The point is not that qualifications are unimportant (for those with high qualifications, 1990 unemployment only increases proneness to unemployment sixfold, i.e. from 4.3% to 25%), but rather that its importance is only seen clearly in the context of (i.e. 'in interaction with') the historical information.

Unemployment 2 years previously is, of course, just one among many alternative ways of indicating a history of unemployment, but the same depressing result emerges whichever indicator we use: an unemployment history is the best predictor of present unemployment. In short, previous unemployment is a very good predictor of subsequent unemployment. Our view of the impact of education on unemployment – or perhaps of the mechanism through which it operates – is substantially changed once we introduce information about personal employment histories.

Of course, the finding begs more questions than it answers; it raises issues about deskilling, employers' selection procedures, regional differences and motivational effects, among other matters. However, this is precisely the point: only once we have extensive access to information about various aspects of peoples' history – not only descriptions of previous employment (and marital and other family circumstances) but previous living arrangements and locations, attitudes and activity patterns – can we begin to develop an adequate understanding of their present circumstances. This is why we collect longitudinal data.

Net and gross change

Table 1.6 and Figures 1.1 and 1.2 illustrate the general point about the difference between being able either to discuss *net change* or to estimate population parameters *via* a repeated survey and being able to discuss *gross change* and other components of individual change (i.e. to

Table 1.6 Employment status for men, BHPS 1991–3

	1993		
	Employed (%)	*Unemployed (%)*	*1991 Totals (%)*
1991 Employed	86.7	5.0	91.7
1991 Unemployed	5.1	3.2	8.3
1993 Totals	91.8	8.2	100

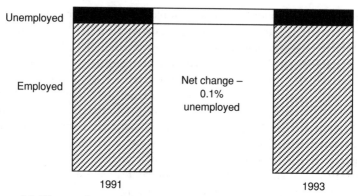

Figure 1.1 Changes in employment status: cross-sectional

disaggregate net change) *via* a panel study. Table 1.6 shows data on employment status for males in the BHPS in the years 1991 and 1993.

If we imagined that these data had been taken from two separate samples (i.e. if they were data from a repeated cross-sectional survey rather than from a panel survey), the picture of change they would offer is that illustrated in Figure 1.1.

Figure 1.1 shows a net aggregate change of only 0.1%. However, because the data are drawn from a panel survey, we can see the pattern of individual or micro-change. This is shown in Figure 1.2 and reveals an overall change far greater than the one we see in Figure 1.1. Whereas the first figure showed only the changes in the proportions of those employed and unemployed in 1991 and 1993, Figure 1.2, because it contains individual level data, demonstrates much more detail. For example, we can see that 5% of the sample changed their employment status from employed to unemployed and only 3% constituted a hard core of unemployed. The amount of individual change exceeds 10%.

Where Figure 1.1 shows only the pattern of net change, Figure 1.2 shows gross individual change. Not only do we see the *stocks* of employed and unemployed (as revealed by the margins of Table 1.6) but the *flows* between them too (what we see inside the cells of Table 1.6). This is vital to any analyses which attempt to explain why these changes take place. When linked with other information about the sample, we could begin to explore, say, who constitutes the hard core unemployed or the types of people who become unemployed and why this happens. In this way, we can study not only the changes but the *changers* (see Farber, 1994). Thus, because panel surveys follow the *same* individuals across time, we can examine not only the stocks of relevant phenomena (for example proportion in poverty or unemployed, etc.) but also the *flows* between these states, which reveal the true extent of change. Further

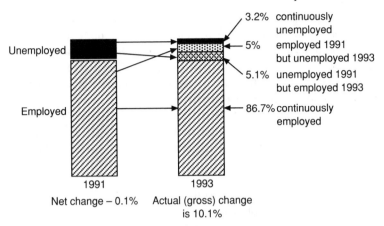

Figure 1.2 Changes in employment status: panel information

examples of these types of analysis and of others are to be found in the chapters in Part III.

Household panel surveys and social policy

If the ability to perform these types of analysis is important to academic researchers attempting to understand social dynamics, it is equally important to policy-makers (Smeeding and Burkhauser, 1999). The current need for household panel studies, and the reason why so many countries have invested in them, stems in large part from the political perception that the last 20 years have witnessed apparently major changes in Western societies. These changes are arguably as great as those experienced in the nineteenth-century transition from an agricultural to an industrial economy. However, the causes and effects of these changes, and the directions in which they are leading, are imperfectly perceived. This is a problem for public policy if scarce resources are to be used most effectively. For example, the 'flexible' labour market has policy and public expenditure consequences (*inter alia*) in terms of more and longer unemployment spells and earlier retirements, whereas the end of 'jobs for life', even apparently for 'organisation men', creates new educational and training needs. Demographic changes also have policy and spending implications with, for example, greater longevity leading to the need for new forms of health care and old-age provision as well as to increased pension and benefit costs, whereas increased divorce rates and more single-parent families result in a greater need for social assistance and housing and so on. These and other features of our society are much debated, but can only be properly understood if they are seen as events which affect families and households rather than isolated individuals. Moreover, we need to analyse the *dynamics* of these events and how they interact. This requires us to follow the changing behaviour and fortunes of households, families and their members across time; it therefore requires us to use the appropriate method for this purpose – the household panel study.

Household panel data allow us to address a range of policy issues which cross-sectional data cannot confront. Among the areas of panel research which have been identified around the world as being of particular concern to policy-makers are the following:

 i   Comparing the economic well-being of the elderly.
 ii Dynamic analyses of labour income.
 iii Poverty, welfare and income dynamics.
 iv Transitions out of the labour force.
 v   Behavioural models of retirement.
 vi Dynamic issues of disability.
 vii Child poverty, child achievement and parenting.
viii Household formation and dissolution.
 ix Social exclusion.
 x   Transitions, e.g.
       – from immigrant to citizen;
       – from youth to adulthood.

Further details on some of these areas are offered by Smeeding and Burkhauser (1999) and some (income dynamics, household change, poverty) are illustrated in Part III. As Smeeding and Burkhauser argue (1999: 1), all the countries that have panel surveys face common social policy concerns, issues and challenges such as those noted above. Policy-makers need to understand the dynamics that underlie the issues of poverty, unemployment, lone parenthood and so on. They also want to know the effects of policies designed to tackle these issues.

Household panels are thus a unique strategic data resource to policy-makers, and the longer a panel study lasts the more valuable and indispensable it becomes. This is particularly so in the case of the US Panel Study of Income Dynamics. Now into its thirty-second year, it is providing data on intergenerational issues such as the 'culture of poverty' and the 'underclass' debate (see, for example, Chapter 3; Duncan and Rodgers, 1988; Altonji, 1994; Mare, 1994).

Household panels in Europe and North America

So much for the mechanics; what of the studies themselves? As Table 1.7 shows, in Europe independent national studies are in operation in Belgium, Germany, Great Britain, Holland, Hungary, Luxembourg and Sweden. In addition, the ECHP is operating in thirteen of the member states (see Barreiros, 1995). In North America, there are PSID and Statistics Canada's Survey of Labor and Income Dynamics (SLID). Not shown in Table 1.7 are other US panels such as the US Census Bureau's Survey of Income and Program Participation (SIPP), the National Longitudinal Surveys of Labor Market Experience and the Health and Retirement Survey conducted by the Survey Research Center, Institute for Social Research, University of Michigan. Finally, the Department of Family and Community Services of the Australian Commonwealth Government is considering proposals for the establishment of a new panel study similar to SLID. Although contents of questionnaires vary to reflect the particular research and policy interests of their practitioners and sponsors, data are routinely collected on matters such as panel members' employment, income, household structure, housing and other major items of consumption, health and social and political values.

Plan and purpose of the book

The next two chapters in Part I provide more detail on some of the issues that I have discussed here. In Chapter 2, Kalton and Citro discuss panel designs and their consequences for data quality, data collection and longitudinal analysis, thus developing the earlier work of Duncan and Kalton (1987) on these issues. In Chapter 3, Duncan offers an overview of the promise and problems of household panels in relation to the analysis of economic and demographic behaviour.

   Part II contains five chapters, each dealing with different aspects of panel data quality. In Chapter 4, Winkels and Davies explore the problem of panel attrition using the example of the Dutch panel. Thereby they expand on the issues of unit non-response discussed above. They reveal the ways in which attrition might bias analyses if not statistically treated. Given that attrition will occur whatever measures are taken to reduce it, what can be done statistically to counter its effects? This is the concern of Kalton and Brick in Chapter 5. They are concerned with the use of statistical weights to adjust for non-response. Statistical weighting is common for all forms of survey, the aim being to compensate for both unequal sample selection probabilities and

Table 1.7 Household panel studies in Europe, the USA and Canada

European Union
European Community Household
  Panel
Eurostat
58,750 households
1994
European Commission and Member
  States
Annual
Purpose: EU policy development
  and monitoring

Belgium
Panel Study of Belgian Households
Universities of Antwerp and Liege
5,000 households
1992
Government
Annual
Purpose: study of social change

Hungary
TARKI/Department of Sociology,
  Budapest University of Economic
  Sciences
2,000 households
1992
Hungarian National Research Fund
  and Hungarian SCO
Annual
Purpose: study of social change

Ireland
The Irish Panel Study
Economic and Social Research
  Institute
3,321 households (4,000)
1987 (1994)
DGV, EC and ESRI
Repeated by ECHP
Purpose: to understand Irish living
  conditions

The Netherlands
Socioeconomic Panel
Central Bureau of Statistics
3,984 households
1984
CBS
Two waves per year to 1990; annual
  since 1990
Purpose: dynamics of income
  distribution

Sweden
Household Market and Non-market
  activities
(HUS)
Department of Economics,
  Gothenberg University
1,531 households
1984
Government and national research
  funds
Every 2 years
Purpose: study of labour supply,
  income and consumption

Germany
Socioeconomic Panel (SOEP)
DIW, Berlin (formerly Sfb-3, Frankfurt)
5,921 households (including gastarbeiter households)
From 1990, additional 2179 households from ex-GDR
1984
Government
Annual
Purpose: study of microsocioeconomic change

Great Britain
British Household Panel Study (Living in Britain)
ISER, University of Essex
5,600 households
1991
ESRC and University of Essex
Annual
Purpose: scientific and policy research on microsocial change

Lorraine, France
Socioeconomic Survey of Lorraine Households (ESEML)
ADEPS, University of Nancy II
2,092 households
1985
Six waves (and finished)
INSEE, CNRS, EC, central and regional government
Annual
Purpose: poverty and social security studies

Luxembourg
Panel Socioeconomique 'Liewen zu Letzeburg' (PSELL)
CEPS/INSTEAD
2,012 households
1985
Government
Annual
Purpose: social policy

USA
Panel Study of Income Dynamics
Survey Research Centre, University of Michigan
5,000 households
1968
NSF and government
Annual to 1999 but now every 2 years
Purpose: socioeconomic change in population

Canada
Survey of Labour and Income Dynamics
Statistics Canada, Ottawa
40,000 households
1993
(Replacement of half sample every 3 years)
Government
Annual
Purpose: labour market experience, income and family circumstances

missing data. In panel surveys, as we have seen, these problems are magnified and thus introduce greater problems for survey statisticians. Kalton and Brick discuss and explain the techniques that have been developed to address the problems.

I noted previously that non-response was not the only source of non-sampling errors in surveys. There is also the problem of measurement error. In Chapter 6, Skinner examines the effects of measurement errors for categorical variables in panel surveys. The problem can be simply stated via an example. Suppose that a person's occupation is recorded as being a housekeeper at wave 1 of a panel and as a cook at wave 2. The data file will record that this person had different occupations at each wave. This will have other consequences. For example, in the UK it would mean that this respondent would be recorded as having changed social class position from one wave to the other. Suppose further, however, that the respondent in fact has the *same* job at each wave, but has described it differently at each interview. At wave 1, when asked for an occupational title, the respondent said 'housekeeper'; at wave 2, the respondent replied 'cook' to describe the same job. The consequence here is a measurement error leading to the recording of a 'spurious' rather than a real change. This is a very real problem for panel surveys and Skinner discusses various analytical approaches to this type of misclassification and their consequences.

In Chapter 7, Hill *et al.* discuss another issue that is particular to panel surveys. We saw previously that although the unit of analysis in panels is the individual, nevertheless we are interested in the family and household relationships of individuals across time. These can become very complex and ideally should be thought through before a panel survey begins so that information is collected in an appropriate way. However, in the case of PSID, basic problems were not anticipated – indeed, it was not anticipated that PSID would have an indefinite life. Eventually, therefore, relationship information on PSID had to be reconstructed to allow analysts to investigate changing family and household structures. Hill and her colleagues relate the history of this project and draw some general conclusions on the collection and processing of demographic survey data.

In the final chapter in Part II, Taylor discusses the documentation and dissemination of panel data. Panels are very expensive undertakings and their resulting data structures are complex. To render useful the results of these considerable investments in research resources requires that they be comprehensively and clearly documented. The design of panel documentation is no less important than the design of the panel itself. Documentation must be user friendly so that the data structures and the data themselves are fully understood by analysts. Taylor discusses general documentation issues and how these relate to panel datasets.

Part III is concerned with the analysis of panel data. The five chapters in this section are thus concerned with what panels can uniquely reveal. The examples discussed in the final part of the book deal with income and household dynamics. Analysis of income dynamics has always been one of the most important academic and policy uses of panel data. How income changes, how this is related to other events such as unemployment, births, marital splits and so on, and the lengths of the effects of such changes are all of equal concern. Panels are also important for the study of transitions between states – employment to unemployment, married to divorced, single to married. Thus, panel studies come into their own when we are concerned with data for which recall would be a problem for other types of survey. If we are interested in the changing economic circumstances of individuals, as when we examine income dynamics, or if we are concerned with events for which we need accurate timing of information (as with household transitions), data must be collected contemporaneously. The chapters in Part III are precisely concerned with such issues.

Chapter 9, by Muffels, sets the scene for panel analyses of income dynamics by offering examples of poverty analyses using different types of Dutch survey data. In this way, he is able to show exactly what sorts of information a panel can uniquely provide. Among his findings is a high degree of income mobility which has the consequence of higher rates of poverty risks than the analysis of cross-sectional data would imply. In the following chapter, Jarvis and Jenkins investigate low-income dynamics in Britain as shown by the first four waves of the BHPS. Like Muffels for The Netherlands, they show that there is a high level of income turnover or 'churning'. Although only a small proportion of people is permanently poor from wave to wave, there are large numbers of low-income escapers and entrants every year. The characteristics of these two groups are examined.

In Chapter 11, Ashworth *et al.* also examine poverty dynamics. However, their concern is with the overemphasis in longitudinal analysis on poverty spells (i.e. poverty as an event), rather than on those individuals and households that experience poverty, and what that experience means. Their 'new approach' to the dynamic analysis of poverty emphasises its temporal distribution, thus recognising that there is more than one kind of poverty. Poverty is not only about duration (how long?) but about prevalence (how much?) and severity (how bad?).

The final two chapters each have a demographic focus. In Chapter

12, Ermisch demonstrates the use of panel data in the analysis of household and family dynamics. He shows that although techniques such as event history analysis may be applied to retrospective survey data on demographic events, there are severe limitations on what can be achieved. Many of the problems here arise from measurement errors due to inaccurate recall of past events by respondents. We have seen that such recall errors are less likely in panels. Ermisch uses BHPS data with hazard models to estimate the competing risks of certain events, such as entry into first partnership, partnership duration and leaving the parental home.

Finally, in Chapter 13, Buck uses BHPS data to investigate patterns of migration and residential mobility. His analysis indicates the importance of an issue referred to at the beginning of this chapter: the need to relate change at the individual or micro-level to change at the societal or macro-level. Again, Buck's analysis involves a consideration of different types of data, cross-sectional, retrospective and panel, their relative merits for migration research and how panel data may be used to improve understanding of migration processes.

It might be objected by some that no room has been found in Part III for analyses of labour market dynamics as this is another major area of panel research. However, the aim of Part III is not to cover all the areas in which panel data can improve our comprehension of social and economic processes. As with Parts I and II, the chapters in Part III are designed to assist in an understanding of panel surveys, the purposes to which they may be put, their aims and objectives, strengths and limitations, techniques and mechanics. This is a book designed to help the panel novitiate to come to grips with the complexities and potentials of household panels. Its aim is to provide a comprehensive and comprehensible introduction to the study of social and economic change using panel data.

We have seen in this chapter the reasons why panel studies are important for a richer comprehension of social, economic and demographic issues. Essentially, panel data allow us to distinguish between transitory and persistent aspects of phenomena such as poverty and unemployment. They allow us to examine gross change – the flows as well as the stocks. As they mature, panels provide vital information on intergenerational issues, e.g. social mobility. Panel data can also illuminate the effects of changes in status, e.g. what happens to the economic position of family members consequent on divorce. However, these advantages only emerge if panel surveys are well designed and are maintained so that the disadvantages inherent to panels – panel conditioning, wave non-response, attrition – are minimised. If this volume encourages readers to make greater use of the panel data resources now available to them, it will have served an important function.

Notes

1 The support of the Economic and Social Research Council (UK), the European Science Foundation and the University of Essex is gratefully acknowledged. Some of the work reported in this book arises from the activities of the European Science Foundation's Scientific Network on Household Panel Studies, which was co-ordinated by the ESRC Research Centre on Micro-social Change (now ISER), University of Essex. This chapter, and those by Buck, by Jarvis and Jenkins, by Ermisch and by Taylor are part of the scientific programme of the ISER. This chapter has been developed in part from earlier work that I undertook with Nick Buck and Louise Corti and their contribution is thus acknowledged.

2 These points, and others relevant to the concerns of this volume, are all examined in greater detail in standard texts and papers on longitudinal analysis. A large number are cited here to provide references from different disciplines and substantive areas at various levels of sophistication: Wall and Williams (1970), Crider *et al.* (1973), Social Science Research Council (1975), Markus (1979), Nesselroade and Baltes (1979), Coleman (1981), Kessler and Greenberg (1981), Schulsinger *et al.* (1981), Allison (1984), Chamberlain (1984), Duncan *et al.* (1984), Mednick *et al.* (1984), Tuma and Hannan (1984), Elder (1985a,b,c), Heckman and Singer (1985), Hsiao (1985, 1986, 1995), Nesselroade and Von Eye (1985), Plewis (1985), Crouchley (1987), Duncan and Kalton (1987), Galler and Poetter (1987), Mayer and Tuma (1987), Uncles (1988), Blossfeld *et al.* (1989, 1991), Huebler (1989), Hujer and Schneider (1989), Kasprzyk *et al.* (1989), Hagenaars (1990), Huebler and Gerlach (1990), Magnusson and Bergman (1990), Gerlach and Schasse (1991), Kemp (1991), Winkelmann and Zimmermann (1991), Bird *et al.* (1992), Merkle and Zimmermann (1992), Mueller *et al.* (1992), Petersen (1993, 1995), Dale and Davies (1994), Hamerle and Ronning (1995) and Gershuny and Buck (2001).

3 I am grateful to Jonathan Gershuny for permission to reproduce these analyses.

2 Panel surveys

Adding the fourth dimension[1]

Graham Kalton and Constance F. Citro

Introduction

As we saw in Chapter 1, survey populations are constantly changing over time, both in composition and in the characteristics of their members. Changes in composition occur when members enter the survey population through birth (or reaching adulthood), immigration, or through leaving an institution (for a non-institutional population) or leave through death, emigration, or through entering an institution. Changes in characteristics include, for example, a change from married to divorced, or from a monthly income of US$2,000 to one of US$2,500. As also discussed in Chapter 1, these population changes give rise to a range of objectives for the analysis of survey data across time. This chapter reviews survey designs that produce the data needed to satisfy these various objectives.

The chapter is divided into two parts. The first part contains a general review of designs for surveys across time and the types of analyses they will support, expanding on Rose's discussion in Chapter 1. The second, and main, part of this chapter discusses the considerations involved in designing, conducting, and analysing panel survey designs. The final section provides some concluding remarks.

Surveys across time

In Chapter 1, Rose has described several designs for surveys across time and has discussed the types of analyses they can support (see Table 1.2). This section, which builds on Chapter 1, provides a more detailed treatment of these issues. It supplements the material in Chapter 1 and should be read in conjuction with that chapter. Six designs for surveys across time are considered here. The three main designs – *repeated surveys*, *panel surveys*, and *rotating panel surveys* – have been discussed in Chapter 1. The other three – *repeated panel surveys*, *overlapping surveys*, and *split panel surveys* – are described below. After that, the section examines the analytical uses of the various designs, relying heavily on the paper by Duncan and Kalton (1987).

A repeated panel survey is made up of a series of panel surveys each of a fixed duration. There may or may not be overlap in the time periods covered by the individual panels. Strictly, a repeated panel survey with overlap is equivalent to a rotating panel survey. Both limit the length of a panel and have two or more panels in the field at the same time. However, it seems useful to distinguish between the two designs because they have different objectives. Rotating panel surveys are widely used to provide a series of cross-sectional estimates and estimates of net change (for example, of unemployment rates and changes in such rates), whereas repeated panel surveys with overlaps also have a major focus on longitudinal measures (for example, durations of spells of unemployment). In consequence, repeated panel surveys tend to have longer durations and have fewer panels in operation at any given time than rotating panel surveys.

Like a repeated survey, an overlapping survey is a series of cross-sectional surveys conducted at different time points. However, whereas the repeated survey does not attempt to secure any sample overlap from the survey at one time point to the next, an overlapping survey is designed to provide such overlap. The aim may be to maximise the degree of sample overlap while taking into account both the changes desired in selection probabilities for sample elements that remain in the survey population and also changes in population composition over time. A split panel survey is a combination of a panel survey and a repeated survey or rotating panel survey. At each wave, part of the sample comes from the panel survey component and part from the repeated survey or rotating panel survey component.

The choice of design in a particular case depends on the objectives to be satisfied. As we saw in Table 1.2, some designs are better than others for some objectives but are poorer for other objectives. Some designs cannot satisfy certain objectives at all (for a detailed discussion, see Duncan and Kalton, 1987).

The strength of a repeated survey is that it selects a new sample at each time point, so that each cross-sectional survey is based on a probability sample of the population existing at that time. A panel survey is based on a sample drawn from the population existing at the start of the panel. Although attempts are sometimes made to add samples of new entrants to a panel at later time points, such updating is generally difficult to carry out and thus is carried out imperfectly. Moreover, non-response losses from a panel as it ages heighten concerns about non-response bias when the panel sample is used to estimate cross-sectional parameters for later time points. For these reasons, repeated surveys are stronger than panel surveys for producing cross-sectional and average cross-sectional estimates [objectives (a) and (b) in Table 1.2]. With average cross-sectional estimates, another factor to be considered is the correlation between the values of the survey variables for the same individual at different time points. When this correlation is positive, as it generally is, it increases the standard errors of the average cross-sectional estimates from a panel survey. This factor thus also favours repeated surveys over panel surveys for average cross-sectional estimates.

The superior representation of the samples for a repeated survey at later time points also argues in favour of a repeated survey over a panel survey for estimating net change (assuming that the interest in net change relates to changes in both population composition and characteristics). However, in this case, the positive correlations of the values of the survey variables for the same individuals across time decrease the standard errors of estimates of net change from a panel survey. Hence, the presence of this correlation operates in favour of the panel design for measuring net change.

The key advantages of the panel design are its abilities to measure gross change and also to aggregate data for individuals over time [objectives (d) and (e) in Table 1.2]. Repeated surveys are incapable of satisfying these objectives. The great analytical potential provided by the measurement of individual changes is the major reason for using a panel design.

Repeated surveys can collect data on events occurring in a specified period [objective (f)] and on durations of events (for example, spells of sickness) by retrospective questioning. However, retrospective questioning often introduces a serious problem of response error in recalling dates and therefore the risk of telescoping bias. A panel survey that uses a reference period for the event that corresponds to the interval between waves of data collection can eliminate the telescoping problem by using the previous interview to bound the recall (for example, an illness reported at the current interview can be discarded if it had already been reported at the previous one). Similarly, a panel survey can determine the duration of an event from successive waves of data collection, limiting the length of recall to the interval between waves.

Repeated data collections over time can provide a vehicle for accumulating a sample of members of a rare population [objective (g)], such as persons with a rare chronic disease or persons who have recently experienced a bereavement. Repeated surveys can be used in this manner to generate a sample of any form of rare population. Panel surveys, however, can be used to accumulate only samples of new rare events (such as bereavements) but not of stable rare characteristics (such as having a chronic disease). If a sample of members with a rare stable characteristic (for example, persons with doctoral degrees) has already been identified, a panel survey can be useful for maintaining the sample over time, with suitable supplementation for new entrants at later waves (for an example, see Citro and Kalton, 1989).

Rotating panel surveys are primarily concerned with estimating current levels and net change [objectives (a) and (c)]. As such, elements are usually retained in the panel for only short periods. For instance, sample members remain in the monthly Canadian Labour Force Survey for only 6 months. The extent to which individual changes can be charted and aggregation over time can be performed is thus limited by the short panel duration. A special feature of rotating panel surveys is the potential to use composite estimation to improve the precision of both cross-sectional estimates and estimates of net change (see Binder and Hidiroglou, 1988, Cantwell and Ernst, 1993; for an alternative method of using past information in forming estimates from a rotating panel design, see Fuller *et al.*, 1993).

Like rotating panel surveys, overlapping surveys are primarily concerned with estimating current levels and net change. They can also provide some limited information on gross change and aggregations over time. Overlapping survey designs are applicable in situations where some sample overlap is required and where the desired element selection probabilities vary over time. This situation arises in particular in establishment surveys, in which the desired selection probability for an establishment may vary from one cross-sectional survey to the next to reflect its change in size and type of activity. In such circumstances, a Keyfitz-type procedure can be applied to maximise the retention of elements from the previous survey while taking account of changes in selection probabilities and population composition (see, for example, Keyfitz, 1951; Kish and Scott, 1971; Sunter, 1986). The US Internal Revenue Service Statistics of Income Division's corporate sample provides an example of an overlapping survey design (Hinkins *et al.*, 1988).

By combining a panel survey with a repeated survey or a rotating panel survey, a split panel survey can provide the advantages of each. However, given a constraint on total resources, the sample size for each component is necessarily smaller than if only one component had been used. In particular, estimates of gross change and other measures of individual change from a split panel survey will be based on a smaller sample than would have been the case if all the resources had been devoted to the panel component.

In comparing alternative designs for surveys across time, the costs of the designs need to be considered. For instance, panel surveys avoid the costs of repeated sample selections incurred with repeated surveys, but they face costs of tracking and tracing mobile sample members and sometimes costs of incentives to encourage panel members to continue to co-operate in the panel (see p. 43). If two designs can each satisfy the survey objectives, the relative costs for given levels of precision for the survey estimates need to be examined.

Panel surveys

As we saw in Chapter 1, the repeated measures over time on the same sampled elements that are obtained in panel surveys provide such surveys with a key analytical advantage over repeated surveys. The measurements of gross change and other components of individual change that are possible with panel survey data form the basis of a much greater understanding of social processes than can be obtained from a series of independent cross-sectional snapshots. The power of longitudinal data derived from panel surveys has long been recognised (see, for instance, Lazarsfeld and Fiske, 1938; Lazarsfeld, 1948), and panel surveys have been carried out in many fields for many years. Subjects of panel surveys have included, for example, human growth and development, juvenile delinquency, drug use, victimisations from crime, voting behaviour, marketing studies of consumer expenditures, education and career choices, retirement, health and medical care expenditures.[2] In recent years, there has been a major upsurge in interest in panel surveys in many subject matter areas, and especially in household economics. The ongoing US Panel Study of Income Dynamics (PSID) began in 1968 (for a description of the PSID, see Hill, 1992) and similar long-term panel studies have been started in the past 20 years in many European countries. The US Bureau of the Census started to conduct the Survey of Income and Program Participation (SIPP) in 1983 (Nelson *et al.*, 1985; Kasprzyk, 1988; US Bureau of the Census, 1990) and Statistics Canada introduced the Survey of Labour and Income Dynamics (SLID) in 1993. The growth in interest in panel surveys has also given rise to an increase in literature about the methodology of such surveys, including such recent texts as Kasprzyk *et al.* (1989), Magnusson and Bergman (1990) and van der Pol (1989).

This section reviews the major issues involved in the design and analysis of panel surveys. The treatment is geared towards repeated panel surveys of fixed duration such as the SIPP and SLID, but most of the discussion applies more generally to all forms of panel survey.

Design decisions for a panel survey

The time dimension adds an extra dimension of complexity to a panel survey as compared with a cross-sectional survey. In addition to all the decisions that need to be made about the design features of a cross-sectional survey, a wide range of extra decisions needs to be reached for a panel survey. Major design decisions are as follows.

Length of the panel

The longer the panel lasts, the greater is the wealth of data obtained for longitudinal analysis. For instance, the longer the panel, the greater the number of spells of unemployment starting during the life of the panel that will be completed before the end of the panel, and hence the greater the precision in estimating the survival function for such spells. On the other hand, the longer the panel, the greater the problems of maintaining a representative cross-sectional sample at later waves because of both sample attrition and difficulties in updating the sample for new entrants to the population.

It can sometimes be beneficial to vary the length of the panel between different types of panel members. Thus, for instance, when the analytical objectives call for it, panel members with certain characteristics (for example, members of a minority population) or who experience certain events during the course of the regular panel (for example, a divorce) can be retained in the panel for extended periods of observation.

Length of the reference period

The frequency of data collection depends on the ability of respondents to recall the information collected in the survey over time. Thus, the PSID, with annual waves of data collection, requires recall of events occurring in the previous calendar year, whereas SIPP, with 4-monthly waves of data collection, requires recall for the preceding 4 months. The longer the reference period, the greater the risk of recall error.

Number of waves

In most cases, the number of waves of data collection is determined by a combination of the length of the panel and the length of the reference period. The greater the number of waves, the greater the risk of panel attrition and time-in-sample effects and the greater the degree of respondent burden.

Overlapping or non-overlapping panels

With a repeated panel survey of fixed duration, a decision needs to be made as to whether the panels should overlap across time. Consider, for instance, a repeated survey of 4 years' duration. One possibility is to run each panel for 4 years, starting a new panel when the previous one finishes. Another possibility is to run each panel for 4 years, but to start a new panel every 2 years. Yet another possibility is to run each panel for 4 years, starting a new panel every year.

The design of non-overlapping panels has the benefit of simplicity as only one panel is in the field at any one time. It also produces a large sample for longitudinal analysis for a specific period; for instance, the panels with the non-overlapping design can be roughly twice the size of those with the design that has two overlapping panels at any one time. However, this increase in sample size for non-overlapping panels does not apply for cross-sectional estimates because the data from the panels covering a given time point can be combined for cross-sectional estimation. Also, the cross-sectional estimates for a time period near the end of a panel with the non-overlapping design are at greater risk of bias from attrition, time-in-sample bias and failure to update the sample fully for new population entrants than is the case with an overlapping design, in which one panel is of more recent origin. Moreover, the overlapping design permits the examination of such biases through a comparison of the results for the two panels for a given time period, whereas no such examination is possible with a non-overlapping design. Another limitation of the non-overlapping design is that it may not be well positioned to measure the effect of such events as a change in legislation. For instance, if legislation takes effect in the final year of a non-overlapping panel, there will be little opportunity to evaluate its effect by comparing the situations of the same individuals before and for some period after the legislation is enacted. With overlapping panels, one of the panels will provide a wider window of observation.

Panel sample size

For a given amount of annual resources, the sample size for each panel is determined by the preceding factors. A larger panel for longitudinal analysis can be achieved by lengthening the reference period and by using a non-overlapping design. The sample size for cross-sectional estimates can be increased by lengthening the reference period, but not by using a non-overlapping design.

The above list determines the major parameters of a panel survey design, but there still remain a number of other factors that need to be considered. These other factors are discussed below.

Mode of data collection

As with any survey, a decision needs to be made as to whether the survey data are to be collected by face-to-face interviewing, by telephone or by self-completion questionnaire, and whether computer-assisted interviewing [computer-assisted personal interviewing (CAPI) or computer-assisted telephone interviewing (CATI)] is to be used. With a panel survey, this decision needs to be made for each wave of data collection, with the possibility of different modes for different waves (for instance, face-to-face interviewing at the first wave to make contact and establish rapport, with telephone interviewing or mail question-naires at some of the later waves). When modes may be changed between waves, consideration needs to be given to the comparability of the data across waves. Sometimes a change in mode may involve a change in interviewer, as, for instance, would occur with a change from face-to-face interviewing to a centralised CATI operation. Then the effects of a change of interviewer between waves on the respondent's willingness to continue in the panel and on the comparability of responses across waves also need to be carefully considered.

Dependent interviewing

With panel surveys, there is the possibility of feeding back to respondents their responses at earlier waves of data collection. This dependent interviewing procedure can secure more consistent responses across waves, but risks generating an undue level of consistency. The ease of application of dependent interviewing depends on the length of the interval between waves and the mode of data collection. Processing the responses from one wave to feed back in the next is easier to accomplish if the interval between waves is a long one and if computer-assisted interviewing is used. Edwards *et al.* (1993) describe the use of dependent interviewing with CAPI in the Medical Care Beneficiary Survey, a survey which involves three interviews per year with each respondent.

Incentives

Monetary or other incentives (for example, coffee mugs, calculators, lunch bags) may be offered to sampled persons to encourage their participation in a survey. With a panel survey, incentives may be used not only to secure initial participation but also to maintain co-operation throughout the duration of the panel. There is an issue of when are the best times to provide incentives in a panel survey (for example, at the first wave, at an intermediate wave, or at the last wave of the panel). Panel survey researchers often send respondents a survey newsletter, frequently giving some recent highlights from the survey findings, at regular intervals, both to generate goodwill for the survey and to maintain contact with respondents (see below). Birthday cards sent at the time of the respondents' birthdays are also often used for these purposes.

Respondent rules

Survey data are often collected from proxy informants when respondents are unavailable for interview. With a panel survey, this gives rise to the possibility that the data may be collected from different individuals at different waves, thus jeopardising the comparability of the data across waves. The respondent rules for a panel survey need to take this factor into account.

Sample design

The longitudinal nature of a panel survey needs to be considered in constructing the sample design for the initial wave. Clustered samples are commonly used for cross-sectional surveys with face-to-face interviewing to reduce fieldwork travel costs and to enable frame construction of housing unit listings to be performed only for selected segments. These benefits are bought at the price of the increase in the variance of survey estimates arising from the clustering. The optimum extent of clustering depends on the various cost factors involved and the homogeneity of the survey variables in the clusters (see, for instance, Kish, 1965). With a panel survey, the use and extent of any clustering should be determined in relation to the overall panel with all its waves of data collection. In particular, the benefit of reduced fieldwork costs disappears for waves of data collection that are conducted by telephone interviewing or by mail questionnaire. Also, the migration of panel members to locations outside the original clusters reduces the benefit of the initial clustering for fieldwork costs at later waves. (However, some benefits of the initial clustering still operate for the large proportion of mobile persons who move within their own neighbourhoods.)

Oversampling of certain population subgroups is widely used in cross-sectional surveys to provide sufficient numbers of subgroup members for separate analysis. Such subgroups may, for instance, comprise persons with low incomes, minority populations, persons in a specified age group, or persons living in certain geographical areas. Such oversampling can also be useful in panel surveys, but caution is needed in its application. With long-term panels, one reason for caution is that the objectives of the survey may change over time. Oversampling to meet an objective identified at the start of a panel may prove harmful to objectives that emerge later. Another reason for caution is that many of the subgroups of interest are transient in nature (for example low-income persons, persons living in a given geographical area). Oversampling persons in such subgroups at the outset of the panel may be of limited value for later waves: some of those oversampled will leave the subgroup whereas others not oversampled will join it. Third, the definition of the desired subgroup for longitudinal analysis needs to be considered. For instance, SIPP data are used to estimate durations of spells on various welfare programmes. Since such estimates are usually based on new spells starting during the life of the panel, it may not be useful to oversample persons already enrolled on welfare programmes. (For a discussion of oversampling for the SIPP, see Citro and Kalton, 1993.)

When oversampling of a certain subgroup of the population (for example, a minority population) is desired for a panel survey, the oversampling may require a large screening operation. The assessment of the cost of such screening should be made in the context of the full panel with all its waves of data collection. An expensive screening operation at the first wave may well be justifiable in this context.

Updating the sample

When the sole objective of a panel survey is longitudinal analysis, it may be sufficient to adopt a cohort approach that simply follows the initial sample selected for the first wave. However, when cross-sectional estimates are also of interest, it may be necessary to update the sample at each wave to represent new entrants to the population. Updating for all types of new entrants is often difficult, but it is sometimes possible to develop fairly simple procedures to account for certain types of new entrants. For instance, in a panel of persons of all ages, babies born to female panel members after the start of the panel can be included as panel members. The SIPP population of inference comprises persons aged 15 and over. By identifying in initially sampled households persons who are under 15 years old but who will attain that age before the end of the panel, by following them during the panel, and by interviewing them after they reach 15 years of age, a SIPP panel can be updated for this class of new entrants (Kalton and Lepkowski, 1985).

Attention also needs to be paid to panel members who leave the survey population. For some, the departure is clearly permanent (for example, deaths), but for others it may be only temporary (for example, going abroad or entering an institution). If efforts are made to keep track of temporary leavers, they can be readmitted to the panel if they return to the survey's population of inference.

Panel surveys such as SIPP and PSID collect data not only for persons in original sampled households but also for other persons – non-sampled persons – with whom they are living at later waves. The prime purpose of collecting survey data for non-sampled persons is to be able to describe the economic and social circumstances of sampled persons. The issue arises as to whether any or all non-sampled persons should remain in the panel after they stop living with sampled persons. For some kinds of analysis, it is useful to follow them. However, to follow them would eat significantly into the survey's resources.

When data are collected for non-sample members, these data may be used simply to describe the circumstances of sample members, in which case analyses are restricted to sample members, with non-sample members being assigned weights of zero. Alternatively, non-sample members can be included in cross-sectional analyses. In this case, appropriate weights for sample and non-sample persons need to be developed to reflect the multiple ways in which individuals may appear in the dataset. Huang (1984), Ernst (1989) and Lavallée and Hunter (1993) describe the fair share weighting approach that may be used for this purpose.

Tracking and tracing

Most panel surveys encounter the problem that some panel members have moved since the last wave and cannot be located (Laurie *et al.*, 1999). There are two ways to try to handle this problem. First, attempts can be made to avoid the problem by implementing procedures for tracking panel members between waves. One widely used procedure when there is a long interval between waves is to send mailings, such as birthday cards and survey newsletters, to respondents between waves, requesting the post office to provide notification of change of address if applicable. Another tracking device is to ask respondents for the names and addresses or telephone numbers of persons close to them (for example, parents) who are unlikely to move and who will be able to provide locating information for them if they move.

The second way to deal with lost panel members is to institute various tracing methods to try to locate them. With effort and ingenuity, high success rates can be achieved. Some methods of tracing may be specific for the particular population of interest (for example, professional societies for persons with professional qualifications) whereas others may be more general, such as telephone directories, computerised telephone number look-ups, reverse telephone directories for telephone numbers of neighbours, mail forwarding, marriage licence registers, motor vehicle registrations, employers, and credit bureaux. It can be useful to search death records for lost panel members, particularly for long-term panel surveys. Panel members found to have died can then be correctly classified, rather than being viewed as non-respondents. Methods of tracing are discussed by Eckland (1968), Crider *et al.* (1971), Clarridge *et al.* (1978) and Burgess (1989).

Problems of panel surveys

Panel surveys share with all surveys a wide range of sources of non-sampling error. This section does not review all these sources, but rather concentrates on three sources that are unique to panel surveys, namely wave non-response, time-in-sample bias and the seam effect. Measurement errors are discussed by Skinner in Chapter 6.

Wave non-response

The non-response experienced by panel surveys at the first wave of data collection corresponds to that experienced by cross-sectional surveys. The distinctive feature of panel surveys is that they encounter further non-response at subsequent waves. Some panel members who become non-respondents at a particular wave do not respond at any subsequent wave whereas others respond at some or all subsequent waves. The former are often termed attrition cases and the latter non-attrition cases. The overall wave non-response rates in panel surveys increase with later waves, but with well-managed surveys the rate of increase usually declines appreciably over time. For example, with the 1987 SIPP panel, the sample loss was 6.7% at wave 1, 12.6% at wave 2 and it then increased slowly to 19.0% at wave 7 (US Bureau of the Census, 1990). The tendency for the non-response rate to flatten off at later waves is comforting, but nevertheless the accumulation of non-response over many waves produces high non-response rates at later waves of a long-term panel. For instance, in 1988, after twenty-one annual rounds of data collection, the PSID non-response rate for individuals who lived in 1968 sampled households had risen to 43.9% (Hill, 1992).

The choice between the two standard general purpose methods for handling missing survey data – weighting adjustments and imputation – is not straightforward for wave non-response in panel surveys. For longitudinal analysis, the weighting approach drops all records with one or more missing waves from the data file and attempts to compensate for them by weighting adjustments applied to the remaining records. This approach can lead to the loss of a substantial amount of data when the data file covers several waves. On the other hand, the imputation approach retains all the reported data, but requires conducting wholesale imputations for missing waves. A compromise approach uses imputation for some patterns of wave non-response (for example those with only one missing wave, when data are available from both adjacent waves) and weighting for others (see, for example, Singh *et al.* 1990). For cross-sectional analysis, separate data files may be created for each wave. These files can comprise all the respondents for that wave, with either weighting adjustments or imputations for the wave non-respondents. In Chapter 5 of this volume, Kalton and Brick consider weighting issues in more detail. Kalton (1986) and Lepkowski (1989) discuss general methods for handling wave non-response, Lepkowski *et al.* (1993) discuss imputations for wave non-response in the SIPP, and Michaud and Hunter (1993) describe plans for handling wave non-response in the SLID.

With wave non-response, there is the possibility of collecting some or all of the data for the missing wave at a subsequent interview. However, the quality of the retrospective data collected in this way needs to be carefully assessed. An experiment was conducted to examine the utility of this approach with the 1984 SIPP panel, using a missing wave form to collect responses for a skeleton set of core questions for the missing wave (Huggins, 1987; Singh, 1993). The analyses showed substantially fewer transitions in receipt of income, assets, and government assistance from the missing wave form than from benchmark data. In consequence, the use of the missing wave form was discontinued. Administrative records may sometimes provide another possible source of skeletal data for missing waves.

Time-in-sample bias

Time-in-sample bias, or panel conditioning, refers to the effect that panel members' responses at a given wave of data collection are affected by their participation in previous waves. The effect may reflect simply a change in reporting behaviour. For example, a respondent may recognise from previous interviews that a 'yes' response to a question leads to follow-up questions, whereas a 'no' answer does not. The respondent may therefore give a 'no' answer to avoid the burden of the extra questions. Alternatively, a respondent may learn from previous interviews that detailed information on income is needed, and may therefore prepare for later interviews by collecting the necessary data. The time-in-sample effect may also reflect a change in actual behaviour. For example, a SIPP respondent may enrol in the food stamp programme as a result of learning of its existence from the questions asked about it at earlier waves of data collection.

An experimental study of panel conditioning in a 4-year panel study of newlyweds found some evidence that participation in the study did affect marital well-being (Veroff *et al.*, 1992). However, that study used in-depth interviewing techniques that are more intrusive than those used in most surveys. A number of studies of panel conditioning that have been conducted in more standard survey settings have found that conditioning effects do sometimes occur, but they are not pervasive (Mooney, 1962; Ferber, 1964; Traugott and Katosh, 1979; Waterton and Lievesley, 1989).

A benefit of rotating and overlapping panel surveys is that they enable estimates for the same time period obtained from different panels to be compared. Such comparisons have clearly identified the presence of what is termed 'rotation group bias' in the US and Canadian labour force surveys (for the US Current Population Survey, see, for example, Bailar, 1975, 1989; US Bureau of Labor Statistics and US Census Bureau, 2000; for the Canadian Labour Force Survey, see, for example, Ghangurde, 1982). Rotation group bias may reflect non-response bias and conditioning effects. In analyses comparing the overlapping 1985, 1986 and 1987 SIPP panels, Pennell and Lepkowski (1992) found few differences in the results from the different panels.

Seam effect

Many panel surveys collect data for subperiods within the reference period from the last wave of data collection. The SIPP, for instance, collects data on a monthly basis within the 4-month reference period between waves. The seam effect refers to the common finding with this form of data collection that the levels of reported changes between adjacent subperiods (for example, going on or off of a welfare programme from one month to the next) are much greater when the data for the pair of subperiods are collected in different waves than when they are collected in the same wave. The seam effect has been found to be pervasive in SIPP and to relate to both recipiency status and amounts received (see, for example, US Bureau of the Census, 1990; Kalton and Miller, 1991). It has also been found in PSID (Hill, D., 1987). Murray *et al.* (1991) describe approaches used to reduce the seam effect in the Canadian Labour Market Activity Survey.

Longitudinal analysis

As Rose noted in Chapter 1, there is a substantial and rapidly expanding literature on the analysis of longitudinal data, including a number of texts on the subject (for example, Goldstein, 1979; Markus, 1979; Kessler and Greenberg, 1981; Hsiao, 1986, 1995; Dale and Davies, 1994; Gershuny and Buck, 2001). This treatment cannot be comprehensive, but rather identifies a few general themes.

Measurement of gross change

As has already been noted, a key analytical advantage of a panel survey over a repeated survey is the ability to measure gross change, i.e. change at the individual level. The basic approach to measuring gross change is the turnover table that tabulates responses at one wave against the responses to the same question at another wave. A severe limitation to this form of analysis is that changes in measurement errors across waves can lead to serious bias in the estimation of the gross change (for further discussion, see Chapter 6; Abowd and Zellner, 1985; Chua and Fuller, 1987; Kalton *et al.*, 1989; Rodgers, 1989; Fuller, 1990; Skinner 1993).

Relationships between variables across time

Panel surveys collect the data necessary to study the relationships between variables measured at different times. For instance, based on the data collected in the 1946 British birth cohort, the National Survey of Health and Development, Douglas (1975) found that children who were hospitalised for more than a week or who had repeated hospitalisations between the ages of 6 months and 3.5 years exhibited more troublesome behaviour in school and lower reading scores at age 15. In principle, cross-section surveys may use retrospective questions to collect the data needed to perform this type of analysis. However, the responses to such questions are often subject to serious memory error and, potentially, to systematic distortions that affect the relationships investigated.

Regression with change scores

Regression with change scores can be used to avoid a certain type of model misspecification. Suppose that the correct regression model for individual i at time t is:

$$Y_{it} = \alpha + \beta x_{it} + \gamma z_{it} + \varepsilon_{it}$$

where x_{it} is an explanatory variable that changes value over time and z_{it} is an explanatory variable that is constant over time (for example, sex or race). Suppose further that z_{it} is unobserved; it may well be unknown. Then β can still be estimated from the regression on the change scores:

$$Y_{i(t+1)} - Y_{(t)} = \beta(x_{i(t+1)} - x_{it}) + \varepsilon_{i(t+1)} - \varepsilon_{it}$$

Further information may be found in Rodgers (1989) and in Duncan and Kalton (1987).

Estimation of spell durations

The data collected in panel surveys may be used to estimate the distribution of lengths of spells of such events as being on a welfare programme. In panel surveys such as the SIPP, some individuals have a spell in progress at the start of the panel (initial-censored spells), some start a spell during the panel, and some spells continue beyond the end of the panel (right-censored spells). Thus, not all spells are observed in their entirety. The distribution of spell durations may be estimated by applying survival analysis methods, such as the Kaplan–Meier product limit estimation procedure to all new spells (including right-censored new spells) starting during the life of the panel (for example, see Ruggles and Williams, 1989).

Structural equation models with measurement errors

The sequence of data collection in a panel survey provides a clear ordering of the survey variables that fits well with the use of structural equation modelling for their analysis. This form of analysis can make allowance for measurement errors and, with several repeated measures, can handle correlated error structures (for example, see Jöreskog and Sörbom, 1979).

Conclusion

The datasets generated from panel surveys are usually extremely rich in analytical potential. They contain repeated measures for some variables that are collected on several occasions and also measures for other variables that are asked on a single wave. Repeated interviewing of the same sample provides the opportunity to collect data on new variables at each wave, thus yielding data on an extensive range of variables over a number of waves. A panel dataset may be analysed both longitudinally and cross-sectionally. Repeated measures may be used to examine individual response patterns over time and they may also be related to other variables. Variables measured at a single wave may be analysed both in relation to other variables measured at that wave and to variables measured at other waves.

The richness of panel data is of value only to the extent that the dataset is analysed, and is analysed in a timely manner. Running a panel survey is like being on a treadmill: the operations of questionnaire design, data collection, processing and analysis have to be undertaken repeatedly for each successive wave. There is a real danger that the survey team will become overwhelmed by this process, with the result that the data are not fully analysed. To avoid this danger, adequate staffing is needed and a well-integrated organisation needs to be maintained.

In addition, it is advisable to keep the panel survey design simple. The survey design should be developed to meet clearly specified objectives. Adding complexities to the design to enhance the richness of the panel dataset for other uses should be critically assessed. Although persuasive arguments can often be made for such additions, they should be rejected if they threaten the orderly conduct of any stage of the survey process.

As noted earlier, measurement errors have particularly harmful effects on the analysis of individual changes from panel survey data. The allocation of part of a panel survey's resources to measure the magnitude of such errors is therefore well warranted (Fuller, 1989). Measurement errors may be investigated either by validity studies (comparing survey responses with 'true' values from an external source) or by reliability studies (for example, reinterview studies). The results of such studies may be then used in the survey estimation procedures to adjust for the effects of measurement errors.

Notes

1 This chapter is extracted from a paper that was originally published in December 1993 by Statistics Canada in *Survey Methodology* 19, 2, 205–15, catalogue number 12-001. Reproduced by authority of the Minister of Industry, 1996. Readers wishing further information on data provided through the co-operation of Statistics Canada may obtain copies of related publications by mail from Publications Sales, Statistics Canada, Ottawa, Ontario, K1A 0T6, or by calling (+1) 613 951 7277 or toll free (+1) 800 267 6677. Readers may also facsimile their order by dialling (+1) 613 951 1584.

2 See Wall and Williams (1970) for a review of early panel studies on human growth and development, Boruch and Pearson (1988) for descriptions of some US panel surveys, and the Subcommittee on Federal Longitudinal Surveys (1986) for descriptions of US federal panel surveys.

3 Using panel studies to understand household behaviour and well-being[1]

Greg Duncan

Introduction

Following the downfall of Communism, a new spectre is now haunting social scientists – the spectre of household panel surveys. Not content with cross-sectional surveys (i.e. surveys that collect information from different individuals or households at a single point in time), academic groups and national statistical offices have launched household panel surveys in most European countries as well as in North America. Panel surveys, which periodically gather economic and demographic information about the *same* people over a number of years, have the potential to provide much richer information about economic and demographic behaviour. But they also appear to have voracious appetites for severely constrained resources from national science foundation budgets and may suffer from a number of technical problems as well. Under what conditions, if any, are household panels worth the effort and expense?

The purpose of this chapter is to build on some of the comments in the first two chapters and thus to provide an assessment of the promise and problems of household panel surveys as sources of data for analyses of economic and demographic behaviour. I will begin by repeating the good news noted earlier by Rose and by Kalton and Citro: data from high-quality panel surveys make it possible for analysts to: (i) make the crucial distinction between transitory and persistent characteristics (for example poverty); (ii) study gross flows between states (for example unemployment) or across important boundaries such as those defining the middle class; (iii) conduct studies of the intergenerational consequences of phenomena such as poverty and dependence; (iv) estimate changes surrounding events of interest; and (v) estimate more sophisticated behavioural models.

However, as we have also seen, panel surveys are not without their analytical disadvantages, and a balanced assessment of panel and cross-sectional surveys must take note of a number of possible drawbacks: (i) the absence of data from respondents lost during the panel period may impart substantial bias to inferences drawn from information provided by surviving respondents; (ii) panel data on change may contain more measurement error than cross-sectional data on level; and (iii) respondent participation in panels may affect behaviour.

If disadvantages are to be minimised and advantages maximised, the most important steps for conducting a household panel survey project are to (i) ensure that the initial sample is of the highest possible quality; (ii) use the proper rules about whom to follow and interview; (iii) minimise bias due to panel attrition; (iv) use feedback techniques during interviewing and check for cross-wave inconsistencies to minimise errors in the measurement of change; and (v) whenever possible, gather continuous measures throughout the panel period.

The structure of household panel surveys

Household panel surveys begin just like cross-sectional ones – with the selection of a set of individuals to be interviewed. If properly selected and sufficiently co-operative, these individuals, whether part of a cross-sectional survey or the initial wave of a panel survey, represent the larger population from which they are drawn. Given the proper set of questions about income or labour force status, for example, the selected individuals provide data for producing reliable estimates of the proportion of individuals who are poor or unemployed in the larger population and for drawing a demographic profile of the poor or unemployed at the time the survey is taken.

Panel surveys differ from cross-sectional ones in that they continue to follow and interview sampled individuals at regular intervals. Adhering to the basic 'following rules' regarding whom to contact and interview, household panel surveys produce data on *changes* in the economic and demographic conditions of its sample members.

The simplest kind of panel studies are those of birth cohorts of individuals in the population, in which 'following rules' amount to attempting interviews with as many sampled individuals as possible. Disregarding non-response and immigration, these panels represent their cohorts as they age and gradually lose their representation of the original age range.

Panel designs of the US Panel Study of Income Dynamics (PSID) and many European panels represent *all* individuals and households in the population and contain a mechanism for representing new entrants – both individuals and families – into the population. The panels start with a representative set of households and, more importantly, a representative set of individuals residing in those households. If 'following rules' for such panels call for attempted interviews with *all* households containing members of the original sample and individuals born to such original sample members, then such a panel survey continues to provide representative cross-sectional snapshot information of the larger (non-immigrant) population over the life of the panel.[2]

Analytical advantages of panel surveys

High-quality panel data provide a number of analytical advantages relative to cross-sectional data (Chapter 2; Duncan and Kalton, 1987). These advantages are explained here using illustrations from various panel household surveys.

Transitory versus persistent components of economic well-being

Successive cross-sections from income surveys typically show little change from one year to the next in both the numbers of poor households and the characteristics of poor households. This has created the impression that the same households are poor from one year to the next. A recent study of poverty dynamics (Duncan *et al.*, 1993a) shows the extent of transitory and persistent poverty among families with children in the mid-1980s in eight countries – Canada, France (the Lorraine province), the Federal Republic of Germany, Ireland, Luxembourg, The Netherlands, Sweden and the USA.[3]

Poverty in a given country was defined by whether, after tax, family size-adjusted family income exceeded 50% of the median size-adjusted income of that country.[4] As median income-based poverty lines are drawn relative to each country's own median, the resulting poverty estimates reflect the degree of inequality of the distribution of size-adjusted family income.

The first column of Table 3.1 shows the single-year incidence of poverty in the various countries. Although drawn from household panels, these data amount to cross-sectional estimates of poverty and are similar to those found in the cross-sectional Luxembourg Income Study (LIS) datasets (Smeeding and Rainwater, 1992). Rates of median income-based poverty varied widely across countries, with Canada, foreign residents of Germany, Ireland and the USA having double digit rates, and all continental countries having rates of less than 10%. Nearly half of all Black families in the USA were poor by this definition, reflecting

Table 3.1 Poverty rates and transitions for families with children (mid-1980s)

Country	Single-year poverty rate[a] (%)	Three-year poverty rate[b] (%)	Poverty transitions among _all_ the poor[c] (%)	Poverty transitions among the _near_ poor[d] (%)
Canada	17	12	11	21
Lorraine, France	4	2	28	32
Germany (West)	8	2	26	24
Foreign residents only	18	4	20	23
Ireland	11	n.a.	25	22
Luxembourg	4	1	26	29
The Netherlands	3	1	44	23
Sweden	3	n.a.	37	45
USA	20	14	14	22
Blacks only	49	42	8	15

Source: Duncan *et al.* (1993a).

Notes

a Per cent with income <50% of given country's median income in a single year.

b Per cent with income <50% of given country's median income for all 3 years of a 3-year period.

c Of families with income <50% of median in t, per cent with income >60% of median in $t+1$.

d Of families with income 40–50% of median in t, per cent with income >60% of median in $t+1$.

n.a., Not available.

the much worse economic position of US Blacks than Whites relative to the median for Blacks and Whites taken together.

The second column of Table 3.1 takes advantage of the panel nature of the data by presenting poverty estimates using a 3-year window. Specifically, the estimates are of the fractions of the populations of the six countries with appropriate data that failed to enjoy incomes at least 50% of the median in all 3 of the years.[5] For the continental European countries – the Lorraine province of France, Germany, Luxembourg and The Netherlands – the combination of only modest inequality and extensive mobility among the poor left virtually no families with persistently low relative incomes. However, many families in both Canada and the USA had incomes that were less than 50% of the median in all 3 years: about one in eight Canadian and one in seven American (and two in five Black American) families were persistently poor over the 3 years by this definition.

The third column of Table 3.1 shows for each country the fraction of poor families in a given year who make the transition out of poverty by the following year. To minimise the effects of measurement error, Duncan *et al.* (1993a) required that transitions involve income changes of at least 20% – from below 50% of median in year *t* to above 60% of median in year *t* + 1.[6]

There are striking differences in rates of transitions out of poverty. In The Netherlands and Sweden, the fraction of poor climbing out of poverty exceeds one-third, whereas in the USA the comparable fraction was only one-seventh for the entire population of US poor and one-twelfth for Blacks.

A closer look at the first and third columns of Table 3.1 shows a marked inverse relationship between the estimated incidence of poverty and escape rates. Countries with larger fractions of their populations below the poverty line have lower escape rates. This is only logical because, everything else being the same, the higher the poverty threshold then the farther away the average poor family is from that line and the higher the income increase required to escape poverty. In fact, the typical annual income of poor families in the USA was only about 70% of the median income-based poverty line, compared with an average of about 80% for the other countries.

The fourth column of Table 3.1 adjusts for distance to the poverty line by taking families with year *t* incomes between 40% and 50% of the median with, as before, a transition defined as having year *t* + 1 incomes of 60% of the median or higher. Transition rates among families close to the poverty line are strikingly uniform across the countries, with rates for the USA and Canada being quite similar to those found in Germany, Luxembourg and The Netherlands. Blacks in the USA have lower transitions rates, whereas Swedes generally have higher than average rates. Supplemental calculations of the distribution of family income changes among poor families (not shown in Table 3.1) confirm that the typical amount of such change is very similar across the eight countries.

Thus, household panel data paint the following picture of poverty across the eight countries in the study: the relative economic position of families varies widely across countries, with substantial numbers of families in the USA and Canada quite badly off. Although favourable income changes among low-income families with children were widespread and remarkably similar across the eight countries in our study, the very low starting position of the typical poor family in the USA and Canada could not elevate the living standards of a substantial number of families to a level that was half that enjoyed by a typical family. Further analyses of poverty dynamics will be found in Chapters 9–11.

Gross flows

Poverty transitions are but one example of the more general ability of longitudinal data to describe gross change. Cross-sectional surveys measure net changes of phenomena of interest – poverty and unemployment rates, income shares, etc. In providing measures of gross flows, panel data can provide a crucial additional dimension to the analyst. This is useful, for example, in accounting for America's declining middle class (Duncan *et al.*, 1993b).

By nearly any measure, the size of America's middle class is smaller today than 15 years ago. Data from the US Census Bureau's Current Population Survey show a slow but steady decline in the fraction of middle-income households (defined as households with incomes between $15,000 and $50,000 in 1991 US dollars) from nearly 60% in the late 1960s to about 51% in the late 1980s. Some commentators argue that we should celebrate the decline of America's middle class, since it reflects a boom not bust, as a product of the growth years of the 1980s that saw many formerly middle-income families graduate to the ranks of the affluent. A more pessimistic view is that the middle class is shrinking because increasing numbers of workers are losing good jobs and facing unemployment or, at best, a disastrous skid to lower paying jobs.

Panel studies are well suited to assist in this debate because they can show the gross flows into and out of the middle class that produce the net changes. To study such gross flows with the PSID, Duncan *et al.* (1993b) drew samples of men and women aged 25–50 years in the first year of the 5-year period over which possible income transitions are observed.[7] They set the lower boundary of the middle class at $18,500 (after tax) in 1987 and the upper boundary at US$55,000. These income boundaries classify roughly 20% of US adults as 'low income' and 10% as 'high income', leaving about 70% in the middle.

Table 3.2 shows changes in the fraction of the sample experiencing the four transitions into and out of the middle class before and after 1980. On the positive side, more middle-income American adults became affluent during the 1980s than before (row 1). Before 1980, an average of 6.3% of the middle class achieved upper income status over any given 5-year period. In the 1980s, this average jumped to 7.5%, a highly significant difference. This difference persisted even after adjustments for changes in the demographic composition of families and macroeconomic conditions.

But the bad news was that more Americans fell from the middle- into low-income status, and it became more difficult for low-income families to climb into the middle class. During the years between 1967

Table 3.2 Per cent of US adults making key income transitions

	Before 1980 (%)	After 1980 (%)
High-income transitions		
Per cent of middle-income individuals climbing up	6.3	7.5
Per cent of high-income individuals falling out	31.1	27.1
Low-income transitions		
Per cent of low-income individuals climbing up	35.5	30.4
Per cent of middle-income individuals falling out	6.2	8.5

Source: Duncan *et al.* (1993b).

Note
Boundaries of high and low income are $55,000 and $18,500 respectively. Income is after-tax total family income in 1987 dollars.

and 1980, 6.2% of middle-income individuals fell into the lower income group over a typical 5-year period. After 1980, this number had increased to 8.5%, also a highly significant difference that persisted even after adjustments for changes in the demographic composition of families and macroeconomic conditions.

An even larger – and also unfavourable – change took place in the extent of mobility up into the middle class. Before 1980, an extraordinary fraction – some 35.5% – of low-income adults typically made the transition into the middle-income group. Upward mobility was less frequent in the 1980s; the fraction of low-income adults making the transition fell to 30.4%. As with the favourable transitions, these differences in transition rates across the lower boundary of the middle class before and after 1980 persisted after adjustments for changes in the demographic composition of families and macroeconomic conditions.

In this case, a household panel provides data on the four gross flows across middle-income boundaries and shows that *all* changed in a way that emptied out the middle class in the 1980s. A *simultaneous* increase in both upward and downward mobility accounts for America's shrinking middle class.

Intergenerational transmission of economic status

A wide array of theories in the social sciences address issues of parental influences on their children's abilities, achievements and behaviours as grown adults. Tests of the theories rely either on measurement of the strength of association between parental status and children's adult status or on identification of the mechanism by which transmission of socioeconomic status takes place. Longitudinal data are favoured for these types of analysis since the data contain measures of second-generation outcomes such as earnings, welfare dependence and educational attainment as well as parent-reported first-generation economic and demographic circumstances.

Much of the recent research focuses on two crucial parameters related to intergenerational transmission of economic status: (i) brothers' (or sisters') correlations in economic status and (ii) father–son (or mother–daughter) correlations in economic status.

Sibling correlations are taken as a summary measure of the proportion of the population variance in long-run economic status that is attributable to family background. Parent–child correlations are taken as a measure of the strength of the intergenerational linkage.

Following closely on the exposition of Corcoran *et al.* (1990), let y_{ij} denote the long-run economic status of the jth son from the ith family. Partition y_{ij} into orthogonal components:

$$y_{ij} = a_i + u_{ij}$$

where a_i is the component shared by sons from the same family and u_{ij} is the idiosyncratic component. The population variance in y_{ij} (σ^2_y) is the sum of $\sigma^2_a + \sigma^2_u$.

The brother correlation in economic status (ρ) can be expressed as:

$$\rho = \sigma^2_a / (\sigma^2_a + \sigma^2_u)$$

whereas the intergenerational income correlation (β) between y_{ij} and x_i, the long-run economic status of the ith father, is defined from the regression:

$$a_i = \beta x_i + z_i$$

(z_i are background characteristics orthogonal to x_i). Assuming $\sigma^2_x = \sigma^2_y$, ρ and β are related as follows:

$$\rho = \beta^2 + \sigma^2_z / \sigma^2_y$$

There are two important sources of bias in attempts to estimate ρ and β. First, samples used in previous studies (for example Mormon brothers, White twins who served in the armed forces) tend to be peculiarly homogeneous, resulting in smaller estimates of σ^2_a and, under plausible assumptions, ρ in the sample than in the population. And second, single-year proxies for long-run economic status (y_{ij} and x_i) contain transitory fluctuations that, under plausible assumptions, impart a downward bias to the estimates of ρ and β.

Using data from the PSID, Solon *et al.* (1991) show that increasing the measurement interval from 1 to several years causes the estimate of ρ for brothers' earnings to jump from 0.25, a number consistent with most past studies, to 0.45; and Solon (1992) shows that estimates of β from the PSID data jump from about 0.3 using a single year of earnings data to over 0.4 when transitory and permanent components of earnings are properly accounted for. This latter intergenerational correlation is roughly double the value typically estimated by other researchers. Thus, intergenerational economic mobility appears to be substantially lower and family resemblance substantially higher than had been depicted in studies based on homogeneous samples and single-year measures of income or earnings.

Estimates of change surrounding events of interest

If interesting events occur during the period in which panel data are being collected, then the data can be used to describe and evaluate the effects of those events. An example of an endogenous event is marital disruption, where it is of interest to describe income changes surrounding a separation or divorce for the family members undergoing it. Cross-sectional data comparing married couples and divorced or separated individuals are potentially misleading because married couples who will divorce may differ and cannot be separated from perpetually intact couples.

Burkhauser *et al.* (1991) use panel data from the US PSID and German SOEP to compare the economic position of men and women in the two countries 1 year before and 1 year after marital disruption. PSID data confirm the conventional wisdom about separation and divorce in the USA: the size-adjusted family income of women drops substantially (the median change is –24%); US men, on the other hand, do much better, with a median change of only –6%. Surprisingly, the situation in Germany is even worse for women. The typical German woman suffers a drop in income of 44%, whereas the typical German man undergoing a marital separation experiences very little income change (–7%), at least in the first year following the initial separation.[8]

An example of an important exogenous event of interest is the dismantling of internal market barriers in the European Community in 1992. By collecting data on an ongoing basis, household panels provide a vehicle for assessing the short-run effects of 'natural experiments', such as the policy changes associated with '1992' or macroeconomic fluctuations (see Barreiros, 1995). They do this in several ways.

First, they provide direct 'before and after' observations on the employment and wages of sample households and individuals surrounding the change in policy or economic environment. The short-run distributional impact of policy changes can thus be observed directly (although the change measures will be confounded by other economic, political and sociodemographic developments occurring at the same time). For example, if it is of interest to know to what extent the economic benefits of 1992 are shared by owners, managers and workers, panel data gathered before and after 1992 will provide the necessary information on the income changes and employment experiences of each group.

Second, panel surveys also provide critical details to help to understand the implications of observed changes. For example, suppose that, in 1992, one finds that average wages fall (or lag behind economy-wide increases) in some affected industries. One interpretation is that those working in these industries have suffered a significant wage loss. An alternative is that those working in these industries moved to other industries that were positively affected by the change and their place is taken by new workers who earn less because they are less experienced. Moreover, even if we know that the workers involved suffered non-trivial losses, the case for compensation might depend on whether they were earning significantly more than workers with similar skills in other industries in the first place.

Analytical advantages for estimating behavioural models

Apart from simple descriptions of the components of change, analysts may also wish to use panel data to estimate behavioural models. There are several potential analytical advantages to panel data for this purpose.

First, panel surveys enable one to collect a great deal of reliable economic and demographic information on a more or less continuous basis. Continuous information can be cast as event histories and used in a variety of event history models (for example, see Tuma and Hannan, 1984). Continuous measurement provides information about the distribution of spells and makes possible much richer analyses of phenomena such as poverty, unemployment, employer-specific work, lone-parent status and geographical mobility. Although event history data can also be collected retrospectively in cross-sectional surveys, the shorter recall period and possibilities for feeding back information collected in previous waves (Neter and Waksberg, 1964) argues for large potential measurement advantages for panel surveys (see below).

A second analytical advantage of panels is seen in a comparison of (i) cross-sectional models in which the level of a particular dependent variable is related to the level of a series of independent variables and (ii) models of change, in which the confounding effects of persistent and unmeasured interpersonal differences can be eliminated in some cases.

An example is the wages of blue collar workers, which are generally assumed to depend on their skill, reliability, etc. and on whether their workplace is covered by a union contract. Often, we have limited indicators of skill and no indication of subtler personal characteristics, which must therefore remain unmeasured, and we have reason to suspect that these unmeasured characteristics are correlated with union coverage. Models relating *change* in wages to *change* in union status can, under certain conditions, eliminate the effects of the unmeasured personal characteristics and provide a less biased estimate of the effects of unionisation (Freeman, 1984).

Aside from eliminating the biases caused by unmeasured and unchanging explanatory factors, panel models of change are helpful in instances where measurement error persists over time (for example, see Duncan and Holmlund, 1983, who relate change in earnings to change in working conditions) and where measures of change in explanatory variables are more reliable than retrospective cross-sectional reports of level of the explanatory variables (for example, see Mincer and Ofek, 1982, who regress earnings change on work experience segments constructed from panel data).

Data from several waves of a panel survey also enable the estimation of considerably more sophisticated models of lagged effects of dependent and independent variables and of the dynamic components of error variance (for example, see Lillard and Willis, 1978). However, panel models are no panacea – they still require analysts to make a series of untestable assumptions (Heckman and Robb, 1985).

We can illustrate some of these advantages with research on labour supply. Although static models continue to be an important undertaking (see, in particular, Mroz, 1987, for a detailed evaluation of the effect of specification choices on female labour supply estimates), labour supply models based on the assumption that individuals maximise utility over time have benefited in a more fundamental way from the availability of panel data.

Altonji (1986) assumes that lifetime utility is a discounted sum of individual period utilities and that utility in each period depends only on current consumption and leisure (or labour supply). Choosing a convenient form for this within period utility function gives the log of labour supply in period t as a linear function of the log of the period t wage and the marginal utility of consumption in period t. With these conventional simplifications, prior and expected future wages and prices enter the period t labour supply equation only through this marginal utility term λ_t. Now one need 'only' solve for λ_t.

One solution is to make fairly strong assumptions about individuals' information (for example perfect foresight), in which case $\Delta\lambda_t$ is a constant and the change in log hours supplied is a linear function of the change in log wage (see Heckman and MaCurdy, 1980; MaCurdy, 1981). Another is to observe that optimal consumption at time t also depends on λ_t (and not on wages in *any* period, given λ_t), and use (food) consumption in period t as a proxy for λ_t. Altonji (1986) finds that, whichever approach is taken, the estimate of the intertemporal labour supply elasticity is positive but less than 0.35.

While most empirical work on intertemporal models of labour supply is based on males, Jakubson (1988) estimates such a model for women. Because of the higher rates of non-participation among women, he uses a panel data generalisation of the Tobit model. Both the fixed effects (conventional) and the random effects (unconventional) are allowed to be correlated with the explanatory variables; the random effects estimator specifies that these individual effects be normally distributed. He finds that the two panel methods produce strikingly similar results. Both show appreciably smaller effects of young children on labour supply than do cross-sectional methods and both show supply elasticities of 1.1–1.7, larger than those found in studies of male labour supply.

Possible disadvantages of panel surveys

Panel surveys are not without their analytical disadvantages, and a balanced assessment of panel and cross-sectional survey should take note of these problems as well, with a view towards steps that might be taken to eliminate them.

Panel attrition may impart unacceptable biases

No household panel survey can succeed in following all members of its initial sample households. However, analytical problems caused by attrition are much more closely linked to the *nature* than to the *amount* of such attrition. If truly random, a 50% or even 75% attrition rate harms only the efficiency of estimates made from the panel data. On the other hand, if non-random in unmeasured ways, even a very small amount of attrition may produce unacceptable bias. For example, suppose that one was interested in using a household to estimate the size of a nation's 'underclass', defined by persistently low economic resources. Suppose further that the panel had experienced only 5% attrition. Random attrition would produce no bias in the resulting estimates of persistent poverty. Similarly, non-random attrition that is linked only to *measured* initial wave characteristics would produce no bias as long as weighting or other adjustments were made. However, if the 5% attrition is non-random, heavily concentrated among the persistently poor, and not linkable to measured characteristics, then the surviving 95% of the sample might produce seriously biased inferences about the size of the 'underclass'.

It is difficult to know for what purposes attrition may be 'acceptable' or 'not acceptable'. Using first-wave characteristics to distinguish subsequent response and non-response cases provides some clues, as do comparisons of subsequent waves of data with independent demographic information or financial aggregates. One can also estimate behavioural models using initial wave data and test whether the parameter estimates differ between subsequent respondents and non-respondents (Becketti *et al.*, 1988). The issue of attrition is explored in more detail in the next chapter.

Panel data on change may contain more error than cross-sectional data on level

It is generally accepted (although not necessarily true) that measurement error leads to more dire consequences for analyses of change than of level. A complete treatment of this topic is beyond the scope of this chapter (see, for example, Chapter 6; see Fuller, 1987), but an intuitive explanation of the point can readily be seen in the susceptibility of analyses of gross flows into and out of poverty to measurement errors. A spuriously low-income report in one period will create two spurious poverty transitions – one from non-poverty to poverty and one from poverty to non-poverty. It is often difficult or impossible to identify spurious transitions; such errors of measurement are typically assumed to produce overestimates of the number of transitions and interfere with attempts to estimate models of these transitions. More generally, the 'signal-to-noise ratio' is lower for a change measure than a corresponding level measure: (i) as the correlation across time in the 'true' measure increases and (ii) as the correlation across time in the error decreases.

It is generally assumed that correlations in 'true' conditions are fairly high whereas cross-time correlations in measurement errors are typically assumed to be zero. However, validation studies that compare interview reports of employment information such as earnings and work hours to the 'truth' as revealed by highly accurate company or Social Security records generally find only slightly lower signal-to-noise ratios for change than level measures, although results for earnings per hour were less reassuring (Bound *et al.*, 1990).

This is illustrated in Table 3.3, using data from a validation study of the PSID questionnaire in which survey responses from a sample of workers from a single firm were compared with detailed company payroll records and with data from responses to the Current Population Survey that were matched to Social Security earnings records.

In the classic case of regression-related measurement error in a single independent variable, the ratio of error-to-total variance of that independent variable indicates the downward bias due to measurement error. (Specifically, one minus the ratio of error-to-total variance is the ratio of the expected value of the estimated regressions coefficient to the true regression coefficient.) Ratios of error-to-total variance from the two surveys for ln earnings *levels* were in the range 0.30–0.15 – appreciable but not alarming.[9]

We usually teach that the bias from change measures is likely to be greater than for level measures because it is presumed that the true values of the independent variables are highly correlated across time whereas the error of measurement is not. In both of the validated datasets, the correlation in true earnings was surprisingly modest – 0.45 for a 4-year change in the payroll records of PSID validation study and 0.64 for a 1-year change in Social Security earnings records. On

Table 3.3 Error-to-total variance in measures of earnings level and change

Data source	Earnings variable	Ratio of error to total variance
PSID validation study	ln 1986 annual earnings	0.30
	ln 1982 annual earnings	0.15
	4-year change in ln annual earnings	0.29
Current population survey – Social Security records	ln 1977 annual earnings	0.22
	ln 1976 annual earnings	0.21
	1-year change in ln annual earnings	0.32

Sources: Bound *et al.* (1990) and Bound and Krueger (1991).

the other hand, measurement error correlations were relatively high in the Current Population Survey responses – 0.37 over the 1-year period. This correlation indicates that respondents who over-reported in the first year tend to over-report the next – hardly surprising but almost never assumed to be the case in measurement error models involving change.

All in all, the error-to-total variance of the measures of *change* in ln earnings was not much higher – 0.29 in the PSID validation study and 0.32 in the CPS Social Security match data – than in the measures of earnings level.

There is little doubt that panels have the potential for improving the quality of event history data. Evidence of often severe bias in episodic recall of seemingly salient events such as unemployment or doctor visits is very troubling. This is illustrated in Table 3.4, using data from a validation study of the PSID questionnaire in which survey responses from a sample of workers from a single firm were compared with detailed company payroll records (Mathiowetz, 1985). About two-thirds of the unemployment spells reported in the company records were *not* reported in the interview, although the reporting was considerably more accurate if the interval between the unemployment spell and the interview was shorter.

Problems with episodic recall are well documented in the literature. In recent research, Loftus *et al.* (1992) found that less than 40% of specific visits to doctors in the past 12 months were recalled accurately, although estimations of the total number of such visits (without providing details of their timing) were much less biased and recall of specific medical procedures were actually overestimated. Abelson *et al.* (1992) designed question-wording experiments in an attempt to reduce reporting error in a voter survey but still found that between one-sixth

Table 3.4 Fraction of actual unemployment spells <u>not</u> reported in interview

	Per cent of spells <u>not</u> reported in interview
All unemployment spells recorded in company records	66
Length of time between unemployment spell and interview	
– 8 months or less	51
– 19 months or more	75

Source: calculated from Mathiowetz (1985: Table 1).

and one-half of reported votes were erroneous if the recall period was between 2 weeks and 3 months. Doubling the recall period doubled the false positives in two of his three experiments. Although methods have been developed to improve episodic reporting, some are often too time-consuming to implement in production interviewing (Means and Loftus, 1991), whereas others – in particular feeding back information collected in prior waves – are readily implemented with computer-assisted interviewing methods.

Although panel surveys hold the promise of providing more reliable data on episodic events, they can introduce additional problems as well. As we saw in Chapter 2, in longitudinal data such as the Survey of Income and Program Participation, analysts find implausibly high transition rates (for example from employment to unemployment, or the reverse) at the 'seam' which occurs at the beginning of one survey's reporting period and the end of that of the previous one (Jabine, 1990).

Panel data also place a much greater burden on the data collectors to ensure that cross-wave linkages are correct and that apparent inconsistencies are checked to ensure that errors in coding or other stages of data processing have not produced errors. They also place greater burdens on analysts to make judgements about how to deal with apparent inconsistencies that cannot be resolved by the data collectors and to make sure that extreme change values, however 'truthful', do not dominate one's results.

Participation in the panel may affect behaviour

There is ample evidence that participation in a panel survey affects responses to that survey (for example Bailar, 1989; Corder and Horvitz, 1989; Silberstein and Jacobs, 1989; Waterton and Lievesley, 1989). Whether this is due to changed *behaviour* or merely changes in *responses* to questions about behaviour is a matter of considerable debate (Kalton *et al.*, 1989: section 3).

Evidence of changed behaviour is seen most clearly in panel studies of voter behaviour, in which participation in the survey study appears to have increased respondent interest and participation in elections (Traugott and Katosh, 1979). However, it is more difficult to believe that participation in a survey about demographic and economic matters would affect decisions about work or marriage and, indeed, there is no evidence of these possible effects.

It is also possible (and perhaps even more likely) that participation in a panel survey *improves* the quality of the data. Methodological studies have shown the importance of motivating respondents, especially when they are asked to do tasks such as recalling dates or financial details that require cognitive work. A panel provides the opportunity to show respondents the uses to which the information they provide is being put as well as to inform them in advance of the interview of question areas for which they might want to consult financial records. Sudman and Ferber (1979) conclude that, after the initial wave, general purpose panels are unlikely to be distorted by 'conditioning' effects.

Avoiding the disadvantages: elements of high-quality panel data

Household panel data have the *potential* for providing a number of analytical advantages relative to cross-sectional data. However, they are also susceptible to the various problems listed above. Only panel datasets that avoid these problems can be considered of sufficient quality to warrant analysis. 'Quality' has many dimensions, including the nature of the initial sample, success in following households during the course of the panel, questionnaire design and data processing. Panel data that do not meet high quality standards provide few analytical benefits and are arguably inferior to cross-sectional data drawn from fresh samples. The following are crucial to high-quality panel data.

A high-quality initial sample

The best insurance against the myriad problems of attrition during the course of a panel is a high-quality initial probability sample from the population of interest. Problems in the initial wave with non-random non-response or departures from probability sampling methods are often impossible to remedy in a satisfactory manner. (In contrast, as we shall see in Chapter 5, non-response *subsequent* to the first wave is somewhat easier to handle, for example through weighting for differential non-response or other means, because so much more is known about such non-response households.)

Proper following rules

As pointed out above, a properly designed household panel survey can provide continuous representation of the larger population from which it is drawn. This is true because changes such as births, divorces and children leaving their parents' homes that add individuals and households to the larger population are reflected in a probability sample in the same proportion as in the population at large. To produce this result, the panel study must adhere to the proper rules regarding whom to follow and must make the proper adjustment of weights. Briefly stated, the basic rule is that all members of original sample households (and all individuals born to original members) be followed in the panel survey.

Success in following sample members across time

Crucial to the quality of household panel surveys is the gathering of time series information about a substantial fraction of initially sampled household members. As pointed out above, the definition of 'substantial fraction' is tricky as the analytical problems caused by attrition are much more closely linked to the nature than the amount of such attrition.

That non-response in a panel survey can be kept to a minimum has been demonstrated repeatedly. Cumulative response rates (among sampled units successfully interviewed in the first wave) are between 85% and 92% for (i) the British National Survey of Health and Development after 26 years; (ii) the US National Longitudinal Survey of Youth (NLSY) after 12 years;[10] and (iii) a demographic panel study of women residing in the Detroit area after 15 years (Duncan and Kalton, 1987: 107). Cumulative response rates in the US PSID was about 50% after 24 years owing in large part to its unfortunate (but largely reversible) rule of not attempting interviews with prior wave non-respondents.

Experiences from a number of panel surveys (for example Freedman *et al.*, 1980; Burgess, 1989) suggest a variety of methods by which response rates can be maintained at reasonably high levels. Those successful for the PSID include (i) a substantial field period to allow for tracking of mobile sample members and persuasion of reluctant ones; (ii) respondent payments after the interview; (iii) an interesting and highly readable respondent booklet summarising how information obtained in prior waves is being analysed and used in policy debates; (iv) personalised persuasion letters for reluctant potential respondents; (v) requests, at the end of each interview, for the names and telephone numbers of friends or relatives who would know their location; (vi) a staff person with ready access to this information who helps interviewers 'troubleshoot' difficult cases; (vii) continuity of interviewer–respondent matches, if possible, especially in the early years of the survey; (viii) the offer of either a telephone or personal interview, depending on the respondent's preferences; (ix) close monitoring on the performance of new interviewers in the early weeks of fieldwork; (x) the formation of a small set of 'elite' interviewers, midway through the field period, who assume exclusive responsibility for the remaining fieldwork and for countries in which addresses are not registered; and (xi) periodic mailings (checks, respondent reports, announcement of the upcoming interview), spaced throughout the period between interviews, that produce changes of address for mobile respondents.

Feeding forward data from prior waves during interviewing and checks for cross-wave inconsistencies to minimise errors in the measurement of change

There is a saying that a man with one watch always knows the correct time but the man with two watches never does. By providing multiple observations on the same individuals, panel data offer abundant opportunities for inconsistent responses across waves. Apparent inconsistencies stem from many sources: genuinely inconsistent responses of respondents, interviewer recording errors, coding errors and errors in the information used to link data records across time. Inconsistencies may produce measurement error that imparts large bias at the analysis stage.

Computer-assisted telephone and personal interviewing (CAPI and CATI) are revolutionising the technology associated with the interviewing process. In addition to routing interviewers through complicated skip logic, these systems enable researchers to feed forward information from previous interviewing waves and improve the consistency of data across waves. The feeding forward of information is not without problems, however, because the earlier information may have been erroneous and, if the questionnaire is not carefully designed, the respondent may become defensive, confused or intimidated if confronted with prior information that contradicts his current response. Although these problems should be kept in mind, they are small relative to the large potential benefits of having previous wave data available during the interviewing process.

Minimisation of cross-wave measurement error may also require that resources be devoted to data cleaning when information from several waves is linked. Such consistency checking is best carried out when checkers have access to original interview protocols.

Continuous measurement during the panel period

Panel survey interviewing is always conducted at discrete points, often at intervals of 1 year. While much of the information gathered in panel surveys refers to conditions at the time of the interview (for example employment and marital status of household members, housing conditions), panels also, as explained above, make it possible to collect a great deal of economic and demographic information on a more or less continuous basis. In the case of demographic events involving births, marriage or other household composition changes, for example, this amounts to gathering information on the dates of births, marriages, divorces and other departures of household members. In the case of labour market events, this means gathering information on the timing of job changes and periods of unemployment. For household income, this means gathering information on the timing of the receipt of various sources of household income.

If people's memories were more dependable, all of this continuous information could be gathered in a single retrospective interview. As we have seen, however, episodic recall information is badly reported, especially if the events took place more than a year before the interview. High-quality continuous information can best be provided by panel surveys that gather short-term retrospective information in each panel wave. Even here, as we noted earlier, evidence that reported transitions cluster at the 'seams' between surveys provides grounds for concern.

Conclusion

Panel datasets offer great promise for understanding economic and demographic behaviour and the impact of government upon it. However, the analytical potential of panel surveys can only be realised if the surveys are conducted properly. 'Proper' conduct in this case includes a very good initial probability sample, following rules designed to keep the sample representative across time, continuous measurement of phenomena of interest and considerable resources devoted to checking the consistency of data across time. If it was also possible to achieve consistency in the way in which data were gathered across the various countries conducting panel surveys, then the analytical benefits of multicountry panel data would be large indeed.

Notes

1 An earlier version of this chapter was presented at the International Conference on Social Science Methodology, Trento, Italy, 22–6 June 1992. Charles Brown, Dorothy Duncan, Nancy Mathiowetz and Willard Rodgers provided many helpful suggestions.
2 To see why this is true, suppose one begins with a probability sample from the population. Over time, the population changes as births and

immigration add individuals to the population while events such as divorce and the departure of children from their parents' homes add new households. Except for immigration, all of these events are reflected in a probability sample in the same proportion as in the population at large. (Immigration has to be handled with supplemental samples or some other means.) Thus, births to a probability sample of households constitute a probability sample of births in the population. Similarly, new households formed in a probability sample through divorce or the departure of children from their parents' households constitute a probability sample of newly formed households in the population. If proper rules are observed regarding whom to follow and the adjustment of weights, and if attrition is modest and 'properly behaved', a household panel survey can thus provide a continuous representation of the population. In this sense, there is no trade-off between panels and successive cross-sections; properly designed and executed household panels can provide both kinds of information. Surprisingly, the field costs of panel surveys appear to be lower than the costs of a series of similar cross-sectional surveys. Duncan *et al.* (1984) compared actual field costs of a wave of the PSID and a similar cross-sectional survey and found that the latter were 30–70% higher, depending on the length of the cross-sectional interview. Most of the added costs were due to the additional time needed by interviewers to contact and persuade potential cross-sectional respondents to participate.

3   The data sources are Canada, the Longitudinal Administrative Database; Federal Republic of Germany, the Socio-economic Panel (SOEP), using only its West German sample; Ireland, a two-wave household panel study conducted by the Economic and Social Research Institute; Luxembourg, the Liewen zu Letzebuerg household panel; France, the Lorraine Household Panel; The Netherlands, the Dutch Socio-economic Panel Project (SEP); Sweden, the Household Income Survey (HINK); USA, the Panel Study of Income Dynamics (PSID).

4   The measure of family economic status was total family income, including social assistance and other government and private transfers, but excluding income and payroll taxes. Samples drawn from all countries consisted of families with minor children. Median income-based poverty thresholds were obtained using an equivalence scale that gave respective weights of 1.0, 0.7 and 0.5 to the first adult, subsequent adults and children in the family. The distribution of size-adjusted family income was then estimated for the entire population of each country each year. A family was defined to be in 'median income-based poverty' if its size-adjusted income was below 50% of the median in that year.

5   The Swedish and Irish panels spanned only 2 years and could not be used for this 3-year calculation. Note that the 3-year figures are problematic estimates of 'long-run' poverty because a family poor in, say, the first of the 3 years could have just ended a very long spell of poverty. Rather, the estimates should be taken for what they are – poverty estimates for each country over a 3-year period in the mid-1980s.

6   Assumptions about measurement error are crucial for transition analyses of this kind since it is easy to show that uncorrelated measurement error in reports of a truly unchanging income between time t and $t + 1$ can produce many erroneous transitions. These conclusions are misleading at

best as their assumption of uncorrelated measurement error is contradicted by validation studies of income reporting (see below). Once correlated measurement error is allowed in these models then it is possible to either overstate or understate the number of true transitions. Our requirement that transitions involve income changes of at least 20% provide some insurance against overstating real transitions; our ability to compare transitions based on presumably less erroneous administrative records (from Sweden and Canada) and survey-based reports (from the other countries) is another.

7 Data were gathered from annual interviews conducted from 1968 to 1987, which cover income received in calendar years 1967 through 1986. Income transitions are defined over all possible periods of 5 consecutive years observed in the data. Each sample adult's 'initial' household economic position is defined by the 2-year average household income over the first 2 years of the 5-year interval. A 'final' position is defined by household income averaged over the fourth and fifth years of the interval. Two-year averages are used in order to provide a more reliable picture of change in economic status. A transition occurs if average income in the fourth and fifth years was different enough from average income in the first 2 years to cross over one of the two thresholds that bound our middle-income category. Aside from using 2-year accounting periods, Duncan *et al.* departed from the conventional measurement of household income in two ways – including the US dollar value of food stamps as a component of household income and subtracting estimates of federal income taxes and Social Security payroll taxes from each household's income.

8 German courts typically take several years to adjudicate a divorce, but their more rigorous enforcement of court awards may lead to an improvement in women's economic well-being several years after the initial separation.

9 A closer look at the measurement errors in earnings level and earnings change revealed that each was negatively correlated with observed level and change. This correlation is typically assumed to be zero in classic measurement error models. Such a negative correlation reduces the regression-related bias associated with the measurement error. In the case of earnings level, the range of bias was 8–24%. In the case of earnings change, the range of bias was 21–23%.

10 Because the NLSY surveys ask prior wave non-respondents to provide information (for example employer event histories) missing from previous waves, their effective response rate is even higher than their nominal 91.8% rate.

Part II
Panel data quality

4   Panel attrition

Jeroen W. Winkels and Suzanne Davies Withers

Introduction

Although the advantages of longitudinal over cross-sectional data
sources are amply discussed elsewhere in this book and in the wider
literature, most of these advantages are dependent on the continual
participation of members in the panel (Boruch and Pearson, 1988). As
previous chapters have noted, high levels of attrition can turn elegant
research designs into a nightmare of too few subjects suitable for
analysis. High levels of attrition over time are generally found within
most panel surveys. Lillard (1989: 449), for example, indicates that
only 60% of the original sample of the Panel Study of Income Dynamics
(PSID) were present after fourteen waves (1968–81). Wagner *et al.* (1991:
39) report a similar proportion (61%) remaining in the German
Socioeconomic Panel (SOEP) after seven waves (1984–90). In the Dutch
Socioeconomic Panel (SEP), 42% of the original sample persons are
present after seventeen waves within the period 1984–94.

Any analysis using panel surveys must contend with the influences
of attrition on sample representation over time. Attrition affects the
results of longitudinal analysis by reducing the sample size, thereby
diminishing the efficiency of estimates. More importantly, attrition may
be of a selective nature and thereby increase the bias of certain
estimates. Attrition may be biased with respect to the characteristics
of non-response individuals or with respect to the recent behaviour of
individuals. For example, household composition changes are the
outcome of numerous demographic shifts and processes. Panel data
potentially are rich sources of information about the causes and
conditions which stimulate such changes. Consequently, knowledge of
the sequence of transitions will lend insight into the demographic
processes in evidence (Richards *et al.*, 1987). An assessment of both
characteristic and behavioural selectivity in attrition rates is an
important preliminary stage for longitudinal studies of household
dynamics.

The aim of this chapter, therefore, is to provide an example of the analysis of attrition with respect to both characteristic and behavioural selectivity. Specifically, how is the description of household composition change using panel data affected by panel attrition? There are two reasons for selecting household composition change as a substantive area for an analysis of non-response bias. Contending with household transitions over time is problematic within all longitudinal surveys. In addition, many substantive research issues use the household as the basic unit of analysis. For example, residential mobility, household income dynamics and household expenditures are areas of panel research which commonly use households as the unit of analysis, as we shall see in Part III. Therefore, any bias in attrition which may change the sample of households over time needs to be investigated. In general, the quality of both descriptive and explanatory models using panel data will be substantially improved when tests of the effects of attrition on the various variables is included in the analysis.

Attrition – the panel researcher's nightmare?

Surveys experience different types of missing data. To recapitulate on points made in previous chapters, one important type of missing data is unit non-response, the focus of this chapter. The other is item non-response, which occurs because people are not able or not willing to answer certain questions. Unit non-response in panel surveys can be further divided into two types: temporary non-response, which means that persons are re-entering the panel sometime after a non-response period, and permanent non-response, when persons never re-enter. Temporary non-response may occur when the interviewers found no one at home on a number of occasions or may occur because of personal circumstances such as illness. Unit non-response can also be subdivided to distinguish between a situation whereby all persons from a household do not respond and one in which one or more persons do not respond while others of the same household do. With respect to attrition, the former situation is only important for analyses at the level of households. However, both cases are linked to the attrition of persons. When other persons in panel households keep participating, there is always a chance that persons who refused to participate for a couple of waves change their minds and re-enter the panel.

The fundamental issue with respect to attrition is selectivity. If the characteristics of those members who drop out of the panel differ systematically from the characteristics of those who are retained then attrition is selective and leads to a bias in estimates due to the resultant change in the sample composition over time. Studies of the PSID have indicated that individual characteristics such as race, income, age, unemployment and mobility are each associated with exit from the panel. Specifically, non-Whites, lower income groups, the elderly, the unemployed and movers leave the panel at higher rates, according to Lillard (1989).

Because of the frequent exit and entry of both original and new panel members, it is difficult to speak of a single measurement of attrition *per se*. In principle, numerous distinctions can be made. First, attrition can be divided into two categories: permanent and temporary. Attrition also can be measured with respect to the original sample members from the first wave. Or, attrition can be measured from wave to wave. Further, attrition rates can refer to all persons that were respondents in a select base time period other than the original date of the survey. Moreover, attrition rates are complicated by the fact that both natural increase and sample renewal differ from wave to wave. This further complicates the measurement of an attrition rate since attrition is likely to be linked to the length of participation. Population dynamics are also of concern for attrition rates. Rates of death and emigration should be estimated as part of attrition which stems from population changes. These sample changes reflect real changes in the population which influence the dynamics of the sample over time.

If attrition is generally interpreted to mean non-response then measurement rates can also depend on the model selected for analysis. For example, event history analyses consider the duration of distinct spells and require information on the initial state at the beginning of the spell and for the interval of time before a change in state. If temporary attrition occurs, leading to non-response over part of the interval, then spells become right censored. The variety of methods for deriving attrition rates indicates the complexity of defining a longitudinal sample due to sample dynamics over time. Several weighting procedures are used to correct some of the missing data caused by unit non-response (see Chapter 5; see Bailar *et al.*, 1978; Lepkowski, 1989). Weighting procedures that satisfy both cross-sectional and longitudinal aims are especially appropriate (van der Pol, 1993).

Attrition – does it make a difference?

Overview of analysis and data

Our analysis of attrition is conducted in two stages. The first stage (in this section) assesses the magnitude of attrition over time. Selectivity in non-response is tested for a number of individual characteristics using discriminant analyses. The models are designed to test whether certain individual attributes are closely correlated with panel non-response over time. This approach both serves as a general description of attrition rates and provides an overview of the influence of attrition on sample dynamics for the period of the panel. The second stage of the analyses (in the next section) specifically assesses the variability in rates of household composition change over the period of the panel. Household composition change is an event which is commonly related to panel attrition because of its frequent association with residential mobility on the part of some, if not all, of the members of a household. Since interviewing procedures require continuous contact with panel members, it stands to reason that non-response, at least on a temporary basis, may be related to this common event. Specifically, this part of our analysis aims to determine whether household transition behaviour and sample attrition are related to an extent which generates a bias in household types and transition rates over time.

Data are used from the SEP, a survey carried out by Statistics Netherlands (NCBS). From 1984 to 1990, the SEP consisted of two waves a year. Since 1990, the two questionnaires have been combined and are conducted annually in April. The SEP is a sample of private households. Because every member of a household who is over the age of 15 years participates by completing a questionnaire, the sample may also be said to be an individual sample in which every person who is not living in an institution has the same chance of being selected. All persons who have participated in one or more waves are to be included in the next wave with the exception of those who 'leave the population' (by death, emigration, entering an institution) or who refuse to participate ever again. If individuals have left the household to which they belonged at the time of the previous wave and have formed their own households or have joined another, all members of the new households are canvassed, provided they are over age 15. In this way, persons are added to the panel by natural increase.

A number of fieldwork procedures are designed to decrease attrition from the panel. NCBS always attempts to send the same interviewer to the same persons in each wave. This is one of the primary mechanisms for keeping attrition low and for tracing as many newly established households as possible. Two fieldwork stages, a main interview stage and a second stage over the next few months, also optimise the participation of individuals over time by enabling interviewers to track newly established households. Often, this second stage captures many individuals who have not only changed residence but also have experienced changes with respect to income, labour and living conditions. In addition, households which participate receive a substantial gift at the end of each wave.

Magnitude of attrition

In this section, we first provide figures on the magnitude of permanent and temporary attrition. Temporary attrition refers to the situation when a household, or an individual, is present in one wave, cannot be found in the subsequent wave and then re-enters the panel in a subsequent wave. The attrition rates are listed in Table 4.1; temporary attrition refers to individuals who return after a period of absence no longer than two waves. Our analysis indicated that non-response for more than two waves is predominantly associated with permanent attrition.

Table 4.1 indicates that the rate of attrition reduces over the panel period, with the exception of waves 13, 16 and especially 14, which have increased rates of attrition. The high attrition rate in wave 14 is

Table 4.1 Temporary and permanent attrition

		No. of persons	Temporary attrition (%)	Permanent attrition (%)	Total (%)
Wave 1	(Apr 1984)	11,809	–	–	–
Wave 2	(Oct 1984)	11,366	1.6	8.6	10.2[a]
Wave 3	(Apr 1985)	9,772	1.6	8.6	10.2[a]
Wave 4	(Oct 1985)	11,838	2.6	6.4	9.0
Wave 5	(Apr 1986)	13,494	3.1	6.6	9.7
Wave 6	(Oct 1986)	14,042	2.2	5.4	7.6
Wave 7	(Apr 1987)	13,577	1.8	5.0	6.8
Wave 8	(Oct 1987)	13,875	1.9	4.0	5.9
Wave 9	(Apr 1988)	13,498	2.2	3.8	6.0
Wave 10	(Oct 1988)	13,772	1.3	3.6	4.9
Wave 11	(Apr 1989)	13,526	1.0	3.6	4.6
Wave 12	(Oct 1989)	13,716	0.4	3.7	4.1
Wave 13	(Apr 1990)	13,404	0.2	4.8	5.1
Wave 14	(Apr 1991)	12,278	0.6	13.1	13.7
Wave 15	(Apr 1992)	13,426	–	–	8.9
Wave 16	(Apr 1993)	13,083	–	–	9.8
Wave 17	(Apr 1994)	13,078	–	–	7.1

Source: NCBS, Socio-economic Panel Survey.

Note
a Mean figures are given, because the second stage of the fieldwork of the first wave was closely linked to the first stage of the second wave.

undoubtedly the result of three factors associated with this wave. First, the period between the waves is a full year instead of 6 months. The influence of a change in fieldwork procedure is thus evident in these response rates. Lillard (1989) has remarked that response rates that are based on the proportion of requested respondents per survey may not be accurate for surveys that change their fieldwork procedures. This holds true for the SEP response rates in 1991.

Second, and of greater influence, is the fact that the fourteenth wave of the SEP was the first to be conducted using computer-assisted personal interviewing (CAPI). Information was gathered by interviewers, entered into hand-held computers during the interview procedure and then downloaded by telephone lines to the NCBS databanks. This has led to some technical problems with tracing both persons and households and, inevitably, to higher numbers of non-respondents. Third, in previous waves, strong efforts were made to send the same interviewer to households in the sample. This procedure was not followed as strictly in the fourteenth wave and appears to have further influenced response rates. This effect was also found in the German SOEP by Rendtell (1990: 292). Because of these special circumstances, for the subsequent analysis of the selectivity of attrition, we only use the waves which have been conducted with the more traditional paper and pencil interview (PAPI).

To some extent, Table 4.1 also illustrates how an important indicator of the quality of a panel dataset is related to organisational change. In this specific case, the change in wave periodicity, the introduction of technological innovations and the relaxation of fieldwork procedures were each related to organisational change. A long-running panel always faces the serious risk that methodological, technological and financial decisions (that almost inevitably occur with time) have negative consequences for the quality of the data.

Tests for selectivity

To analyse the selectivity of attrition, we use numerous indicators in our models, such as income, socioeconomic status, education, type of dwelling, the size of the household, age and position in the household. Income is measured in a number of ways. First, an objective measure is used to test the association of income level and non-response. In addition, income satisfaction is used to allow for the inclusion of a more subjective income measure. The highest and lowest levels of income are also included in the analysis to test for the association with extreme cases. Education was also tested in a way which considers whether the extremely lowly or extremely highly educated individuals are more likely to drop out of the panel.

For the analysis of the selectivity of attrition, we select the fourth wave as the base year and select only panel individuals over the age of 15 years in this time period. Attrition is measured by questionnaire response since the analysis requires sociodemographic information derived from the survey. The main reason for selecting the fourth wave as the base year is that a large number of households are required for the analysis of the dynamic relationships between attrition and household composition to be robust.

Preliminary bivariate analysis of socioeconomic and demographic attributes indicated that the difference between subjects within the temporary attrition group and the permanent attrition group were negligible, particularly in comparison with the differences between the group of non-response individuals and response individuals. In general, the rather small differences with respect to household position, income, socioeconomic status, sex and education between the permanent and the temporary attrition groups did not support the use of this distinction within the analyses of selectivity characteristics in attrition in this specific case.

We chose a discriminant analysis procedure because it both provides an explanation of attrition in past waves and permits us to investigate the possibilities of predicting attrition in future waves. The discriminant analysis procedure has an option to classify the sample from a selected wave with respect to response or non-response in a future wave for which scores are unknown. If a high proportion of the variance between these categories is associated with the independent variables then predictions of future likelihoods of non-response are possible. However, the results of the analyses indicated that the proportions of explained variance were sufficiently low to prevent reasonable predictions from being estimated.

To test for selectivity in attrition, two moments in time are compared within a single discriminant analysis. Because, potentially, the results are dependent on the interval of time over which non-response can occur, all analyses were repeated for four different periods of time: (i) wave 4 with wave 5 measuring attrition within 6 months; (ii) wave 4 with wave 6 measuring attrition within 12 months; (iii) wave 4 with wave 10 measuring attrition within 36 months; (iv) wave 4 with wave 13 measuring attrition within 54 months.

The dependent variable in the discriminant analyses is dichotomous with a value of 1 if an individual participated in both of the waves is being compared and with a value of 2 if the individual had not responded within the last wave. The background variables are all measured in the base year. Initially, it became clear that the distinction between renters and owners, some of the financial characteristics and evaluations of the financial situation of households had *ceteris paribus* no association with attrition. Therefore, these variables were dropped from the subsequent analyses which are discussed in detail below.

For all the discriminant analyses, we used a stepwise introduction of relevant variables. Each of the four analyses show some significant associations between attrition and the socioeconomic variables in the base year. Yet, in most cases, the strength of the associations is not sufficiently strong to be relevant. The proportions of explained variance of our dependent variable are quite low, ranging from 0% to 3%. In our view, the findings indicate that the relationships among income, education and socioeconomic status and attrition are very weak. In some waves, attrition is somewhat higher in the extreme categories, such as in the lowest and highest income deciles. In other wave comparisons, it is not. If all associations, whatever their strength, pointed in the same direction within each of the four analyses, then the effects of the attributes should be explored in detail because the total cumulative effect across the entire panel period would become pronounced. The findings indicate that this is not the case: the cumulative effects are small.

However, with respect to household composition, certain associations with attrition were found. These findings suggest that although attrition is not selective with respect to the characteristics of individuals it may be related to specific behavioural aspects. Specifically, three of the four models resulted in a sizeable coefficient for the variable which indicates individuals who live with their parents. Individuals who live with their parents represent the largest single attrition group after the fourth wave of the panel. Also, individuals in the oldest age group, who are primarily pensioners, show greater levels of attrition as the period of observation increases. In contrast, individuals in the age group 35–44 years show lower levels of attrition. While attrition in the higher age groups is likely to be associated with population dynamics (death and entrance into institutional residences), attrition among young individuals, particularly of those living with their parents, is likely to be associated with fieldwork procedures. The last reflect the difficulties which persist when individuals are tracked over time using a household register of addresses. The dynamic nature of households is problematic for surveys which follow individual members of households over time. These associations need to be investigated in greater depth.

In the analyses of the four interwave comparisons of attrition rates, the rates varied from 10% to 30%, depending on the length of the observation period. As this figure is fairly high compared with figures from the PSID and the SOEP, it indicates that a number of individuals cannot be used for longitudinal analysis.

The nature of attrition is not especially selective. This contrasts with findings from the USA, based on the PSID. In the Dutch case, income, socioeconomic status, education and the type of dwelling are not (or are only very weakly) associated with continued participation or non-response. Some of the demographic variables indicate a relationship with exit from the panel. However, the position in the household and the age of individuals never explained more than 3% of the difference between the response and non-response groups. The difference in the findings may reflect basic differences between the American and Dutch societies. Not only is the White/non-White racial distinction different within the Dutch context, but the distributions of income and education are less extreme in The Netherlands than they are in the USA. In sum, the lack of a sizeable specific characteristic associated with attrition may well in part reflect the comparative lack of diversity within The Netherlands relative to the USA.

Nonetheless, these results suggest that although attrition may not be biased with respect to the characteristics of non-response individuals it may well be linked to their recent behaviour. The findings further suggest that any use of a panel for a longitudinal analysis of demographic processes requires an exploration of the association between attrition and household composition change.

Attrition – is it associated with behaviour?

Overview and classification of persons into households

The purpose of this section is to establish whether the description of household composition change is affected by panel attrition. Specifically, this section tests whether individuals become non-respondents at random or whether there is a correlation between the likelihood of becoming a non-respondent and the likelihood of experiencing a particular type of household transition. The analysis is conducted in three stages. First, the magnitude and sequence of household transitions are examined for a longitudinal sample over the panel period. This procedure illustrates the differential non-response by household type. Therefore, the second stage of the analysis tests the association between temporary attrition and household transitions. This procedure provides an indication of whether attrition is related to the behavioural process itself. Finally, two waves are compared in more detail to determine further the extent of bias caused by differential rates of non-response. Before presenting our results, however, we need to make some remarks about the problem of classification of persons into households with respect to the study of dynamics using panel data.

Households are relatively straightforward units of analysis when we have cross-sectional data but are more problematic in the case of longitudinal data. At a single moment in time, the concept of a 'family' or 'household' poses relatively few analytical problems. A rather unambiguous set of household types or families can be defined on the basis of rules about shared living arrangements, relatives, household size, composition, marital status and so forth. Placing a static definition of a household or family into a dynamic context is problematic, however, and has the potential to minimise the measures of change.

Within the literature, several attempts have been made to develop a longitudinal household definition. While a number of cross-sectional/ dynamic hybrids have been posed (McMillen and Herriot, 1985), each is based on a set of continuity rules based on the substantive area of concern. Many of the alternatives create as many problems as they solve. Duncan and Hill (1985) suggest that the most fortuitous strategy for longitudinal studies is to use the individual as the unit of analysis and the household as the unit of measurement. We have adopted this attribute-based approach to measuring household composition over time by constructing a variable which depicts the household development from an individual perspective. In every wave, each individual's household circumstances are analysed with respect to the individual's relationship to the other members of the household. Hence, this key variable is a time-varying characterisation of the cohabitation relationship from the perspective of the individual member of the household. The six categories used in this analysis are (i) person is living in multiperson household as a child; (ii) person is living alone; (iii) person is living with unmarried partner and without children; (iv) person is living with married partner and without children; (v) person is living with partner (married or not) and children; and (vi) person is living with children but without a partner.

Longitudinal analysis to test for selectivity

The analyses in the previous section compared two moments in time. However, panel surveys are particularly advantageous for behavioural research because they follow individuals over time. Non-response, whether permanent or temporary, can have far-reaching implications for longitudinal analyses of behavioural processes. Permanent non-response removes an individual from the panel sample, thereby truncating the period of observation. The bias of permanent attrition for longitudinal analysis depends on the substantive area of research. Of prime importance is the relationship between the behaviour under study and the factors related to attrition. If attrition is directly, or indirectly, related to the process under study, transition rates will be biased and underestimated. Temporary attrition is also problematic for longitudinal research because it creates a period of time for which no observations are available. If the event in question occurs during the non-response interval, there will be a bias in transition rates and a potential bias in the association of explanatory factors with the event under study. Even if the event does not occur, the status of individuals during the non-response period is unknown. For both permanent and temporary attrition, it must be determined whether they are missing at random or whether there is a systematic aspect to non-response.

To arrive at an estimate of household transition rates, and the types of household composition changes over the panel period, a longitudinal sample of individuals aged 16 years and over was traced from the fourth wave through to wave 13. In this analysis, permanent and temporary attrition were treated in a similar manner: once individuals become non-respondents, they are removed from the sample. The rationale for this treatment is based on issues of censoring and being at risk. Six risk sets were established based on the six household types in the first period of observation for this longitudinal sample (wave 4). Individuals were followed over the period of the panel. Once a household type transition occurs, the individual is no longer in the original risk group. If at any time the individual becomes a non-respondent, the individual is right censored. In other words, an event (non-response) other than the event of interest (a household type change) has removed them from being at risk by removing them from observation.

Table 4.2 provides a matrix of origin household types by destination household types over the panel period. It also lists the proportion of individuals who experience no change over the duration of the panel, as well as the level of attrition for each origin household type. Proportions, both including and excluding attrition, are listed in Table 4.2.

Table 4.2 illustrates the variability in attrition rates by household type. Of individuals who live with their parents, 50% drop out of the panel before a change in household type is observed. In contrast, 24% of these individuals survive to the end of the panel period without experiencing a change in living arrangements. About the same

Table 4.2 Household composition transitions (treating all attrition as permanent)

Original household composition wave 4 (1985)	Destination household composition wave 13 (1990)						No change	Attrition	Total	No. of obs.
	Living with parents	Living alone	Living with partner	Living with married partner	Living with partner and children	Living with children				
Proportions										
Living with parents	–	0.1349	0.0717	0.0470	0.0023	0.0008	0.2421	0.5012	0.1457	1297
Living alone	0.0111	–	0.0765	0.0101	0.0121	0.0081	0.4391	0.4431	0.1116	993
Living with partner	0.0055	0.0773	–	0.3536	0.0608	0.0028	0.2099	0.2901	0.0407	362
Living with married partner	0.0005	0.0422	0.0019	–	0.1410	0.0005	0.4486	0.3653	0.2319	2064
Living with partner and children	0.0000	0.0088	0.0020	0.1077	–	0.0172	0.5420	0.3223	0.4444	3956
Living with children (no partner)	0.0000	0.2358	0.0044	0.0000	0.1092	–	0.3144	0.3362	0.0257	229
Total	0.0016	0.0426	0.0204	0.0702	0.0397	0.0089	0.4458	0.3709	1.0000	8901
Number of observations	14	379	182	625	353	79	3968	3301		8901
Proportions of transitions										
Living with parents	–	0.5255	0.2793	0.1832	0.0090	0.0030				
Living alone	0.0940	–	0.6496	0.0855	0.1026	0.0684				
Living with partner	0.0110	0.1547	–	0.7072	0.1215	0.0055				
Living with married partner	0.0026	0.2266	0.0104	–	0.7578	0.0026				
Living with partner and children	0.0000	0.0652	0.0149	0.7933	–	0.1266				
Living with children (no partner)	0.0000	0.6750	0.0125	0.0000	0.3125	–				
Total	0.0086	0.2322	0.1115	0.3830	0.2163	0.0484				

Source: NCBS, Socio-economic Panel Survey.

proportion experience a change in household type, primarily by making the transition to living alone. The transition figures suggest that individuals living with parents are equally as likely to experience a household transition as not. However, these figures must be interpreted with caution since the behaviour of half of these individuals is not observed. Because individuals living with their parents are most likely to make the transition to living alone, establishing residential independence in adulthood, there is little doubt that the non-response of this group is closely associated with the behaviour under study, yielding biased transition rates. It is evident that longitudinal analysis with these data is inappropriate for studies of the move to adulthood as this behaviour is associated with attrition.

The situation is somewhat different when tracing individuals who live alone. An equal number of individuals survive to the end of the panel without a change in living arrangements as drop out as a result of non-response. Transition rates are therefore quite low for this group. Of those individuals who experience a change, 65% start living with an unmarried partner. Individuals living with a partner have the lowest attrition rates and the highest transition rates of all the household types. Only 29% drop out over time, and only 20% experience no change in living arrangements over the panel period. This is the only household type for which the majority of members experience a transition. Of those making a change, the vast majority (70%) change to living with a married partner, 15% change to living alone and roughly 12% make the transition to living with their partner and children. Of all the demographic shifts, these are the most reliable because of the relatively low levels of attrition over time.

One-third of individuals living with a partner and children drop out of the survey and 54% survive to the end of the panel period without changing their living arrangements. Of the 20% that make a transition, four-fifths change to living with a married partner. Although 12% become single parents living with children, only 6.5% start to live alone. This strongly suggests that divorce and/or separation leads to non-response on the part of the panel member who leaves the partner and children. Tracing these individuals as they move out of the household residence has the same problem as tracing adult children as they move out of the parental home. Household composition changes which involve a dissolution of the members of the household of origin imply residential mobility.

The sequence of household transitions reflects the life cycle of household evolution over the stages of family development. However, two factors must be addressed when considering the reliability of these rates of household composition change. First, differential non-response rates occur by household type. Second, household composition changes which generally are less likely to be related to residential mobility have the lowest levels of attrition. Changes which are generally related to residential mobility appear to be closely related to attrition. For example, the move to independent living has the highest attrition level. More partners with children are retained after a separation. Frequently, upon separation, one partner moves out while the other remains in the same residence with the children. Conversely, the transition to living with a married partner from living with a partner is frequently more of a legal transition than a change in living arrangements. Not surprisingly, this group has the lowest levels of attrition. Also, the fact that attrition rates are higher for married partners than unmarried partners is likely to be an artefact of the timing of residential mobility. Couples tend to move in anticipation of the changing housing needs associated with having children. Therefore, the results suggest that certain demographic transitions are associated with non-response over the duration of the panel when they are related to residential mobility.

Attrition and household transitions

One manner of testing whether temporary attrition is related to a change in household type is to compare the living arrangements of individuals before and after the interval of non-response. Temporary attrition usually occurs for only one wave. Therefore, for all individuals who did not respond for only one wave of the panel, we compared their household types immediately before and after the wave of non-response.

A total of 1,088 individuals dropped out of the panel for a period of only one wave. Of those that did have a household change, the most likely group were individuals who lived with their parents. After returning from one wave of non-response, many have started to live on their own. For the entire panel period, on average, 37% of temporary non-response individuals living alone returned having experienced a change in household type. The next highest group on average were individuals living with a partner to whom they were not married, with 21% having a change in household type. Of the married partners and the married partners with children, only 15% returned as a different type of household. Figures for individuals living alone and single parents were both below 10%. These results suggest that an analysis of household transitions which does not include temporary attrition will provide underestimates. It also confirms that temporary attrition is primarily a function of household composition changes which are associated with mobility.

Although there is little doubt that both permanent and temporary attrition are related to household type changes, the effect of this behavioural non-response on estimates differs across the transition types. To determine the extent of this bias, measures of household composition changes and attrition were calculated for an interwave period of 5 years (1985–90).

Table 4.3 compares wave 4 with wave 13. This table analyses the same period of time as Table 4.2, but the treatment of attrition differs. While Table 4.2 was a longitudinal sample of households over time treating all attrition as permanent, Table 4.3 allows for re-entry into the panel. The increased interval of time again changes the rates of household stability and attrition because of the increased period of risk. By the thirteenth wave, 51% of the sample had experienced no change in household type, 31% had dropped out and almost 18% had a change in household type. The comparison of two waves over a period of almost 5 years does not register changes within the interval and therefore will provide underestimates of transition rates. The longitudinal sample indicates 44% had no change in household type, 37% dropped out and 18% had a change in household type. Since the proportion experiencing a change is so similar, and yet the cross-sectional comparison underestimates change because changes over the interval are not measured, it suggests that panel attrition is closely associated with household changes.

A comparison of the types of changes, calculated from the longitudinal sample and the sample of survivors to wave 13, further indicates that the loss of individuals is closely associated with mobility. The differences in the figures are not great. The household type sequences associated with the development of families over the life course is still in evidence. An interesting difference is the number of transitions from living with a partner initially to living with a married partner and children by wave 13. The transition to living with a married partner occurs within the interval.

Conclusion

The longitudinal analysis of household type changes indicates behavioural non-response. However, it is not household changes *per se* which are associated with non-response but the residential mobility associated with these changes. In other words, there is not a great deal of variability in non-response by household type provided these

Table 4.3 Household composition transitions (allowing for re-entry)

Original household composition wave 4 (1985)	Destination household composition wave 13 (1990)						No change	Attrition	Total	No. of obs.
	Living with parents	Living alone	Living with partner	Living with married partner	Living with partner and children	Living with children				
Proportions										
Living with parents	–	0.1265	0.0733	0.0671	0.0239	0.0031	0.2901	0.4159	0.1459	1296
Living alone	0.0050	–	0.0433	0.0192	0.0292	0.0030	0.5494	0.3508	0.1117	992
Living with partner	0.0000	0.0559	–	0.1536	0.2346	0.0000	0.2430	0.3128	0.0403	358
Living with married partner	0.0000	0.0393	0.0034	–	0.1320	0.0024	0.5117	0.3112	0.2320	2060
Living with partner and children	0.0000	0.0091	0.0015	0.0986	–	0.0150	0.6125	0.2633	0.4443	3946
Living with children (no partner)	0.0000	0.2052	0.0087	0.0000	0.0961	–	0.3930	0.2969	0.0258	229
Total	0.0006	0.0392	0.0172	0.0619	0.0493	0.0080	0.5145	0.3093	1.0000	8881
Number of observations	5	348	153	550	438	71	4569	2747		8881
Proportions of transitions										
Living with parents	–	0.4304	0.2493	0.2283	0.0814	0.0105				
Living alone	0.0505	–	0.4343	0.1919	0.2929	0.0303				
Living with partner	0.0000	0.1258	–	0.3459	0.5283	0.0000				
Living with married partner	0.0000	0.2219	0.0192	–	0.7452	0.0137				
Living with partner and children	0.0000	0.0735	0.0122	0.7939	–	0.1204				
Living with children (no partner)	0.0000	0.6620	0.0282	0.0000	0.3099	–				
Total	0.0032	0.2224	0.0978	0.3514	0.2799	0.0454				

Source: NCBS, Socio-economic Panel Survey.

households remain stable. There is a selectivity to non-response for certain types of household transitions. Changes associated with the dissolution of the original sample households frequently lead to non-response on the part of the members who leave the original home. Moves out of the parental home and from living with a married partner and children were associated with non-response. Residential mobility is also the most likely reason for the differential non-response of married partners and cohabiting partners. Married partners often move in anticipation of having children, and this would imply that the number of transitions to having children is underestimated for married partners who remain in the sample.

In sum, it appears that some conditioning in the panel will occur over time in the direction of lower household transition rates as a result of an association between non-response and household composition changes. However, the magnitude of this conditioning only becomes serious for a longitudinal analysis of the behaviours which are associated with residential mobility. To some extent, the use of modelling techniques which incorporate censored observations, such as event history analysis, can minimise this impact. However, it is evident that panel conditioning over time is biased towards residentially stable households, which has implications for all substantive issues of a related nature (such as labour and income mobility).

5 Weighting in household panel surveys[1]

Graham Kalton and Michael Brick

Introduction

This chapter discusses an issue referred to in all the previous chapters – the development of weights to be used in the analysis of a household panel survey. In general, weights are used in survey analysis to compensate for unequal selection probabilities and to attempt to compensate for certain types of missing data. The basic approach for developing weights for a panel survey is essentially the same as that for a cross-sectional survey but there are a number of additional complexities to address.

The development of survey weights is often performed in three stages. The first stage is the *computation of base weights* which compensate for the unequal selection probabilities that may have occurred because certain elements have been deliberately oversampled or because of imperfections in the sampling frame. (We use the term 'element' to refer to the unit of analysis, which in household panel surveys is usually an individual but may also be a household.)

The second stage of weight development is usually termed a *non-response adjustment*. This adjustment attempts to compensate for total non-response, when no survey data are collected for a sampled element. Total non-response occurs when a sampled element refuses to co-operate in the survey, when the element cannot be contacted, or for a variety of other reasons.

As a third stage, the non-response-adjusted weights may be further adjusted so that the weighted sample distributions for certain variables conform to known population distributions for those variables. This third stage is often termed *post-stratification* or *population weighting*. It serves to compensate for non-coverage, which occurs when an element in the population of inference for the survey is missing from the survey's sampling frame and consequently has no chance of selection for the sample. It also serves to compensate for total non-response and to improve the precision of the survey estimates.

The three stages of weight development described above are widely applied in all types of surveys, although sometimes only the first two stages are used. The development of the weights at each stage can become complex in some surveys, and may involve more than one component. General discussions of weights and weight development are provided by Oh and Scheuren (1983), Kish (1992), Kalton (1983), Kalton and Kasprzyk (1986), Elliot (1991), Little (1986) and Chapman *et al.* (1986).

An important feature of weighting is to attempt to compensate for missing data arising from total non-response and non-coverage. As we have seen previously, another type of missing data is item non-response, which occurs when a sampled element participates in the survey but fails to provide acceptable responses to one or more of the survey items. Item non-response is often treated by imputation, i.e. by assigning values for the missing responses. A variety of imputation methods have been developed for assigning values for missing responses in a manner that takes account of responses given to other items in the survey, including the widely used hot deck and regression-based methods (see, for example, Sande, 1982; Kalton, 1983; Kalton and Kasprzyk, 1986; Little, 1988).

Item non-responses generally occur as a small number of missing responses among a large number of valid responses for a sampled element, whereas with total non-response all the element's responses are missing. In between these two types of non-response lies what may be termed partial non-response, when a sampled element participates in the survey but fails to provide responses to a substantial proportion of the survey items. Partial non-response can, for example, occur in a telephone survey when a respondent breaks off the interview in the middle, or when the data collection consists of two or more phases (for example, a screening interview and a follow-up interview) and the sampled element fails to provide data for all the phases. As discussed later, partial non-response occurs in panel surveys when a sampled panel member provides data for some but not all waves of data collection for which the member is eligible. There are two alternative ways of handling partial non-response in survey analysis. One is to treat the situation as one of numerous item non-responses, with imputation being used to assign values for the missing responses. The other is to drop the partial non-respondents from the analysis, using weighting adjustments in compensation. The choice between these two alternatives for wave non-response is discussed in the next section (see p. 98 ff.).

In developing weights for a panel survey, four main complexities arise beyond those encountered with a cross-sectional survey. One concerns the variety of populations of inference that are appropriate for different types of analyses of panel survey data. These data can be analysed cross-sectionally to provide estimates for the populations at the time of each wave and longitudinally over two or more waves to provide estimates for the appropriate longitudinal populations. A second complexity concerns wave non-response and how it should be handled. The following section discusses populations of inference and the treatment of wave non-response.

A third complexity arises when weighting adjustments are used to compensate for wave non-response, as is often done in practice. In this case, a great deal of information is available for the wave non-respondents from their responses on other waves. The issue of how to make best use of this information in making the weighting adjustments is discussed in the section beginning on p. 103.

In household panel surveys, a fourth complexity concerns how persons living with panel sample members, but who are not themselves panel sample members, are to be treated in the survey analysis. Many household panel surveys collect the survey data for these non-panel members, or cohabitants, while they are living with panel members in order to obtain family- or household-level data for the panel members. Given this practice, it is natural to seek ways to include cohabitants in survey analyses in order to improve the precision of the survey estimates. A weighting scheme for incorporating cohabitants in cross-sectional analyses of a household panel survey is outlined in the section beginning on p. 109. Finally, the chapter presents some concluding remarks.

Wave non-response

Non-response occurring at the initial wave of a panel survey is similar to that in a cross-sectional survey. Often, no attempts are made to contact initial wave non-respondents at subsequent waves of a panel. They thus become total non-respondents for the panel, providing no data for any wave.

Non-response also occurs at each of the subsequent waves of the panel. In addition to refusals and non-contacts, another cause of later wave non-response is a failure to trace sampled persons who have moved. A question arises as to how non-respondents at one wave should be treated in the fieldwork for the following waves. Fieldwork procedures may differ by type of non-response and also differ across surveys. For example, persons who cannot be traced and persons giving adamant refusals at one wave may not be reissued for data collection at subsequent waves, whereas non-contacts may be reissued. Some panels do not attempt to contact any wave non-respondents at subsequent waves, some attempt to contact some types of wave non-respondents for one more wave but drop all cases that have failed to provide data for two successive waves, and some use other forms of wave non-response following rules.

In discussing wave non-response, a careful distinction needs to be made between wave non-respondents and elements leaving the survey universe. Panel members who die or who leave the survey population (emigrate or, in the case of household surveys, enter an institution) are not wave non-respondents and should not be treated as such. In particular, procedures used to compensate for wave non-response should treat leavers from the survey universe as respondents. One complication that arises is that it is sometimes not possible to distinguish between leavers and unlocated non-respondents. Another is that some leavers (for instance, some persons entering institutions) re-enter the survey universe later and hence should return to the panel at that time.

To facilitate the discussion of methods for handling wave non-response, consider the example of a panel with four waves of data collected on an annual basis. In general, such a panel gives rise to the sixteen patterns of response (X) and non-response (O) listed in Table 5.1. Here, X denotes either a response at a given wave or that the sampled individual was not in the survey universe at that wave and O denotes non-response either because a sampled individual assigned for interview did not provide the survey data or because the individual was not assigned for interview at that wave. The response patterns are classified into four groups: total respondents, who provide data on every wave; attrition non-respondents, who drop out of the panel at some wave after the first and remain out of the panel for all subsequent waves; non-attrition non-respondents, who return to the panel after missing one or more waves; and total non-respondents, who provide data for none of the waves.

In practice, depending on the rules adopted for following wave non-respondents at later waves, some of the non-attrition response patterns will not occur. In particular, response patterns 9–15 will not occur if first-wave non-respondents are not assigned for interview in later waves, and none of the non-attrition response patterns will occur if non-respondents at one wave are not assigned for interview at subsequent waves.

Either weighting or imputation, or a combination of the two, may be used to handle wave non-response. With weighting, records with incomplete data for a particular analysis are dropped from that analysis, and weighting adjustments are made to compensate for the dropped

Table 5.1 Response (X)/non-response (O) patterns for a four-wave panel

Response pattern	Year 1 2 3 4	Description
1	XXXX	Total respondents
2	XXXO	Attrition non-respondents
3	XXOO	
4	XOOO	
5	XXOX	Non-attrition non-respondents
6	XOXX	
7	XOOX	
8	XOXO	
9	OXXX	
10	OXXO	
11	OXOX	
12	OOXX	
13	OOOX	
14	OOXO	
15	OXOO	
16	OOOO	Total non-respondents

records. For example, for an analysis that requires data for all four waves of the panel, only response pattern 1 in Table 5.1 would be retained and all the records with partial data would be dropped. With imputation, responses are assigned for all the items asked on waves for which the individual was a non-respondent, thus creating complete records for all individuals who respond to at least one wave (total non-respondents being handled by a weighting adjustment). Imputation thus has the attraction of retaining all the reported data. However, it is extremely difficult to carry out the mass imputation of all the items in a missing wave in an effective manner that does not distort some of the cross-sectional and longitudinal associations between variables. Therefore, weighting is usually the preferred method for handling wave non-response in household panel surveys. A possible compromise is to use imputation for some response patterns and weighting adjustments for others. For instance, in the 1991, 1992, and 1993 panel files of the Survey of Income and Program Participation (SIPP), imputation was used for single wave non-response where the non-responding wave falls between two responding waves (for example in the XOXX response pattern), whereas weighting adjustments were used for other types of wave non-response (Huggins and Fischer, 1994; Tremblay, 1994). Henceforth, this chapter will consider only weighting adjustments for wave non-response.

Further discussion of the weighting and imputation alternatives for wave non-response is provided by Kalton (1986) and Lepkowski (1989).

The data collected in household panel surveys are generally analysed for many different purposes, involving both cross-sectional estimates for each individual wave and longitudinal estimates for various combinations of waves. For each such analysis, it is desirable to retain all the records that contain the requisite data. However, that implies the need for a multitude of weights. For example, cross-sectional estimates for year 1 are based on records in response patterns 1–8, whereas cross-sectional estimates for year 4 are based on response patterns 1, 5–7, 9 and 11–13. Longitudinal estimates involving data from years 1–4 are based on response pattern 1 alone, whereas longitudinal estimates from years 1 and 4 only are based on response patterns 1 and 5–7. In each case, the base weights of the records in the response patterns included in the analysis are adjusted to compensate for the records in the response patterns that are excluded. In general, as many as $2^t - 1$ sets of weights are needed to allow for analyses of all possible combinations of waves in a panel of t waves.

Dealing with wave non-response by means of a multitude of weights is unattractive both because of the effort required to develop the weights and because of the complexity for the survey analyst. The number of alternative weights needed can be substantially reduced by restricting the wave response patterns to the attrition patterns. If wave non-respondents are not assigned for interview at later waves, the only form of wave non-response is attrition non-response. Otherwise, non-attrition patterns can be converted to attrition patterns by dropping responding waves after the first non-responding wave (for example, converting the non-attrition pattern XXOX to the attrition pattern XXOO). This conversion involves some loss of data, but greatly simplifies the weighting process. When all wave non-response is in the form of attrition non-response, only t sets of weights are needed for a panel of t waves.

The simplicity of the weighting procedures with only attrition non-response makes this approach one that is often adopted. A common procedure is first to compute cross-sectional weights for wave 1 that compensate for the total non-respondents. At wave 2, the wave 1 weights are adjusted to compensate for the wave 2 non-respondents; at wave 3, the wave 2 weights are adjusted to compensate for the wave 3 non-respondents; and so on. The wave t weight is the appropriate weight to use for cross-sectional analyses of wave t and for longitudinal analyses involving data from wave t as the latest wave. This attrition weighting scheme is particularly well suited to the needs of panel surveys that are analysed serially as each wave of data is collected because the scheme's sequential process routinely provides the weights needed for this purpose. It is thus an attractive scheme for household panel surveys with lengthy intervals between waves (for example annual data collections) and with no fixed duration.

As noted in Chapters 1 and 2, a complication of household panel surveys is that the composition of the survey population changes over time. Some individuals leave the population through death, emigration, or entering an institution whereas others enter the population through birth, immigration, or leaving an institution. If the survey population is confined to adults, 'birth' can be defined as reaching the minimum age of eligibility for the survey. For cross-sectional analyses at a panel wave after the first, say, wave t, the population of inference should in general comprise both persons present at the time that the panel sample was selected and persons entering the population between that time and wave t. The former group of persons is represented in the panel by the panel members who still remain in the population. However, supplementation of the panel sample is needed to represent the new entrants.

A sample of births can be readily obtained by defining the panel sample to comprise both original sample persons and children born to these persons since the start of the panel. If the definition is restricted to mothers, then the children born since the start of the panel can be simply assigned their mother's weight. If the definition includes both parents, then allowance needs to be made for possible duplication of selection probabilities. This allowance can be achieved by assigning children born since the start of the panel the average weight of their parents (where a non-panel parent is assigned a zero weight). If birth is defined as reaching the minimum age for survey eligibility then a sample of births can be obtained by identifying underage persons in sampled households at the initial wave, following those that will pass the minimum age during the course of the panel, and collecting data from them once they become age eligible (Kalton and Lepkowski, 1985).

It is generally very difficult to supplement the sample of a household panel survey to give representation to immigrants and persons leaving institutions. As a result, often no efforts are made to do so. In consequence, the cross-sectional samples at later waves do not provide complete coverage of the population. Population weighting adjustments can be used to attempt to compensate for this non-coverage, but these adjustments cannot be expected to handle the problem fully. In many cases, and particularly early in a panel's life, the proportion of these types of new entrants is small, so that the risk of appreciable bias in the survey estimates is negligible. However, if the proportion is sizeable, consideration needs to be given to the magnitude of the bias in the survey estimates that the non-coverage may cause.

Weighting methods

This section describes the procedures that may be used to apply the attrition non-response weighting adjustment scheme described in the previous section. We consider here a weighting scheme that applies only to panel members (including births to panel members), i.e. excluding cohabitants. The next section describes weighting schemes that include cohabitants as sample members in making cross-sectional estimates. The attrition non-response weighting adjustment scheme starts with the initial weights for the first wave. A brief description of the development of those weights is presented before discussing the additional complexities associated with subsequent wave non-response.

The computation of base weights is straightforward because with probability sampling all the sampled elements have known selection probabilities. The base weight for a sampled element is simply made equal to, or proportional to, the inverse of the element's selection probability. Base weights are computed for all sampled elements, including both respondents and non-respondents. Sometimes, the sample design for the panel requires sampling different strata at different rates, e.g. sampling a certain region of the country at a higher rate to produce separate regional estimates of adequate precision. The base weight assigned to a panel member selected from that region compensates for this oversampling. If the panel member moves later in the life of the panel to another region, that does not affect the base weight. Base weights are determined by original selection probabilities and are not altered by subsequent changes in the circumstances of panel members.

The possibilities for non-response adjustments at the first wave are usually severely limited by the paucity of information available about the non-respondents. Often, little is known about these non-respondents other than geographical and sample design variables such as the strata and primary sampling units (PSUs) and, perhaps, type of dwelling unit and race/ethnicity. A common procedure for developing first-wave non-response adjustments is to partition the sample into weighting classes based on the information known for both respondents and non-respondents, and then to compute an adjustment factor for each class that is given by the ratio of the sum of the base weights for the eligible sample members in the class to the sum of the base weights for eligible respondents in the class. The adjusted weight for a respondent is then the product of the respondent's base weight and this adjustment factor.

The non-response-adjusted weights may be further modified to make the weighted sample distributions for certain key variables conform to known population distributions for these variables available from recent censuses, large-scale surveys or administrative records. An advantage of this population weighting is that data corresponding to the population characteristics are needed only for respondents. However, care needs to be taken that these characteristics are measured in an exactly comparable way by the panel and by the external source. Population weighting adjustments can be made within weighting classes (often termed post-stratification) or by means of raking or other calibration methods (Deville and Särndal, 1992; Fuller *et al.*, 1994). Population weighting adjustments are used primarily to compensate for non-coverage, but they are also valuable for reducing non-response bias and improving the precision of the survey estimates. As an example, the British Household Panel Survey used population weighting to make the sample distributions at the first wave conform to Census distributions for tenure, household size and number of cars owned at the household level, and for age and sex at the person level (Taylor, 1994).

For the second and later waves of a household panel survey, the situation is very different because the responses from the prior waves can be used in making the adjustments for subsequent non-response. The responses from prior waves provide extensive data that can be used to classify both the respondents and the non-respondents at a particular wave. These data can be used to form non-response adjustments that may be much more effective than the non-response adjustments formed at the first wave. Before addressing ways of selecting variables to form the adjustments and the methods used to adjust the weights, we briefly discuss the issue of population weighting for later waves.

One issue with population weighting at later waves concerns the type of analysis to be conducted. For cross-sectional analyses of wave t data, the appropriate population weighting relates to population distributions at time t. On the other hand, most longitudinal analyses for the time interval from wave 1 to wave t are concerned only with individuals who exist in the population throughout that interval, excluding entrants and leavers. For such analyses, population weighting of wave 1 characteristics of panel respondents (including leavers) to population distributions at wave 1 is appropriate. Thus, two different sets of population weighting adjustments, and hence two different sets of weights, are ideally required if both types of analysis are to be conducted. In practice, a single set of weights may suffice, and in this case the wave 1 population weighting adjustments are likely to be preferred.

Another issue concerns the starting point for developing the weights for later waves. An obvious approach is to start the process with the fully adjusted wave 1 weights that have both wave 1 non-response and population weighting or post-stratification adjustments. However, if this approach is followed, the population weighting adjustments used in wave 1 must then be reapplied after the wave non-response adjustments to ensure that the resultant panel weights are consistent with the wave 1 population totals. A potential disadvantage of adjusting to the population totals a second time is that it may increase the variability of the weights. Variability in the weights typically leads to an increase in the variances of the survey estimates, and the variance increase can become large if the variability in the weights is substantial (Kish, 1992).

An alternative approach is to apply the panel non-response adjustments to wave 1 weights that have been adjusted for wave 1 non-response but have not been subjected to population weighting adjustments. In this case, the base weights are adjusted for initial and subsequent wave non-response and then the population weighting is applied at the end of the process. This approach is less susceptible to increasing the variability of the weights, but it may not be as effective in reducing the bias due to panel non-response.

We now focus on adjustments for wave non-response. The next two subsections discuss the choice of variables from prior waves to use in making the adjustments and the statistical adjustment methods that may be utilised.

Selecting variables

In contrast to the limited number of variables available for making adjustments for non-response at the first wave of a panel, a large number of variables is available for use in making adjustments for subsequent wave non-response. For non-response at wave t, all the variables collected up to wave $t - 1$ are available for use in the adjustments. Because it is impossible to incorporate all these variables into the adjustments, a subset of them needs to be chosen. In principle, variables from any of the previous waves can be included in the adjustments, but in practice the choice usually focuses mainly on variables collected in the previous wave.

Non-response bias is reduced if variables that are related either to response propensity or to the variables under study are used as the auxiliary variables in the adjustment process. As panel surveys collect data on many different variables and are analysed for many different purposes, the selection as auxiliary variables of those related to the survey variables is problematic. Choosing auxiliary variables that are highly correlated to the variables used in one set of estimates might result in small non-response biases in those estimates but leave large biases in other estimates. For this reason, it is common to focus the choice of auxiliary variables on those that are related to response propensity.

If the number of prior wave variables available for possible use in the wave non-response adjustments is very large, some form of screening analysis may be used to eliminate some of the variables from consideration. The goal of the screening is to reduce the number of variables for detailed examination without excluding any variables that might be useful. Screening may be carried out by subject matter experts, by means of simple bivariate tables relating response status at wave t (respondent/non-respondent) to each of the auxiliary variables individually for respondents at wave $t - 1$, with variables showing no or little association to response status being eliminated from further consideration, or by some simple multivariate procedure.

After reducing the potential auxiliary variables to a manageable number, the next step is to select the set of auxiliary variables for use in the wave non-response adjustment. The basic approach is to choose a limited set of variables that is closely associated with response status at wave t among respondents at wave $t - 1$. A natural method for analysing a dichotomous variable such as response status is logistic regression analysis. Logistic regression models with response status as the dependent variable and prior wave data items as the independent variables may be used to assess which combination of variables is highly correlated to response status at wave t. Main effect models and models with two-way interactions have been considered, but more complex models are feasible. Lepkowski *et al.* (1989), Kalton *et al.* (1985) and Rizzo *et al.* (1996) have explored this approach for the Income Survey Development Program (ISDP), a precursor to the SIPP, and for the SIPP.

An alternative method for selecting the set of auxiliary variables is a classification tree algorithm such as SEARCH (Sonquist *et al.*, 1973), CHAID (Kass, 1980) or CART (Breiman *et al.*, 1993). The dependent variable for the tree algorithm is the wave t response status and the independent variables are the potential auxiliary variables. All the independent variables are treated as categorical, with any continuous variables being categorised for use with the algorithm. The algorithm first chooses the variable that is most highly associated with response status according to some criterion. The sample is split into classes according to this variable (in some algorithms, only two classes are possible, whereas in others the number of classes can exceed two). The algorithm next seeks the variable that is most highly associated with response status within each class, with the possibility that different variables are chosen for different classes. Each class is then split into subclasses based on the variables chosen at this second stage. The algorithm continues in this manner until the criterion does not reach a specified level or until further splits would create subclasses that are smaller than a specified minimum sample size. The result is a tree diagram from which the variables most predictive of response status can be identified. Kalton *et al.* (1985) provide an example of such a tree diagram.

Choosing the adjustment method

Once the auxiliary variables have been selected, several different methods may be used to develop the panel non-response adjustments. We consider four adjustment methods: weighting classes, a classification tree algorithm, logistic regression and generalised raking. These methods differ in either how the adjustments are computed or how the observations are grouped in order to form the adjustments.

As with cross-sectional surveys, a common method of non-response adjustment is to form weighting classes as the cells in the cross-classification of the selected set of auxiliary variables. The adjustment in a cell is the inverse of the weighted response rate in the cell. If the sample size in a cell is too small (for example less than 20 or 30) then the cells are collapsed to meet the minimum cell size requirement. To avoid extremely large adjustments, cells may also be collapsed if the adjustment for a cell is much larger than the average adjustment. The wave non-response adjustment is then multiplied by the prior wave weight to create the adjusted weight.

A second method for adjusting for wave non-response is to use a classification tree algorithm not just to identify the set of auxiliary variables to use, as discussed above, but also to define the adjustment cells. The branches of the tree can be extended until subsequent splits would yield cells with sample sizes that are deemed too small for adjustment cells. Once the weighting cells are formed using the algorithm, the formation of the wave non-response adjustment is exactly the same as in the weighting class approach.

A third method of adjustment is based on logistic regression. The logistic regression model of response status on selected prior wave variables is developed as described earlier. However, instead of using the auxiliary variables to define adjustment cells for a weighting class adjustment, the adjustment is based directly on the logistic regression model. The adjustment weight for each respondent is the inverse of that respondent's predicted response probability. If all the auxiliary variables are categorical, this procedure is equivalent to computing the predicted response rate for each cell from the model and to using the inverse of that predicted response rate for the adjustment weight. Thus, in this case, the difference between the logistic regression method and the weighting class method is the use of predicted rather than actual response rates in each adjustment cell. The logistic regression method eliminates the problem of small cell sample sizes by relying on the validity of the regression model.

Alternative ways of computing the adjustments within the basic logistic regression method may be considered to reduce the reliance on the model. If all the variables in the model are categorical, one approach is to use the inverse of the observed response rates in cells that have large enough sample sizes and to use the inverses of the predicted response rates in other cells. Another approach is to collapse together cells with similar predicted response rates and use the inverses of the observed response rates in the collapsed cells as the adjustments.

A fourth method of adjusting for wave non-response is generalised raking. Generalised raking involves modifying the weights to satisfy certain marginal constraints while minimising the distance between the unadjusted and adjusted weights. Deville and Särndal (1992) describe some distance functions that may be used and derive the corresponding raking methodologies. Generalised raking includes the familiar technique of raking or rim weighting that is obtained by means of an iterative proportional fitting algorithm. Upper and lower bounds can be specified for the weighting adjustments in order to limit the variability of the weights. Raking can be applied to force the wave t respondents' marginal distributions for each of the selected auxiliary variables to equal the corresponding distributions for wave t respondents and non-respondents combined. Kalton and Kasprzyk (1986) refer to this method as sample-based raking.

Rizzo *et al.* (1996) present a detailed evaluation of these alternative methods for adjusting for panel non-response in the SIPP. All the methods were applied and the resulting panel weights and estimates were compared. The weights from the different adjustment methods were highly correlated with one another and yielded very similar estimates. No approach was superior in terms of bias reduction. Although these findings may not hold for other studies, all of these adjustment methods should produce reasonable results if they are applied carefully. The similarity of the weights for all the adjustment methods further suggests that greater benefits might be attained by focusing on the choice of the auxiliary variables to be used in the adjustment than on the choice of the adjustment method.

The preceding discussion has considered the development of weights by means of a sequential adjustment process that modifies the weights from one wave to the next. The same general methods can also be applied in a single rather than a sequential adjustment procedure. Consider, for example, the development of weights for wave t in a single operation that compensates for all the attrition non-response up to that time. In this case, the auxiliary variables would be chosen from the variables collected at wave 1 because this is the only wave for which data are available for all response patterns apart from the total non-respondents. Similarly, a single adjustment can be used to compensate for attrition non-response from wave t to wave $t + k$, choosing the auxiliary variables from the wave t responses. If wave-to-wave response rates are very high, it may be adequate to use this approach to make the adjustments every few years rather than every year.

Cross-sectional estimation

Household panel surveys usually start with a sample of households and follow the members of these households, and subsequent births to the household members, for the entire life of the panel or until they leave the survey universe. These originally sampled persons and the births associated with them may be termed 'panel members', 'sampled persons' or 'permanent sample members'.

As we saw in Chapter 4, during the life of the panel, household changes occur. As a result, some panel members leave their originally sampled households to join other households or to create new households, and persons in originally non-sampled households join households containing panel members. In addition to panel members, most household panel surveys also collect information on all the individuals who live with the panel members at each wave. Information is collected on these individuals only while they live with panel members, i.e. they are not followed if they subsequently leave the household containing panel members (hence it is problematic to include them in a longitudinal analysis that begins at some time after the start of the panel). These individuals are variously known as 'cohabitants', 'non-panel members', 'associated persons', 'non-sample persons' and 'temporary sample members'.

The weighting procedures described earlier are appropriate for longitudinal and cross-sectional analyses of panel members. Cohabitants are assigned weights of zero under these procedures, and hence they are ignored in the analyses. Sometimes this means eliminating a sizeable proportion of the interviews at a given wave, particularly with a later wave that occurs long after the start of the panel. For example, in the US Panel Study of Income Dynamics, in 1992, 24 years after the start of the panel, 24% of the individuals interviewed were cohabitants whereas the other 76% were either originally sampled individuals or their children born after the panel started. After only 2 years, cohabitants constituted nearly 13% of the persons interviewed in an SIPP panel. It should, however, be noted that the inclusion of cohabitants in a cross-sectional analysis will not produce as great a proportionate increase in precision as the proportionate increase in sample size because of the increased variability in the weights and the homogeneity of the survey characteristics of persons within households.

If cohabitants are to be included as part of the cross-sectional sample, then the weights must be modified to allow for the fact that some households and individuals could be sampled by more than one route. A household and all its members are included in the sample at wave t if the household contains any panel members. A household composed of two persons at wave t who lived in different households at the first wave would be in the sample if either of the two original households were sampled at the first wave. On the other hand, if the two persons were in the same household at the first wave, only one original household could give rise to the wave t household being selected.

In general, the possibility that elements may be sampled by more than one route is known as a multiplicity problem. The usual solution is to determine the overall probability that an element is sampled, accounting for the multiple ways in which this could occur, and compute base weights as the inverses of these probabilities. This solution is seldom feasible with cohabitants. For instance, in the first example given above, the overall probability of the wave t household being selected depends on the probabilities of selecting each of the original households and the joint probability of selecting both those households at the initial wave. Typically, only one of the households is sampled at the first wave, and the selection probability of the non-sampled household and the joint probability will not be known.

Another approach for incorporating cohabitants into cross-sectional analyses has been called the weight share method by Lavallée (1995). This method adds some random variability over the inverse overall selection probability method; hence, the latter method is to be preferred where feasible. The attraction of the weight share method is that it requires information only on the selection probabilities of panel members, which are always known.

Alternative versions of the weight share method are reviewed in a paper by Kalton and Brick (1995), to which the reader is referred for further details. For cross-sectional analyses of individuals, they describe what they term the equal person weighting scheme in which all individuals in a wave t household (including new entrants to the population) are assigned the same weight, initially, before population weighting. That weight is the average weight of all the household members excluding new entrants, with the weights of panel members being the inverses of their original households' selection probabilities and the weights of cohabitants being zero.

The equal person weighting scheme is used in the SIPP (Huang, 1984; Ernst, 1989) and in Statistics Canada's Survey of Labour and Income Dynamics (Lavallée, 1995). Kalton and Brick (1995) discuss this scheme and an equal household weighting scheme for cross-sectional estimates for persons and households and also discuss how the schemes can be modified to compensate for non-response and non-coverage.

Conclusion

Non-response rates in panel surveys generally increase over successive waves and after a number of waves are often high. As non-response bias is a function of the non-response rate, it is especially important to try to compensate for non-response in panel surveys. Fortunately, unlike the situation with total non-response, a great deal of information is available for wave non-respondents from their responses for the waves at which they did respond. It is worthwhile to devote considerable efforts to using this information in making non-response adjustments in the most effective manner, as discussed in the section 'Weighting methods' (p. 103).

The weights for a household panel survey need to be developed in relation to the types of analyses that will be conducted with the survey data. If non-attrition non-response occurs, all possible types of analyses are to be covered, and full use is to be made of the data collected, then a multitude of weights is needed. The restriction to attrition patterns involves some loss of data, but greatly reduces the number of sets of weights needed and is often preferred. If non-attrition patterns are to be converted to attrition patterns, there is a question as to whether it is worthwhile to follow non-respondents on one wave at any subsequent wave. Subsequent wave data are ignored in the general analyses, and their role is restricted to providing checks on the effectiveness of the attrition weighting scheme.

As discussed in the section on 'Cross-sectional estimation', cohabitants can be included in cross-sectional analyses by developing a special set of weights, probably using the weight share method, with the benefit of producing more precise estimates than would be obtained from the panel members alone. The gains in precision will be limited in the early years of a panel because of the relatively small number of cohabitants involved. The computation of an extra set of weights may therefore not be warranted. However, the number of cohabitants increases as the panel ages. After a number of years, the inclusion of cohabitants may have an appreciable pay-off in precision, thus justifying the development of the extra set of weights.

Note

1   The authors thank Jim Lepkowski for valuable comments on an earlier version of this chapter.

6 Dealing with measurement error in panel analysis[1]

Chris Skinner

Introduction

This chapter discusses further some of the issues surrounding measurement error in panel surveys which Rose discussed in Chapter 1 and to which Kalton and Citro in Chapter 2 and Duncan in Chapter 3 also referred. Non-response and measurement error may be viewed as the two complementary sources of non-sampling error in panel surveys. Survey estimates are functions of the values of variables for the set of responding units. These estimates may differ from the population values they estimate either because the set of units is 'unrepresentative', resulting in sampling error or non-response error, or because the values of the variables are erroneously recorded, resulting in measurement error. The problem of non-response has been addressed in the previous chapters. In this chapter, the problem of measurement error is considered.

Measurement errors are most naturally conceived in terms of the difference between the *measured value* and the *true value* of a variable (Lessler and Kalsbeek, 1992: 370). From the point of view of the data analyst, the measured value is the value recorded in the data file. Thus, the process of measurement, and consequently the nature of measurement error, should be interpreted in a broad sense, reflecting not only the reporting behaviour of the survey respondent but also the recording of this report by the interviewer and any subsequent processing of the recorded value, e.g. the coding of responses to open-ended questions. The definition of the true value of a 'factual' variable, such as employment status, should in principle be clear, but in practice there may often be cases, for example of individuals in irregular forms of economic activity, where the application of the definition is not straightforward. For non-factual variables, such as attitudes, the definition of true value becomes even more complex and issues of latent variable modelling arise (for example Bartholomew, 1987). In this chapter, we shall comment no further on such definitional concerns and suppose that the measured and true values of a variable are well defined for each unit in the population of interest (for further discussion, see Lessler and Kalsbeek, 1992).

We shall consider two broad kinds of measurement and associated panel analysis. In the next section, we consider the classification of a unit's current status into a number of discrete categories at a number of discrete waves of a panel survey. We then suppose that the aim of the analysis is to study transitions between these states. Examples include transitions into and out of a 'poverty' state, transitions between different marital states and transitions between labour force states, such as employed, unemployed and not in the labour force. Such analyses represent perhaps the simplest form of genuinely longitudinal analysis.

The analysis of transitions is dependent on the timing of the waves of the panel survey, which implies a somewhat artificial dependence of the analysis on the times chosen to carry out these waves. To overcome this dependence, some researchers attempt to measure retrospectively the timing of changes of state, e.g. the date of marriage or start of a job. This results in an 'event history' recorded in continuous time. Event histories may be analysed in a variety of ways (Yamaguchi, 1991), most simply by studying the distribution of the durations spent in one specified state before changing to another specified state. Such analyses provide the focus for the third section of this chapter. Retrospective data are well known to be subject to various sources of measurement error and, in particular, we shall consider the effect of errors in recording duration times.

The effect of measurement error on panel analysis for continuous variables will not be considered. For these variables, measurement error can also lead to bias, e.g. in the estimation of serial correlation coefficients (Solon, 1989). Further discussion of the impact of measurement error on the regression analysis of panel data may be found in the work of Hsiao (1986), Griliches and Hausman (1986) and Wansbeek and Koning (1991).

The analysis of transitions between states

The simplest form of measurement error is the misclassification of a unit at a given time into the wrong category of a discrete variable. An example is presented in Table 6.1, taken from Kuha and Skinner (1996). The economic activity of 7,614 individuals recorded in the 1991 Census in England and Wales is cross-classified against the value recorded in the 'quality check' of the Census Validation Survey. This quality check

Table 6.1 Example of a misclassification matrix: economic activity reported in the Census and in Census Validation Survey

| Census | Census Validation Survey | | | |
	Employed	Unemployed	Inactive	Total
Employed	0.976 (5,264)	0.043 (27)	0.033 (53)	(5,344)
Unemployed	0.005 (29)	0.854 (541)	0.043 (69)	(639)
Inactive	0.018 (98)	0.104 (66)	0.923 (1,467)	(1,631)
Total	1.000 (5,391)	1.000 (634)	1.000 (1,589)	(7,614)

Note
Numbers in the table are column proportions and (in parentheses) are cell counts.

used experienced interviewers and may be expected to provide a better approximation to the true value than the original census. The matrix of conditional probabilities, summing to one down the columns, is referred to as a *misclassification matrix* (Kuha and Skinner, 1997). It appears that there is considerable misclassification, most notably of unemployed persons as inactive.

One interesting feature of Table 6.1 is that, despite the presence of considerable misclassification, the estimated proportions in each category are remarkably similar for the two measures. This occurs because the misclassification between states is approximately mutually compensatory. For example, the 69 'truly' inactive who are misclassified as unemployed are ($N = 69$) roughly compensated for by the 'truly' unemployed who are misclassified as inactive ($N = 66$). Although this pattern certainly need not always apply, it seems to be common that misclassification does not lead to substantial biases in such cross-sectional estimates. The same form of misclassification can, however, lead to much more serious bias effects in the estimation of transitions in panel surveys.

Suppose, for example, that the true proportions of persons possessing an attribute at two waves of a panel survey are as shown in Table 6.2 so that, for example, 30% of persons possess the attribute on both occasions.

Now suppose that the misclassification probabilities are determined by the matrix shown in Table 6.3 so that, for example, 15% of those who truly possess the attribute are misclassified.

Then, if the same misclassification probabilities apply to each person and if the classification at each wave is independent then the expected classified table will be as shown in Table 6.4.

Thus, although the misclassification has no biasing effect on the

Table 6.2 Assumed true proportions

| | | Wave 2 | | |
		With	Without	Total
Wave 1	With	0.3	0.1	0.4
	Without	0.1	0.5	0.6
	Total	0.4	0.6	1.0

Table 6.3 Assumed misclassification probabilities

| | | True | |
		With	Without
Classified	With	0.85	0.1
	Without	0.15	0.9
	Total	1.0	1.0

Table 6.4 Implied expected classified proportions

| | | Wave 2 | | |
		With	Without	Total
Wave 1	With	0.24	0.16	0.4
	Without	0.16	0.44	0.6
	Total	0.4	0.6	1.0

marginal proportions at each wave, the off-diagonal entries are severely biased. For example, the true proportion who lose the attribute between waves is $0.1/0.4 = 25\%$, whereas the expected proportion classified as losing the attribute is $0.16/0.4 = 40\%$, implying a severe degree of overestimation. Generally, such severe bias in the estimation of transition rates will occur whenever the misclassification rates are of a similar order to the transition rates. In these circumstances, if we write:

observed change = true change + spurious change

then the spurious change due to misclassification may be expected to be of a similar order to the true change.

Given the occurrence of such severe effects, it is natural to consider approaches to correcting for bias. Two broad approaches may be distinguished. The first may be described as a *two-step* approach. In the first step, an estimate of the misclassification matrix is obtained from external information. Before describing the second step, let us first introduce some notation. Let M be the misclassification matrix, as illustrated in Table 6.1; let P be the matrix for which the element in the ith row and the jth column is the observed proportion of units in state i at the first wave and in state j at the next wave; and let T be the corresponding matrix for the true proportions. Then, provided that misclassification is independent between waves and only depends on current true state, the following matrix equation holds, subject to sampling variation:

$$P = MTM'$$

where M' denotes the transpose of M. It follows therefore that T may be expressed in terms of P by pre- and post-multiplying P by the inverse of M and M' respectively:

$$T = M^{-1}P(M')^{-1} = M^{-1}P(M^{-1})'$$

The matrix P is obtained directly from the observed proportions. Given the estimate $\hat{M}$ of M from the first step, the second step of the method involves substituting $\hat{M}$ for M in the above equation to give the estimate of T as:

$$\hat{T} = \hat{M}^{-1}P\left(\hat{M}^{-1}\right)'$$

The matrix $\hat{M}$ contains estimates of the joint probabilities of being in different pairs of states at the two waves, and these may be transformed to provide estimates of transition rates if required. Further details of this approach and extensions to allow for weaker assumptions are discussed by Abowd and Zellner (1985), Poterba and Summers (1986), Chua and Fuller (1987), Skinner and Torelli (1993) and Singh and Rao (1995).

Let us now return to the first step and consider how an estimate of the misclassification matrix M may be obtained. Two broad approaches may be distinguished. First, a validation study, such as the Census Validation Survey described earlier, may be conducted with the aim of measuring the true values for a subsample of units. If the survey measuring instrument is also administered to this subsample then the misclassification matrix may be estimated directly. Ideally, this exercise would be conducted on a subsample of the panel sample so that the estimates will apply to the same population from which the panel sample was drawn. A problem with this approach, however, is that such a validation study is likely to add to the burden on the panel respondents and this risks increasing attrition in future waves, something that is usually desirable to avoid. Hence, it will usually be more sensible to conduct a validation study on a separate sample.

A more fundamental problem concerns the measurement of 'truth'. One possibility for some factual variables may be to conduct a record check study in which survey responses are compared with values recorded on records. One example is the Panel Study of Income Dynamics Validation Study (Bound *et al.*, 1990) in which survey responses on various labour market variables were recorded for workers in a single large manufacturing company and then these values were compared with company records. This approach is, of course, restricted to variables available on records. It is also likely to require considerable negotiation to overcome confidentiality concerns and thus may be realistic for only a very restricted subpopulation, such as in the PSID study. This may then lead to problems of representativeness. For example, a validation study based on employees in one company can provide no useful information about the probability of an unemployed person being classified as inactive.

Instead of attempting to measure 'truth' in the validation study, an alternative approach is to attempt to replicate the measurement process, either by repeating questions in a single interview or by reinterviewing. Under certain assumptions about the distribution of the errors in the replicated measurements, it is possible to estimate the misclassification matrix M (Chua and Fuller, 1987). The main problem here is how to make appropriate assumptions about the measurement errors. For example, it will rarely be reasonable to suppose that the distribution of errors on the first measurement is the same as on the second. Nevertheless, it may be more realistic to suppose that both measurements are error prone rather than to make the heroic earlier assumption that it is feasible to measure the true value in a validation study.

One problem with the two-step approach is that there will usually be considerable sampling error associated with the estimate $\hat{M}$ of the misclassification matrix and it will generally not be straightforward to incorporate this uncertainty into panel analyses. A second approach is therefore to incorporate all assumptions and information about measurement error in a single corrected analysis. This approach is most naturally carried out using techniques for the statistical modelling of categorical data. The basic model is represented by Figure 6.1(a).

This model involves the combination of a *true model*, relating the true values $X_1, X_2, \ldots$ at the different waves, and a *measurement model*, relating the measured values $X_1^*, X_2^*, \ldots$ to the true values. Without imposing further assumptions, these models are not identified, and no useful estimates of the true transition rates are available. To achieve identification, the approach thus proceeds either by adding information, such as that provided by repeated measurements $X_1^{**}, X_2^{**}, \ldots$ as in Figure 6.1(b), or by imposing assumptions on the relationships between the variables. Examples of possible assumptions are (i) the measured values at different waves are conditionally independent given the true values; (ii) the measurement error depends only on the current true values, not on previous true values; (iii) the distribution of measurement error is homogeneous through time; (iv) the replicated measurements are conditionally independent given the true values; (v) the true values follow a Markov process within subpopulations; and (vi) the distribution of the measurement errors is homogeneous across subpopulations.

Given sufficient assumptions, the model will be identified and the parameters may be estimated using standard statistical methods, such as maximum likelihood estimation. These methods will generate not only point estimates of the parameters of interest (the transition rates) but also standard error estimates which reflect not only sampling error but also the additional uncertainty arising from the measurement error. Some testing of assumptions using likelihood ratio tests will also be

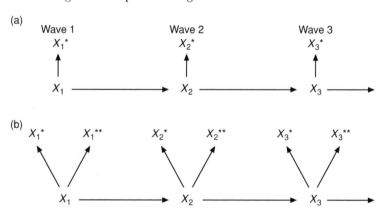

Figure 6.1 (a) Measured and true states in a panel survey. (b) Replicated measurements and true states

possible. The software PANMARK (van der Pol *et al.*, 1991; Humphreys and Skinner, 1994) provides a convenient means of conducting this kind of approach (for some examples, see Langeheine, 1988; van der Pol and Langeheine, 1989). These methods may be viewed as discrete analogies of LISREL models for continuous variables (Jöreskog and Sörbom, 1979). Hagenaars (1990: Ch. 3) provides a discussion which emphasises this analogy.

Event history analysis

The analyses of transitions in the previous section were dependent on the timing of the waves of the panel survey. This dependence may be avoided if event history data are collected retrospectively. For the simplest kind of event histories, we may suppose that for each individual *i* in the population:

    i   an initial event occurs at time I_i;
   ii a terminal event occurs at time $I_i + T_i$;
  iii there is an associated vector of covariates x_i.

The period between I_i and $I_i + T_i$ is the spell and the length T_i of the spell is the duration time for the *i*th individual. The aim of the analysis may be to study the distribution of T_i or to study how T_i depends on the value of the vector of covariates x_i. In this simple situation, the event history for individual *i* is defined just by the values of I_i, T_i and x_i. Some examples of such event histories and associated covariates are shown in Table 6.5.

In panel surveys, data may be collected at the first wave either retrospectively for a fixed initial reference period or as far back as a specific event such as birth or marriage. For subsequent waves, data may be collected retrospectively for the newly completed interwave period. The state (for example employed/unemployed) for each unit at the time of each wave is also collected. From the series of observations, the entire spell (i.e. initial event to terminal event) can be obtained, subject to censoring. If the last wave occurs at time C_i and if $C_i \leq I_i + T_i$ then the duration time is *right censored* and it is only known that the duration is at least $C_i - I_i$. *Left censoring* would occur if I_i, the time the initial event occurs, is not recorded. Following Heckman and Singer (1984: 103), we suppose *left-censored* spells are omitted. If it is assumed that durations are identically distributed given the x_i, this omission of data does not lead to any bias, just some loss of efficiency. Short and Woodrow (1985) present an example of this approach in an analysis of

Table 6.5 Examples of event histories

Initial event	Terminal event	Covariates
Start of first spell of unemployment	End of first spell of unemployment	Age, sex, occupation
Birth	First marriage	Sex, education
First marriage	First birth	Age at first marriage, education
End of full-time education	First full-time employment	Social class, sex, education

unemployment spells from the US Survey of Income and Program Participation.

The measurement of event histories is generally based on the following types of retrospective questions.

  i Has the initial event ever occurred?
 ii When did it occur?
iii Has the terminal event occurred?
 iv When did it occur?

If the answers to (i) and (iii) are 'no' then the remaining questions are skipped. Sometimes the occurrence of the initial event is assumed, e.g. when it is birth. Time in (ii) and (iv) can be measured in several ways, e.g. age at occurrence, date of occurrence or time between occurrence and survey. Any of the measurements may be recorded continuously or grouped into intervals. Errors in the measured responses can occur for any of questions (i) to (iv). Errors in questions (i) to (iii) involve either failure to report an event which did occur or the reporting of an event which did not occur. Errors in questions (ii) and (iv) involve misreporting the timing of an event. There is considerable evidence of the occurrence of errors of each of these kinds.

The US Work Experience Survey (WES) uses a 12-month retrospective reference period. Morgenstern and Barrett (1974) compared estimated person–years unemployed from the WES with estimates from the US Current Population Survey (CPS), which uses a 1-week reference period, and found that the WES tended to understate unemployment by about 3% for men and 23% for women. Horvath (1982) repeated this analysis with later data and found an average understatement of 19%. He also broke down annual estimates into two 6-month estimates and concluded that there was much greater understatement in the WES for a 6- to 12-month recall period than for a 0- to 6-month period. These results do not distinguish, however, between different spells of unemployment. Mathiowetz and Duncan (1988) found in a validation study of the Panel Study of Income Dynamics that measured mean person–years of unemployment again understated the 'true' amount determined from records, but this understatement was minor compared with the error in reported spells. On average, only 34% of all spells of unemployment were reported in the survey, decreasing from 63% of spells of 29 or more weeks to just 25% of spells of 1 week.

Mathiowetz (1985) offers some evidence of telescoping, both backward and forward, of the reported timing of both initial and terminal events. More evidence of such effects comes from studies which ask the unemployed how long they have been unemployed. Bowers and Horvath (1984) and Poterba and Summers (1984) investigated errors in responses to this question indirectly by comparing responses in successive months of the CPS. They found substantial evidence of inconsistency and of a negative relationship between reporting error and duration; short durations seemed to be over-reported, perhaps because unemployment is confused with job search, whereas longer durations may have been under-reported. Related findings for Italian and Canadian Labour Force Survey data were reported by Trivellato and Torelli (1989) and Lemaitre (1988) respectively. Trivellato and Torelli (1989) demonstrated substantial heaping around reported durations of 6 and 12 months and multiples thereof. Horrigan (1987) describes similar heaping in CPS weekly data.

In recognition of the problem of measurement error in retrospective data, one approach for the analyst is only to use data on whether the terminal event occurred between two survey waves but not to rely on the retrospectively reported timing of that event. In other words, the analyst relies on the reported *current status* at each wave of whether a unit has experienced the event. Such information on the terminal event may be used to estimate the parameters of an event history model provided the data on the initial event is assumed reliable. Natural examples arise when T_i is the age at some event, such as menarche, and age is assumed reliably reported. Methods of analysis of current status data are described in Atwood and Taube (1976), with an emphasis on medical/human biological applications, and in Diamond and McDonald (1992), with an emphasis on demographic applications.

Another possible approach to dealing with measurement error is to use discrete time event history analysis. According to this approach, the data on duration T_i are grouped into intervals and discrete time methods (Allison, 1984; Yamaguchi, 1991) are employed. Measurement errors which lead to perturbation of durations within intervals will thus have no effect. In particular, it can be important that the analysis is robust to perturbations of very small durations as these observations may be especially influential (Cox and Oakes, 1984: 84). Nevertheless, this approach will not protect against measurement error which perturbs durations between intervals.

In a numerical study undertaken by Holt *et al.* (1991), it was found, in fact, that the bias of estimation based on grouped durations was just as severe as for estimators based on the original durations. As expected, the bias increases as the amount of measurement error increases. The effect of grouping duration was to increase the variance of the estimators and thus this particular study does not imply any statistical advantage to grouping durations.

Holt *et al.* (1991) conducted a second study assessing the impact of measurement error on the analysis of unemployment durations. In their study, the underlying event history model was estimated from two waves of a panel survey. At the first wave, the duration of unemployment of those unemployed was recorded, and at the second either the duration of the spell was recorded if it was completed or if not the censored duration was recorded. These kind of data, derived from reports from only those experiencing the spell at wave 1, require a different estimation approach, and the conditional maximum likelihood approach of Lancaster (1979) was used. The results of this study suggested that measurement error led to very little bias, especially for the most important parameters, the coefficients of the covariates. The measurement error on the duration of unemployment recorded at the first wave had virtually no effect compared with the measurement error on the duration of the spell reported between the waves. This was so despite the fact that the former duration was potentially much larger than the interwave period. One possible reason for this effect is that the event history model assumed had a fairly flat hazard function and thus the conditional maximum likelihood estimates of the covariate effects were not strongly dependent on the retrospective duration at wave 1.

The effect of measurement error may be assessed in a fairly simple way theoretically if the error acts multiplicatively. A broad class of event history models may be expressed in the logarithmic form:

$$\log T_i = f(x_i) + u_i$$

where u_i is the random variable determining the distribution of the durations T_i. For example, accelerated life models implemented in many standard software packages take this form. If the measurement error is multiplicative so that the measured duration is $T_i^* = T_i E_i$, where E_i is independent of T_i, then the measured durations follow the model

$$\log T_i^* = f(x_i) + u_i^*$$

where $u_i^* = u_i + \log E_i$

In this case, provided the u_i^* are correctly modelled, there will be no bias in the estimation of the systematic part of the model $f(x_i)$. The only bias will arise in the estimation of the distribution of the durations (Skinner and Humphreys, 1999). This result is analogous to that for standard regression models where additive measurement error in the response variable does not lead to bias.

Of course, this result is strongly dependent on the assumed multiplicative error model. One form of measurement error which may lead to biased estimation of $f(x_i)$ is where the measurement error is systematically related to the covariates.

For example, suppose that the logarithm of the measurement error includes a linear dependence γx_i on the covariates x_i so that:

$$\log T_i^* = \log T_i + \gamma x_i + v_i$$

Then if the systematic part of the event history model is also linear in x_i, i.e. $f(x_i) = \beta x_i$, we obtain:

$$\log T_i^* = (\beta + \gamma)x_i + (v_i + u_i)$$

If the error term $v_i + u_i$ is correctly modelled, β will be estimated with bias γ if the measurement error is ignored. In principle, there is no limit to how large this bias could be.

Nevertheless, some empirical studies do suggest that the impact of measurement error will often not be large. Courgeau (1992) compared the results of fitting event history models with residence histories derived from registers with three forms of data derived retrospectively from a survey: from husbands, from wives and from couples together. He found considerable differences between these event histories and thus evidence of considerable measurement error. The main errors seemed to be in the dating of events rather than in their sequencing. The results of Courgeau's analyses were, however, fairly similar in terms of the rough magnitudes of the coefficients and the significance of the covariates.

Conclusion

This chapter has focused on the analysis of panel data on categorical variables. Measurement error can severely distort such analyses by masking true change with spurious change arising solely from misclassification. Some approaches to 'retrieving' the true change have been discussed in two contexts: first, where the aim is to estimate transition rates between the waves of a panel survey; and second, where the aim is to fit an event history model.

There are some circumstances, such as in a log linear event history model with multiplicative measurement error, in which the error will not bias estimates of the primary parameters of interest. In other circumstances, three broad approaches to dealing with measurement error have been distinguished. First, one may use only part of the data which are judged most reliable, as in the analysis of current status data. Second, if available, one can use auxiliary validation data to assess the characteristics of the measurement error process and hence to apply adjustments. Third, one may make modelling assumptions about the relationships between measured variables, enabling the relationships between the latent 'true' variables to be identified and estimated.

Note

1 Research for this chapter was supported by the Economic and Social Research Council award H519255005 as part of the Analysis of Large and Complex Datasets Programme.

7 Tangled webs of family relationships

Untangling them with survey data[1]

Martha S. Hill, Marita A. Servais and Peter Solenberger

Introduction

Social scientists in many fields – demography, sociology, economics, anthropology and social psychology – are interested in the causes and consequences of family formation, dissolution and ties between family members living together or apart. However, conventional approaches to the collection and processing of demographic data relating individuals by blood, marriage or co-residence can hinder examination of issues relating to these topics. Surveys usually collect data on family relationships in one or both of two forms: as relationships of co-residing individuals to the head of the household and as marital, fertility and adoption histories. The problem with these methods is that they may not yield a full account of relationships among all relevant pairs of individuals in the family, including those present in the household and also family members not co-residing.

Relationship-to-head information can leave uncertainty about the identity of important co-residing relatives, such as the parents of grandchildren living in a household along with several children of the household head. In such situations, it is difficult to construct subfamilies. Relationship-to-head data also provide little insight into relationships with family members living elsewhere, yet such relationships are focal to issues such as child support by non-custodial parents or support of frail parents in nursing homes. Marital, fertility and adoption histories can help clarify relationships among persons living apart, but important information of a relationship nature may be missing from an individual's history as well. For example, fertility histories of the current spouse or ex-spouses may be needed to determine the full parentage of children.

This chapter addresses the problem of how to identify fully relationships among family members living together or apart. It examines the issues in light of the experience of the Relationship File Project of the Panel Study of Income Dynamics (PSID) at the University of Michigan in the USA. The project's goal was to identify as clearly as possible relationships among relatives appearing in the study during its first 18 years, whether living in different family units or co-residing. A full 18-year (1968–85) span of data on relationship to head as well as comprehensive marital, fertility and adoption histories gathered in the eighteenth year of observation (1985; hence, after some attrition had occurred) were used to accomplish this goal. Ambiguities in relationships, especially prominent in the early years of the PSID, were clarified using the data collected in the retrospective demographic histories gathered at the end of the observation period along with all (eighteen) waves of PSID data concerning relationship to head.

The Relationship File Project relates, on a pairwise basis and for each of the 18 years 1968–85, individuals who were ever part of, or have derived from, the same original household. Relationship variables were computer derived by devising a set of basic building blocks, or 'primitives' (such as 'biological child' or 'spouse'), and then building relationships with a computer algorithm designed to fit the data. Designing the computer algorithm was a major challenge and so, too, was honing the resulting list of unique relationships down to a manageable set. Hard lessons were taught by the necessity of developing a complex process to construct relationships because the original relationship information was insufficiently comprehensive for important analytical needs. The extensive reprocessing of the data sparked a number of ideas about good versus bad ways to collect and process relationship information in surveys.

This chapter describes the process developed for the file construction, as well as its theoretical roots and compromises imposed by the real world of less than ideal data. Following this introduction, there are six sections to the chapter: defining the problem and the theoretical foundations for a solution; transforming demographic survey data into the basic building blocks of relationships; constructing an algorithm for inferring unknown relationships; reducing a vast set of generated relationships to a manageable set; an illustrative analytical example using the file; and a conclusion with implications for collecting and processing demographic survey data.

Nature of the problem and its treatment

The problem

The Panel Study of Income Dynamics (PSID) conducted at the University of Michigan has been following a sizeable sample of the

American population and its progeny now for three decades, conducting annual (now biennial) interviews on economic status, family composition and a wide range of other topics of interest to social scientists. The PSID has been instrumental in documenting the importance of family structure, even though family structure was not anticipated to be of major importance at the study's start. This lack of anticipation of an important role for family structure resulted in the study's initial measures of relationships among family members being lacking in precision and breadth of coverage (the measures were drawn entirely from information about family members' relationships to head and coded into fewer than ten categories). The precision and breadth of relationship information was enhanced by subsequent revisions in the way PSID's annual relationship-to-head data were coded. Well into the study, the PSID took further steps to clarify relationships by introducing, in addition to its annual relationship-to-head measures, comprehensive fertility, marital and adoption histories. However, by that time, small attrition across the waves had cumulated, leaving a non-trivial number of earlier observed persons (observed but lost to attrition) without comprehensive reports of fertility, marital and adoption histories.

Central to the problem is the fact that the PSID's main data are organised around the concept of a family head (who in husband–wife families is taken to be the husband). At each wave, the head of each family in the sample is identified and then all other individuals in the family are classified according to their relationship to head. Since 1985, retrospective marital and fertility histories have been collected and the data have been summarised on the main files. These summary data, however, omit marriages and births above a certain number as well as the identity of spouses and children.[2] As a result of all of this, the main data files do not optimally accommodate all of the kinds of analyses that involve family structure, either as an analysis topic or for selection of a subsample for analysis.

The PSID's main files do a rather poor job of specifying the family relationships among all pairs of related individuals and in identifying the residential histories of related individuals. Before 1985, certain family relationship information (for example adoptions, parentage of children living elsewhere, sharing a household but not family unit) was simply not available in the PSID because the necessary questions had never been asked or because the required data had not been assembled. Given the importance of living arrangements for family economic status, welfare recipiency and a host of other outcomes, the deficiencies in this regard were particularly unfortunate.

The PSID's main files are also cumbersome for linking individuals who once shared the same dwelling but no longer do so. Analyses of the comparative economic status of ex-spouses are difficult, as are analyses of siblings as a group if those siblings have left the parental household and have formed their own families. PSID's main files also do a poor job of identifying individuals who have left home but who have then returned to it, as with a daughter who leaves home, marries, has a child, is divorced and then returns to the parental home with the child. PSID procedures call for separate interviews with individuals who at some point in the past have been head or wife in their own household even if they have moved back into a parental family, and for years before 1982 the required information to enable an analyst to identify such cases originally was not coded.

The problems are particularly acute for analyses of topics such as (i) the decision of unmarried mothers to live either with their parents or independently; (ii) living arrangements of young children (which can fluctuate between living with biological or step-parents at times and with grandparents, other relatives or family friends at other times); (iii) modelling the ability of non-resident fathers to pay sufficient amounts of child support; and (iv) co-residence with relatives (for example children) of unmarried partners. For these topics, it is important to make distinctions about blood, step- and cohabitational relations, about who is living with whom and when and about who is descended from whom even if they are not currently living in the same household. The PSID's main files have important deficiencies in each of these areas.

Treatment for the problem

The addition to the PSID of comprehensive fertility, marital and adoption histories offered the opportunity to overcome some of these deficiencies. Support from the National Institute of Child Health and Human Development (NICHD) and the Department of Health and Human Services (DHHS) enabled the study in 1985 to interview both household heads and wives (instead of only one person per family as usual) and obtain the necessary demographic information properly to code complex sets of familial relationships that analysts would like to have. These data assisted in cleaning up a great many of the ambiguities surrounding family relationships, establishing important links among related individuals and describing residential histories of those individuals.

Accomplishing this meant constructing a new datafile linking together related individuals in the PSID, showing how each pair of individuals was related in each year of the study and whether the pair shared the same dwelling in each of the years of the study. The new file, termed 'Relationship File', was not intended to replace the PSID's main files but to supplement those files, and analysts could use it in conjunction with the main files to meet their needs better.

The Relationship File links up information on all persons in the same household when the PSID began, persons born to or moving in with someone who was part of that original household or persons they reported as relatives in demographic histories. The file provides a detailed pairwise specification of the relationships among these individuals. A crucial parameter for determining the file design was the wide variation in the number of known relatives of PSID panel members. The total number of persons with the same original (1968) family identifier (ID) ranged from one to fifty. Across the 4,802 distinct original family groupings, there were 512 consisting of only a single person each and one consisting of fifty persons reported as relatives, co-residers or co-residers of a relative at some time during the 18-year time span. A family grouping comprising only one person produces no pairs of related persons, and a family grouping containing fifty persons produces 1,225 pairs of related persons. This wide variation ruled out the possibility of having a file structure that was one person per record with the record consisting of the full string of the person's relatives. A structure consisting of records reflecting the relationship between a pair of individuals offered much more efficient storage possibilities.

The relationship variables are indicators of the ties between a given pair of individuals sharing the same 1968 family ID. The relationship between two individuals can be defined in several ways: blood ties (which remain fixed over time) and ties of marriage, adoption or co-residency (more changeable bonds). To allow for variability in relationships over time, separate year-by-year relationship variables were created over the 18-year period of the PSID (1968–85).

To allow maximal flexibility for analysts in identifying both relationships and persons in relationships, the file contains separate records for each person in any given pair, with the relationship variables in one record coded from one person's perspective and the relationship variables in the other record coded from the other person's perspective. Take the example of a father–son relationship. Call the father 'Ozzie' and the son 'Ricky'. The relationship between them is represented from both the father's (Ozzie's) perspective and from the son's (Ricky's) perspective. This means that the file contains both (i) one record with Ozzie as person X, Ricky as person Y and the relationship of X to Y as 'father' and (ii) one record with Ricky as person X, Ozzie as person Y

and the relationship of *X* to *Y* as 'son'. This helps distinguish both father–son relationships from other types of relationships and fathers from sons.

Theoretical foundations for a solution

The PSID Relationship File Project loosely followed the methodology of the 'ethnogenealogical approach' to the analysis of kinship systems used by some anthropologists. Chad McDaniel suggested this method and provided references explaining it.[3] The procedure applied by the authors in the PSID Relationship File Project, abstracting from problems with the data, was as follows.

i Describe immediate family relationships among individuals in terms of a relatively small number of 'primitive' relationships based on the eight relationships of the traditional nuclear family: wife, husband, mother, father, daughter, son, sister, brother.
ii Describe other family relationships in terms of combinations or chains of these 'primitive' relationships, e.g. 'sister of mother' to describe one variety of 'aunt'.
iii Reduce the large set of relationships derived in (i) and (ii) to a smaller, more manageable, analytically meaningful set of relationships based on conventional American–English definitions of kinship.

The eight nuclear family relationships can be represented as codes as shown, for example, in Table 7.1.

These codes then can be chained to form non-nuclear family relationships as shown in Table 7.2.

Table 7.2 includes thirty-four of the possible sixty-four combinations of the eight 'primitive' codes. The other thirty mathematically possible

Table 7.1 Nuclear family relationships

'Primitive' code	Meaning
W	Wife
H	Husband
M	Mother
F	Father
D	Daughter
S	Son
Z	Sister
B	Brother

Table 7.2 Non-nuclear family relationships

'Chained' code	Literal meaning	Common meaning
WF	Wife of father	Stepmother
HM	Husband of mother	Stepfather
MM,MF	Mother of mother, mother of father	Grandmother
FM, FF	Father of mother, father of father	Grandfather
MW, MH	Mother of wife, mother of husband	Mother-in-law
FW, FH	Father of wife, father of husband	Father-in-law
DW, DH	Daughter of wife, daughter of husband	Stepdaughter
SW, SH	Son of wife, son of husband	Stepson
DD, DS	Daughter of daughter, daughter of son	Granddaughter
SD, SS	Son of daughter, son of son	Grandson
WS	Wife of son	Daughter-in-law
HD	Husband of daughter	Son-in-law
WB, ZW, ZH	Wife of brother, sister of wife, sister of husband	Sister-in-law
HZ, BW, BH	Husband of sister, brother of wife, brother of husband	Brother-in-law
DZ, DB	Daughter of sister, daughter of brother	Niece
SZ, SB	Son of sister, son of brother	Nephew
ZM, ZF	Sister of mother, sister of father	Aunt
BM, BF	Brother of mother, brother of father	Uncle

combinations are either socially or legally impossible in the society of the PSID, such as wife of husband (WH), or less conventional and analytically useful in describing a relationship, such as mother of sister (MZ), which can be described better as wife of father (WF) or stepmother (assuming the relationship is not mother because it would have been specified directly in that case). The incidence of relationships that can be defined in more than one way increases geometrically with the number of links in the 'primitive' chain.

The genealogical method of describing family relationships in terms of 'primitive' codes and chains of codes provides an elegant way to determine relationships among people when only some of these relationships are given. For example, let us assume that we know that Harriet and Ozzie Nelson are married and have a son called David and that David and Janet are married and have a daughter called Kate. What other relationships can we determine from this information?

First, review the known relationships in the Nelson family (see Table 7.3). Notice the symmetry in the relationships. If Harriet is the wife of Ozzie, then Ozzie is the husband of Harriet. Every relationship has a reciprocal relationship. If we know the relationship of A to B and the sex of B, we can determine the reciprocal relationship of B to A.

Table 7.3 'Primitive' relationships in the Nelson family (relationship of person *X* to person *Y*)

Person X	Person Y				
	Harriet	Ozzie	David	Janet	Kate
Harriet	–	W	M		
Ozzie	H	–	F		
David	S	S	–	H	F
Janet			W	–	M
Kate			D	D	–

Table 7.4 'Chained' relationships in the Nelson family (relationship of person *X* to person *Y*)

Person X	Person Y				
	Harriet	Ozzie	David	Janet	Kate
Harriet	–	W	M	MH	MF
Ozzie	H	–	F	FH	FF
David	S	S	–	H	F
Janet	WS	WS	W	–	M
Kate	DS	DS	D	D	–

Using what we know from Table 7.3, we can fill in the missing relationships. For example, we do not know the relationship of Janet to Harriet, but we do know the relationships of Janet to David (W) and David to Harriet (S). From this, we can determine the relationship of Janet to Harriet by chaining the two other relationships to get wife of son (WS), or daughter-in-law. We can determine the relationship of Harriet to Janet by chaining the relationship of Harriet to David (M) and the relationship of David to Janet (H) to get mother of husband (MH), or mother-in-law.

Again, notice the symmetry of relationships. If Janet is the daughter-in-law of Harriet, then Harriet is the mother-in-law of Janet. If we know the relationship chain from one person to another and the sexes of the people involved, we can determine the reciprocal chain by chaining the reciprocal elements in the reverse order: wife of son (WS) becomes mother of husband (MH).

Table 7.4 summarises what we can determine about the relationships in the Nelson family.

We have determined the relationship of Janet to Harriet as wife of son (WS). Another possible way that we might describe their relationship is through Kate and then David: mother of daughter of son (MDS). We have rejected this because it is a less direct relationship. In general, the procedure followed in the PSID Relationship File Project was to choose the 'shortest' possible relationship chain, the one with the fewest and closest links. Conceptually that is, abstracting from data problems this meant the following steps.

  i Build a table of 'primitive' relationships among family members.
 ii Identify missing relationships.
iii Find all third persons to whom both people in the missing relationship are related.
 iv Determine the shortest chain of the known relationships.
  v Fill in the missing relationship.
 vi Repeat steps (ii) to (v) until no more unknown relationships can be filled in or the relationship chain is too long to be of analytical interest. (We chose a limit of no more than four chained elements.)

Step (iv) requires special attention. Often, two people with an undetermined relationship are both related to more than one other person, which means that we must choose the 'shortest' chain. This can be seen in Table 7.2, in which we prefer wife of father (WF) over mother of sister (MZ) to describe stepmother. Our iterative procedure for determining relationships adds one link at a time. To choose the 'shortest' chain among multiple possibilities, we assign a distance to each 'primitive' relationship and then sum the distances of the links. The chain with the smallest total distance is deemed the 'shortest' chain and becomes the designated relationship.

The chaining process can produce large numbers of mathematically possible codes. Our eight nuclear family 'primitives' in combinations of 0–4 'primitive' codes (i.e. from no relationship to, for example, mother of mother of mother of mother) could produce the numbers of generated codes shown in Table 7.5.

Table 7.5 Mathematically possible numbers of chained codes based on eight primitives

Number of codes chained	Number of codes generated
0	1
1	64
2	512
3	4,096
4	32,768
Total	37,441

Even assuming half these codes are impossible or redundant, the codes must be grouped in some way to be comprehended or analysed. The problem is made more difficult by the fact that the eight 'primitive' codes of the traditional nuclear family are quite inadequate to describe the social reality of families in the PSID and the society of which it is part. For example, even apart from ambiguities in the data, the category 'wife' should be broken down into wife, separated wife, divorced wife, widowed wife, deceased wife, female domestic partner and possibly other categories.

The formula for the number of mathematically possible relationship codes is:

$$1 + n + n^2 + n^3 + n^4 + \ldots$$

where n is the number of 'primitive' codes. With a realistic n, the number of possible codes is in the billions and the number that will appear in a relatively large study such as the PSID is in the thousands.

Anthropologists studying kinship systems attempt to develop principles for combining the chained codes that allow them both to reproduce the conventional folk descriptions of the society that they are studying and to analyse underlying social patterns and processes. The same had to be done with the PSID Relationship File Project, grouping the chained codes so that they were manageable but also so that they were intelligible to members of the US society of which the PSID families and individuals are part and useful to analysts of that society. As it could not be sure that the grouping would suit every analyst, 'field notes' were included in the original 'primitive' chains in the Relationship File to allow others to group the chained codes as they pleased.

Building blocks for relationships

Following the theoretical guidelines, the first step in the process of determining relationships with the PSID data involved categorising all readily accessed relations between pairs of people into a set of basic building blocks, termed 'primitives', that could be used as links to construct the chain of ties in relationships not directly observed in the data. The central idea was to identify a moderate size set of 'primitives' that described relationships between pairs of individuals in ways of interest to analysts.

The form of the demographic data and the degree of their specificity are strong determinants of what can be used as basic building blocks ('primitives'). The PSID data came in a variety of forms and levels of specificity. One source was annual data on co-residing family members' relationships to the family head. These data varied in specificity over the course of the study, with the relationship-to-head code taking three different forms at different times: a crude ten-category code in 1968, followed by a different, but still crude, ten-category code during 1969–82, subsequently replaced in 1983 by an expanded thirty-four-category code. Another source of the PSID demographic data was comprehensive fertility, marital and adoption histories collected in 1985. The distinctions about relationships in these demographic histories were more precise, but covered fewer types of basic linkages, than the 1983–5 relationship-to-head codes (they are mostly a variety of spousal and parent–child relations, plus a grandparent–grandchild code).

The wide variation in PSID relationship classification systems complicated the designation of the 'primitives' because the goal was to develop a set of primitives that maintained as much precision in the designation of relationship as possible, while also keeping the number of code elements to a manageable set (in this case approximately 100). The 'primitives' reflect these differences in form and specificity. The 'primitives' based on the fertility, marital and adoption histories represent the highest level of precision in linkages because they clearly distinguish biological, adoptive and step ties and date beginnings and endings of marriages involving specific spouses. The 'primitives' based on the 1983–5 relationship-to-head information (working from thirty-four categories of relations) represent the second highest level of precision, and those based on the 1968–82 relationship-to-head information (working from only ten categories of relations) represent the least precise linkages. A number of assumptions had to be made all along the line in determining relationships, but attempts were made throughout the process to preserve as much specificity as possible.

The original intent was to design 'primitives' to vary with the source of the relationship information in such a way as to serve as markers for the source. This idea was modified for feasibility reasons; preserving the source of the information in this way introduced conflict between designing precise 'primitives' and having a small enough set of 'primitives' to make the design of the computer algorithm for generating unknown relationships a manageable task. The 'primitives' that were developed serve as indicators, but not always unambiguous ones, of data source.

The 'primitives' were designed to be sex specific because common terms for relationships usually convey sex as well as type of tie. When the available relationship information was sex neutral, information regarding the sex was accessed so that all primitives could be defined in sex-specific terms (for example 'mother' instead of just 'parent').

The complete set of primitives consisted of ninety-six elements. A sizeable number of pairs of individuals demonstrated direct linkages via one of those primitives. A much larger number of pairs of individuals did not. To identify the ties for this latter set of pairs, a computer program was developed that attempted to link all pairs of individuals via chains of primitives. The 'primitive chains' consist of a chain of up to four two-digit 'primitives.' A primitive chain of 00315302, for example, represents son (31) of full brother (53) of wife (02); leading zeros are ignored. The reader is referred to the documentation for the Relationship File for details about this and other sets of codes noted in this chapter.

Building the algorithm[4]

The derivation of the 'primitive' and 'primitive chain' relationships required four steps: (i) preprocessing the relationship-to-head data; (ii) processing the relationship-to-head data; (iii) preprocessing the marital–fertility–adoption history data; and (iv) processing the marital–fertility–adoption history data. Steps (i) and (ii) produced relation-to-head relationships, and steps (iii) and (iv) produced distinct history relationships.

We will explain the preprocessing and processing of the relationship-to-head data in some detail to illustrate the complexities of working with real survey data. Because the preprocessing and processing of the marital–fertility–adoption history data were similar, we will not explain it here but instead refer readers to the Relationship File documentation.

Preprocessing the relationship-to-head data

The relationship-to-head program required several types of data from the combined 1968–85 PSID Family Individual Response and Non-response File. The following variables were accessed for all individuals.

  i individual's ID (1968 family number and person number);
 ii individual's sex (to make sex distinctions in relationships);
iii individual's mother's ID (1968 family number and person number);
 iv individual's 1969–85 family number (to distinguish co-resident and separated spouses, as well as co-residency generally);
  v individual's 1968–85 PSID status (to determine attrition and death).

vi   shared dwelling unit ID 1969–85 (to identify any other PSID family
     units in the individual's household);
vii individual's relationship to head 1968–85.

In addition, the following variables were created, based on the
individual's relationship to head 1968–85.

viii reverse relationship (head's relationship to individual 1968–85;
      the reverse of item vii);
  ix distance value for individual's relationship to head 1968–85 (this
      is specific to the type of relationship and provides a relative
      weighting of the closeness of different ties).

Items (i) to (iv) involved no restructuring. Item (v) involved
restructuring of the PSID's 1968–85 sequence number variables. Items
(vii) to (ix) required assigning 'primitive' code values and 'distance'
values based on the individual's 1968–85 relationship-to-head variables.

Processing the relationship-to-head data

The relationship-to-head program essentially created two large three-
dimensional matrices for each set of individuals with the same 1968
family ID: annual values for relationship based on relationship-to-head
information and annual co-residence status. The dimensions of the
matrices were person X, person Y and time. The number of elements
in each matrix was the square of the number of persons X with the
same 1968 family ID (across 1968 families, the number of person X
ranged from 1 to 50) multiplied by the number of years (18).
   The relationship-to-head program filled in values for the relationship
and cohabitation matrices using the following procedure.

  i Access, for all years, the nine data items listed above for all persons
     with the same 1968 family number.
 ii Enter cohabitation codes for persons in the same 1968 family in
     each of the years, based on their 1968–85 family number and PSID
     status.
iii Enter cohabitation codes for persons in the same dwelling unit
     but different family units in each of the years, based on their shared
     dwelling unit IDs.
 iv Enter relationship-to-head, reverse relationship-to-head and
     distance codes for persons in the same 1968 family for each year,
     beginning with 1968.

  v Enter mother–child relationships and distances for persons in the same 1968 family.

  vi Bring forward the previous year's immediate relationships, beginning with 1969. The relationships carried forward were parent–child, sibling, spouse and ex-spouse. A spouse tie was carried forward only from one year to the next, whereas the other three types of relationship were carried forward indefinitely.

  vii Generate the sibling, parent–child and other 'primitive' relationships implied by the information available through above steps (iv) to (vi).

  viii Iterate to derive relationship chains linking persons in more complex ways.

  ix Repeat above steps (iv) to (viii) for each year 1968–85.

  x Output the relationship and cohabitation matrices with two records for each pair of related persons for each year.

Step 8 is the 'algorithm', properly speaking. It involves the following procedure.

  i Examine the relationship matrices for each year to locate undetermined relationships between pairs of 1968 family members.

  ii For each undetermined relationship, check to see whether both persons have one or more determined relationships with another person from the 1968 family.

  iii Select the 'closest' relationship between the two persons with a previously undetermined relationship through a third intermediary person.

  iv Repeat above steps (i) to (iii) for all pairs of persons.

  v Repeat above steps (i) to (iv) until no more relationships can be determined or until the relationships are too distant to be of interest (in our case, mediated through more than three other persons).

Step (iii) used our designated measure of relationship 'distance', which totalled the weighted ties between the pair of individuals. The weighting scheme for 'distance' assigned a number value to each primitive, giving smaller values to primitives reflecting closer, less distant, ties. If the program produced alternative relationship chains for a pair of individuals, the algorithm selected the relationship chain with the smallest total distance. For example, in the 1968 relationship-to-head primitives, the parent and child primitives were assigned a distance of 1, spouse was assigned a distance of 2, sibling was assigned a distance of 3 and 'other relative under age 18' (a single code in that relationship-to-head designation) was assigned a distance of 1504, a value greater than that of any other more specific choice. If our algorithm produced two separate chained linkages between a given pair of individuals, one showing the relationship as 'child of child' and the other showing the relationship as 'other relative under age 18', the program selected the 'child of child' (in common language, 'grandchild') designation because its total combined distance was 2 compared with 1504 for the 'other relative under age 18' relationship. This helps to select the closer relationship.

Merged file

With a similar approach taken for assigning relationships based on marital–fertility–adoption history data, two separate files were generated by the above processes: one showing relation-to-head-based relationships and one showing history-based relationships. These two forms of relationship were preserved as separate sets of variables but merged into one file. The resulting file contained 426,608 records representing the relationship of person X to person Y and the relationship of person Y to person X – two records for each pair of people who were associated with a single 1968 family. In each record, there were thirty-six relationship variables (eighteen relationship variables based on annual relationship to head over the period 1968–85 and eighteen relationship variables based on the 1985 marital and fertility histories over the period 1968–85). In total, across all records, these thirty-six variables contained approximately 10,000 unique primitive chains.

Constructing a manageable set of codes

Building the primitive chains was a challenging task, but there were still further obstacles to producing a product that could be considered useful to most analysts. Having produced roughly 10,000 unique primitive chains, it was imperative to find some method of classifying them into a manageable number of categories. Not only was this much too large a number of relationships for a sane human to evaluate, most of the relationships are not of interest for any particular type of analysis. For instance, if parent–child relationships are of interest, sibling, cousin, etc. relationships need not be considered at all. It was essential that this vast number of disparate relationships be reduced to a much smaller number.

As an initial step, a file was constructed containing the primitive chain, the number of times the relationship occurred from the specified source and a translation of the primitive chain into words. This file proved a critical tool during the struggle with the daunting task of classifying the derived primitive chains in a meaningful and manageable way.

Reducing the number of unique relationships

First, an attempt was made to classify the primitive chains by inspection of them as translated into words. This proved not feasible because of problems of consistency and symmetry in the classification. Ultimately, the primitive chains were successfully classified using a series of machine algorithms to recode them. We devised two different methods. The first method resulted in the classification of the approximately 10,000 primitive chains into just fifty-eight types of relationships. The second method, retaining more detailed information, resulted in the classification of the roughly 10,000 primitive chains into about 1,500 types of relationships. The first method classified the primitive chains using a multistep process. With the following two steps, the chains were altered to consist of only four basic, sex-neutral elements – parent, child, sibling and spouse (in addition to other relative and non-relative). First, some primitives were recoded into more aggregated elements. For example, the wide variety of primitives for different types of spouse – 'wife', 'husband', 'separated wife' and so forth – were recoded into the single element 'spouse'. Second, some primitives were 'expanded' into more basic elements. For example, 'child-in-law' became 'spouse of child'. Third, some extended relationships were 'contracted' to express them more concisely. For example, 'parent of child' became 'spouse', with an underlying assumption that both parent–child ties are blood ties rather than ties by adoption or marriage (steprelations). All of these transformations involved making assumptions to compensate for not knowing the relationships among all persons. Finally, duplicate chains were eliminated and unique chains were assigned codes. This allowed the classification of the original 10,000 or so unique primitive chains into just fifty-eight types of relationships! As an illustration, see Table 7.6 for types of relationships identified along with their unique three-digit codes when persons X and Y are one generation removed.

Massive simplification had been achieved by relying on a number of plausible, simplifying assumptions. However, although the initial task

Table 7.6 Reclassification of primitive chains using the less detailed method (method 1); one generation removed relationships

Code	Relationship of person X to person Y	Code	Relationship of person Y to person X
101	Parent	151	Child
102	Parent-in-law	152	Child-in-law
103	Parent or aunt/uncle	153	Child or niece/nephew
104	Aunt/uncle	154	Niece/nephew
105	Spouse of aunt/uncle	155	Nephew of spouse
106	Aunt/uncle of spouse	156	Spouse of niece/nephew
107	Spouse of aunt/uncle of spouse	157	Spouse of niece/nephew of spouse
108	Cousin of parent	158	Child of cousin
109	Sibling of spouse of aunt/uncle	159	Niece/nephew of spouse of sibling
110	Parent-in-law of sibling	160	Sibling of child-in-law
111	Parent-in-law of sibling of spouse	161	Spouse of sibling of child-in-law
112	Grandparent of child-in-law	162	Parent-in-law of grandchild

of classifying the roughly 10,000 primitive chains had been realised, much useful detail had been eliminated.

Therefore, a second method of classifying the original primitive chains was developed. First, the primitives which were the basic building blocks for the original primitive chains were recoded, this time into twenty-two elements. This set of twenty-two elements made finer distinctions than the set of six elements used in the first method. It retained key distinctions about the types of spouses, children, parents and siblings. For example, current spouse, cohabiting partner and former spouse were made separate elements. Also, some complex relationships (such as aunt/uncle, grandchild and cousin) were specified with distinct codes. Then duplicate chains were eliminated. This resulted in the classification of the original 10,000 or so unique primitive chains into approximately 1,500 types of relationships.

Assigning five-digit relationship codes

The final five-digit code was obtained using a combination of the two methods of classification. The first three digits of the code are based on those obtained from the first method of classifying the primitive chains. The final two digits, the decimal values, are a sequential number beginning with 0.01 for more common types of relationships classified according to the second, more detailed, method and 0.99 for infrequently occurring relationships (ones that occurred fewer than 100 times across all 15,357,888 possible relationship–years). The resulting five-digit code with about 450 unique categories provides an efficient way of identifying the relationships of interest and discarding those that are not.

Modal relationships

As a further means of helping the analyst to select efficiently only the relationship records of interest, we added summary variables to each record to indicate the most frequently occurring relationship between the given pair of individuals. These summary variables, 'modal three-digit relationship' and 'modal five-digit relationship', are based on the inspection of all thirty-six five-digit relationships of person X to person Y. Of the pairs, 6% had more than one three-digit relationship and 23% had more than one five-digit relationship over the 18-year period; 10% of the pairs had no relationship derived at any time during the 18-year period.

An illustrative example of using the file

To illustrate analytical uses for the resulting Relationship File, we focus on co-residency of daughters with their parents. The daughters of interest are themselves unmarried mothers as of 1985, and at issue is the frequency with which they were co-residing with their parents at the time of the 1985 interview. It is possible that some daughters had set up households separate from their parents but then subsequently returned to the parental home. PSID interviewing rules call for continuing to classify such a daughter as the head of her own family unit, and during interviewing her as a separate family unit, even after she returns to her parents' household, it can be difficult to tell that she is back with her parents. This impediment can be overcome by using information about relationships and about co-residence on the Relationship File in conjunction with other data on the PSID's main datafiles.[5]

First, from the PSID's main files, select the subset of unmarried mothers in 1985 and their relevant data, including identification number. Next, turn to the Relationship File to identify their parents and co-residence status. The Relationship File defines relationships in terms of the relationship of person X to person Y. If we think of person Y as a daughter who is herself an unmarried mother, then her parent is a person X with a relationship to person Y of 'father' or 'mother.' We make a subset file of the records in which relationship is 'father' or 'mother'. We then match the identification number for an unmarried mother from the subset of the PSID's main files to the identification number of person Y on the subset of the Relationship File and merge the 1985 co-residence variable from the Relationship File. This co-residence variable indicates whether person X (parent) and person Y (daughter who is herself an unmarried mother) are living in the same household.

Because various variables on the Relationship File indicate relationship with different degrees of specificity and over a variety of time periods, there is a great deal of leeway in how an analyst chooses to define 'father' and 'mother'. All told, there are four relevant relationship variables – the three-digit modal, the five-digit modal, the 1985 relationship to head and the 1985 history variable. For subsetting the records from the Relationship File, the analyst decides which of these variables best suits the purpose at hand.

Summary and conclusion

To circumvent problems in the PSID caused by information about relationships having been collected and/or processed in insufficient detail to satisfy the needs of analysts, a process for generating the required detail was designed and implemented. This process involved designating basic building blocks of relationship ties, designing a computer algorithm to use the known relationships to generate unknown relationships between pairs of individuals and devising a system of recoding the vast number of resulting relationships to a more manageable number of analytically meaningful codes.

The complexities of designing this system to make up for shortcomings in the available demographic survey data spurred considerable thought about better ways to collect and process the data from the beginning (and hence avoid the shortcomings necessitating reconstructive work). Collecting or coding relationships in crude detail clearly poses problems for many types of analysis. Even with highly detailed codes, however, there are major problems with the approach of gathering a household listing that relates each household member to only one household member (for example the household head). Identification of the pairwise relationships between all individuals in the household is a substantial improvement over just relationship-to-head information. However, directly collecting such information is tedious and time-consuming in large and complex households. An alternative, which yields more comprehensive and flexible information, is to identify, for each household member, who (if anyone) in the household is their parent or their spouse. This provides important basic building blocks for constructing relationships with household members.

However, relationships are not confined to co-residing individuals. There are important interhousehold relationships, such as the links between adult children and their parents or an absent father and a child living with his former spouse. Extending questions about parents and spouses of household members to relatives living elsewhere would add considerably to the analytical potential of the demographic survey data. Comprehensive retrospective marital, fertility and adoption histories are quite helpful in identifying blood and legal ties among persons, regardless of where they are currently living. They are most useful if collected right at the start of the panel study and then updated as the panel study progresses through time. If they are gathered for the first time several waves into the study, attrition poses problems; the information would be totally missing for study members leaving the study before the comprehensive histories were first collected.

It is our hope that this description of the complex process that was devised to correct for shortcomings in the data collection and processing will prove useful to the survey research community for circumventing similar problems in other existent data. It is, we think, a process that is intrinsically interesting to demographers, anthropologists and family sociologists. However, it is also our hope that others will benefit from the lessons we learned about improved methods of collecting and processing demographic data from the start, rather than having to rely on complex post-processing methods of deriving needed information.

Notes

1 The authors wish to acknowledge funding assistance from the National Science Foundation, valuable assistance in file design by Chad McDaniel, considerable input from Greg J. Duncan on the Relationship File Project and the very helpful comments of Sandra Hofferth and Wei-Jun Jean Yeung. Special thanks also to Barbara Browne for all of her careful work and headaches resulting from the tedious work underlying the development of the codes for relationships.

2 The full details of the data collected in the retrospective marital and fertility histories are provided on special files that are separate from the main files.

3 C. McDaniel (September 1984), personal correspondence.

4 For details about the various stages of the process summarised here, see Hill *et al.* (1992). Copies are available upon request by e-mailing Martha Hill (hillm@isr.umich.edu) or Marita Servais (servais@umich.edu).

5 For information about obtaining the PSID Relationship File or other PSID files, contact the Inter-university Consortium for Political and Social Research (ICPSR): www.icpsr.umich.edu.

8 Dissemination issues for panel studies

Metadata and documentation

Marcia Freed Taylor

Introduction

This chapter considers an often neglected topic in data quality in books such as this: data dissemination. Although high standards of data documentation and metadata are required if any survey is to be of use to analysts, in the case of household panels it is even more necessary for careful thought to be given and for resources to be devoted to dissemination in all its forms. After all, panel studies, being the social science equivalent of scientific laboratories or observatories, are precisely created to be resources for the wider community of scholars, other users and policy-makers. It is therefore important that those who intend to create these resources, as well as data users, are aware of the basic issues concerning panel data dissemination. This is the purpose of this chapter. Hence, in what follows I first consider general issues concerning documentation and metadata before turning to the particular case of household panel studies.

Why disseminate data?

The importance of dissemination of the results of the research process – and this must include the data collected – has not always been accepted by the social science research community. It has recently come much more to the forefront, however, and is now an integral part of most funded research projects. We can (with the then Secretary of the UK Economic and Social Research Council William Solesbury; Solesbury, 1991) distinguish three major reasons for such dissemination: (i) epistemological: to be true knowledge, the results of the research process must be 'known'; (ii) ethical: those using the scarce resources available for research have a responsibility to make the results of that research known to the wider community; and (iii) economic: research costs are high and we must therefore make the best use possible of resources.

These general principles can be appropriately applied to the dissemination of datasets of all types. The collection of data is an increasingly expensive undertaking and the resulting datasets must be perceived as valuable research resources, which can profitably be analysed by a wider research community; the original research team are rarely able fully to analyse or exploit the data. Dissemination of the data to other researchers ensures that the high costs can be more completely justified. To fulfil the aims of dissemination, the datasets must be documented so that others can properly comprehend – even test and validate – the results of data analyses. This is true whether the data are seen as the by-product of a particular research project or are specifically collected to serve as general research resources, as is the case with most household panel studies. In the latter case, the level and quality of the documentation will be central to the success of any dissemination effort. In fact, we can go so far as to say that the design of the study and the documentation of the data are equally important in the production of well-planned, reliable data for the primary researcher as they are for the secondary researcher who requires access to the untapped information potential inherent in the data.

The case for good documentation of research data

We all recognise the need for good documentation. It is so obviously good research practice that few researchers would deny its importance. In an informal survey carried out by this author among the secondary analysis community, most respondents considered the existence of good documentation to be either 'essential' or 'very important'.

Why then do so many datasets have such sketchy and incomplete documentation? Researchers are, for perhaps understandable reasons, reluctant to spend hard won research time, and that of their research assistants, on documentation of their datafiles. The need to publish quickly and the lack of recognition of a well-documented dataset as a valid 'research output', coupled with the lack of appropriate quality control procedures implemented throughout the life of the project, mean that many datasets are next to useless for reanalysis or validation purposes.

Even if a researcher is, unusually, committed to the production of high-quality documentation, there are currently no available standards or easy to use guidelines for such activity. Some attempts to produce such guidelines are discussed below.

What purpose, then, does documentation serve in the research process? We have stated that good documentation is as useful for the primary researcher as for the secondary analysts. For primary investigators, the process of documenting data is a means of organising their thinking, of focusing on important aspects of the data which might otherwise be ignored, of locating errors or incomplete procedures which might well have an effect on the final outcome of analyses. As most data collection exercises involve more than a single researcher, documenting the data is also a method of ensuring that all members of the primary research team share the knowledge accumulated during the data collection process. It can also serve as an insurance policy against the loss of information over time and the 'disappearing research assistant', who often is the sole fount of detailed knowledge.

For the secondary user of a dataset, the virtues of good documentation are much clearer and more widely accepted. Information about the data, in the form of documentation, is, quite simply, essential. Data documentation should conserve the knowledge developed by the data collector and the initial analysts; it should describe what the dataset contains, how and why it was collected and how it was cleaned and prepared; it should clarify issues of importance to the analyst; it should illustrate how the dataset can be used, its virtues and potential; it should allow multiple views of the same dataset; it should be creative in that it adds new knowledge and suggests ways in which the data can be reanalysed; it should stimulate and inspire new users; and, lastly, it should educate secondary users so that misuse of the data is obviated by clarifying exactly what the data contains and by pointing out potential pitfalls and possibilities of misunderstanding.

Documentation and metadata

Definitions

In the past decade, there has been much talk of 'metadata' and 'meta-information' rather than merely of data documentation. In the end, of course, it matters little what we call the essential information which should accompany a dataset, as long as it is there. To avoid confusion and to provide the structure for what follows, however, a short digression into a discussion of the varying terminology and the distinctions that can be made is in order.

'Metadata' is a generic term that is used in a wide variety of ways. In its broadest sense, it means 'data about data' and has been applied to information as varied as that required by a specific database management system, standard library cataloguing information, codebook information on specific survey variables and to descriptions of data access conditions

Considerable research has been, and is, going on into this area, as the stock of datasets being made available to researchers increases in quantity, if not quality, in size and in complexity. Early work is reported by Tanenbaum and Taylor (1991) and by Sieber (1991). The European Commission has funded several large projects on metadata delivery systems, most notably the DOSES (Development of Statistical Expert Systems) and DOSIS (Development of Statistical Information Systems) schemes in the 1990s, and has held a number of international workshops to present the results of work on metadata standards (Drewett *et al.*, 1989; Hand, 1993; Statistical Office of the European Commission, 1993; European Commission, 1994). This work has concentrated primarily on documentation standards for the statistical data produced by national statistical agencies and has emphasised delivery and handling methods rather than concentrating on definitions of required elements. A series of Metadata Workshops, sponsored by the then European Commission DGXIII between 1997 and 1999, concentrated more on the definition of standards for metadata, which were defined as 'data which describes attributes of a resource and …supports location, discovery, document-ation, evaluation, and selection.'[1] Such data are therefore seen not only as a key to the discovery of information resources but also as fundamental to the effective use of found resources. Three types of metadata format were distinguished:

i   simple format for full text indexing such as those used in Yahoo and Altavista search engines;

ii   structured format with a fairly high level of information, such as that identified as the Dublin Core Metadata Initiative,[2] which recommends a fifteen-element metadataset for describing Web resources; and

iii   rich format with elaborate tagging, international standards used for location and discovery but also for documenting objects or collections of objects and capturing a variety of relationships at different levels, such as that used in the Data Documentation Initiative (see below).

Similar standards defining activities are under way in many major international organisations, including the United Nations and the Organisation for Economic Co-operation and Development (OECD). Considerable and highly competitive work is being carried out by the networking and information industries on metadata standards for indexing information on the Internet. Here, the proliferation of available data and information makes the provision of an efficient and rapid information-finding aid absolutely crucial. (for example Weibel *et al.*, 1995; Sundgren *et al.*, 1996; United Nations Economic Commission for Europe Statistical Division, 1999[3]).

Work is also under way in the academic community to provide guidelines to assist data producers in the production of good and adequate documentation. A Data Documentation Working Group (consisting of representatives of the research, data archive, information science and library communities) began working on *Guidelines for the Documentation of Research Data* some years ago. This should provide the basic structure for future data documentation efforts.[4] The largest data archive in the USA, the Inter-university Consortium for Political and Social Research, has also produced a user guide to documentation, the *Guide to Social Science Data Preparation and Archiving*.[5] The social science data archives have carried out much work in this area in the past, including the production of the Standard Study Description Form and its successors, which from the early 1970s has allowed the collection and dissemination of basic identifying information on all computer-readable holdings of the European data archives in a standardised format (Guy, 1993; Rockwell, 1993).

Recognising that a universally supported standard had not yet emerged from this activity, Richard Rockwell of the Inter-university Consortium of Political and Social Research at the University of Michigan in the USA began the Data Documentation Initiative[6] in 1995. It began work on an international codebook standard using Standard General Markup Language (SGML); in 1997, the standard was made compliant with Extensible Markup Language (XML), which had emerged as a more flexible and effective method of placing information on the Internet.[7] This work was aimed at the definition of Document Type Definitions (DTDs) and of the relationships among them. An assessment of this standard was undertaken in 1999 by the Royal Statistical Society Working Group on Archiving Data Standards for Documenting Data for Preservation and Secondary Analysis, but it found that this system was rather more limited than was desirable (Beedham, 1999). It was argued to be limited in dealing with links between and within surveys and therefore inappropriate for hierarchical data, aggregate files or time series data. It did not deal well with derived variables or presentation of complex routing information; it was difficult to make connections between question text, subsequent questions and those individuals of whom the questions are asked. Links between core and derived variables were not easily documented using the system. At present, therefore, it is not suitable for use with panel studies. A second edition of the DTD is currently in proposal stage; the new version will attempt to resolve the limitations identified and deal also with CATI/ CAPI surveys. In addition to looking towards the development of software to encourage and facilitate the use of the DDT, the new project will also look at interoperability with other standards initiatives such as the National Spatial Data Infrastructure standards.

The result of all of this activity is, therefore, a proliferation of potential standards for data description, but also, and more positively, an increased awareness among researchers of the need to provide metadata and full documentation of their data.

Elements of metadata and documentation

To act as a mediator between the data and the conscientious data user, data documentation must, as we have seen, contain far more than that implied by the ubiquitous term 'metadata' – a description of the data. The user requires a wide range of information about the research project which controlled the gathering of the data, from initial aims to questionnaire design, about the data collection, the data processing and much more. This is the information which gives the data context and meaning.

One approach to defining the elements required in metadata and data documentation is to look at the use to which the information is put. Thus, metadata would be that information required for resource identification and location (i.e. finding out what data exist and how they may be obtained, and other high-level bibliographic information about the dataset). Data documentation is that information required by those who wish to process the data further in some non-trivial fashion (i.e. those who wish to carry out analyses on the data).

Another, perhaps more useful, way of defining the two categories of information would be to consider the class of user of the information. Deecker *et al.* (1993) divide the potential user community into two or three groups with different requirements: the data brokers and data providers require identifying metadata, and the data analysts require more detailed data documentation. Sundgren (1993) makes finer distinctions which can be paraphrased as follows:

i data users (who need to know what and how, with information about the system and its contents, plus global information which allows the merging of different datasets);

ii data collectors (who need reminders of what tasks should be performed and how to perform them and need information for training and introducing new staff to production routines; plus a great deal of information about all aspects of the survey);

iii methodologists and specialists who design and maintain surveys (who need global information to get hints and ideas from the design of others surveys, and local meta-information about the particular survey they are designing, redesigning or maintaining);

iv managers (who need information on costs and revenues and on all quality aspects, user attitudes and usage patterns);

v software component specialists (who need formalised metadata to run the software successfully).

These general types of information are defined in Table 8.1.

When dealing with panel data, all of this information will be required. To ensure good and wide usage, the potential user community must be aware of the dataset's existence, potential and accessibility; metadata, of the descriptive or 'indexing' type, must be made available. For the secondary analyst, more detailed data documentation will be essential to aid in interpretation, to assist in data validation and imputation, to guide in analysis and to assist secondary users. What is generally true for all datasets becomes even more vital when we consider the case of household panel studies.

Documentation of household panels

Household panels, a 'new spectre haunting the social sciences' (Duncan in Chapter 3), are indeed notoriously complex undertakings. They grow rapidly to behemoth proportions. The obvious need for good documentation – for both primary investigators and secondary analysts – is matched by the considerable difficulties and peculiarities of panel studies. In this section, we shall first look at the particular aspects of panel studies which affect the documentation process and then turn to some of the solutions to those problems found and implemented by existing household panels.

Particular characteristics of panel studies

Household panel studies are, in general, specifically designed to be disseminated research resources. This places particular importance on clear and comprehensive accompanying documentation. So what are the particular characteristics of panel studies relevant to documentation issues?

i The *data files* are usually extremely large; the majority of existing household panels have initial samples of around 5,000 households

Table 8.1 Types of information required in data documentation

Information type	Examples of information required
Identifying information	Title, edition statement Producer and distributor information Bibliographic citation and cataloguing information Abstract covering the main features of the dataset
Bibliographies	Publications describing the data origin Publications based on analysis of the data
Background history of the originating project	Description of research questions which determined data collection strategy Sampling and selection procedures Detailed spatial referencing Time references Context information and relationship to other studies
Data processing information	Confidentiality procedures imposed Weighting and imputation procedures used Information on derived variables and other records Procedures taken to detect and correct errors (for example missing data, item non-response, case non-response)
Data management software and file descriptions	Information on type of data management systems in which files were prepared Number of logical records Number of variables Record length Number of files in the collection Data structure diagrams and so on
Data structure information	Formal descriptive elements necessary to collect, process and analyse data by computer Identifying names and numbers of variables Question texts Coding conventions used Interviewer instructions Descriptions of allowed values and formulas to check relationships between fields and to obtain derived variables Missing data definitions Frequencies and summary statistics Identification and documentation of derived variables and so on
Examples of data capture instruments and original documents	Questionnaires Show cards Interviewer instructions Coding instructions

and over 10,000 individuals. Successful navigation through the individual wave and cross-wave files is therefore a complex task and requires careful documentation. This is particularly relevant at the moment, when expertise and experience in longitudinal analysis is not widespread among the social science research community. In general, users will tend to assume that the rules and procedures resulting from their experiences with cross-sectional survey data are relevant for the processing and analysis of longitudinal data. To obviate this, the primary investigator's/ data collector's specific knowledge and expertise in longitudinal research must be made as clear and overt as possible.

ii The *substantive coverage* is usually *broad and interdisciplinary*. The documentation must therefore be clear and concise and must facilitate the widest range of approaches and analytical techniques and the investigation of varying research questions.

iii The *data structure* of panel studies is often extremely complex. Data are collected for different response units and at both the household and individual level, and analysis at both levels must be accommodated. It is important that the data user understands the structure of the datafile and the methods used by the data collector to organise the file. Users might well wish to carry out cross-sectional as well as longitudinal analyses on the dataset. The documentation must carry full instructions on undertaking both types of analysis.

iv Most panel studies carry *new, as well as repeated, questions at every wave*. The documentation must contain the requisite information to trace repeated questions and inform the user whether the repetition is exact, whether questions are similar or different (and in what way) and provide a guide to the relationship of questions across waves. The interdependence of all elements within and across waves of the survey must therefore be made clear.

v *Imputation and coding*: although it is common practice to include the questionnaire/data collection instrument in the documentation to establish context and response alternatives, as well as the sample design to establish probabilities of selection and to allow the calculation of sampling error, it is particularly important that the procedures and algorithms used for imputation and all forms of coding and adjustment in panel surveys are also fully described. A lack of information can lead to errors; for example, changes in variable meaning, different variable labels and other modifications, if not carefully recorded, can lead to errors in interpretation and, at the very least, wasted time and resources on the part of the secondary user.

vi The *same, as well as new, persons are interviewed each year* and sophisticated procedures for tracking these individuals across waves and for linking the relevant data must be in place. These must be carefully documented; the frequent inclusion of carried over baseline statistics must also be described.

vii Because of the longitudinal nature of panels, the *data are constantly updated and changed*. Some of this is the result of retrospective editing (for example where the data collected at a later wave replace data which were imputed in the earlier release, most often the case with income data). Other changes occur when inconsistencies in the data are discovered and resolved before, and after, release. Users need to understand what inconsistencies have been found and what data have been changed, revised or adjusted. The documentation must contain detailed information on the updating and changes made, to allow users of previous waves to repeat or to continue their analyses with each new release of the entire longitudinal file.

viii *Time* causes particular documentation problems. There are three types of time frame within household panels; each value must be carefully linked to the correct time if errors in interpretation are to be avoided. The first of these is the *time of data collection*. This can be extremely important in cases where external events might influence the data collected (for example tax reductions, elections and so on). In panel studies with extraordinarily long data collection periods, this information can be extremely complex in its own right. The second is *reference time*, the time period to which the data actually refer. This may be the past year, the past 10 years, when the respondent was a child (in the case of retrospective data) or the coming year (in the case of data on expectations or plans). Of particular importance for panel studies is the third type – *version time*. As indicated above, panel datasets are frequently adjusted, corrected and updated. Information on the version of each data release, the date of the last alteration, must be clear to all users.

Documenting panel data

David (1991) has identified a number of topics as essential for documentation of a panel dataset (see Table 8.2). The list is based on that provided by Bailar (1984) in relation to assessment of data quality and incorporates David's work on documenting the American Survey of Income and Program Participation (SIPP; see David 1989, 1991; Robbin and Frost-Kumpf, 1992).

Table 8.2 Types of information required in panel dataset documentation

---

Metadata, information about the data collection

---

1 Design of issues of the survey
       Sample
       Questionnaire
       Field procedures
       Coding
       Editing
       Linkage
       Treatment of missing data
       Integrity rules

2 Design of the panel
       Following rules
       Verification of linkage
       Periodicity

3 Facts of the survey
       Consistencies (related to integrity rules)
       Sample reconciliation
       Control tabulations (demographic, design, and linkage)

4 Facts of the panel
       Intertemporal consistencies
       Sample reconciliation
       Control tabulations

5 Analyses

The elements in Table 8.2 differ somewhat in emphasis and specificity from those listed in Table 8.1, as would be expected. Information types (1) and (2) concern the design of the dataset. Integrity rules describe consistencies demanded of the data by the logic of the collection process. Although seldom reported in standard documentation, this information is considered essential by David. Information type (3) records what is known about the data, including inconsistencies and anomalies, whereas (4) relates these particularly to the information which is needed to understand the conditioning of data collected in later waves on data collected in prior waves. Finally, (5) records the completed work already carried out on the data.

Documentation of existing household panels

As Rose has noted in Chapter 1, there are a number of national household panel studies in Europe, the USA and elsewhere. These range in age from the oldest continuous panel, the Panel Study of Income

Dynamics (PSID) based at the Institute for Social Research at the University of Michigan (32 years), through the Luxembourg Household Panel Study (PSELL) based at CEPS/INSTEAD in Luxembourg (15 years) and the German Socio-economic Panel Study (SOEP) (15 years) to the newer Hungarian Household Panel Study (HPS) based at TARKI in Budapest (5 years) and the British Household Panel Study (BHPS) based at the Institute for Social and Economic Research at the University of Essex (8 years). More recently, the European Community Household Panel Study (ECHP), a comparative panel study for twelve of the European Community countries, has been initiated and is now in its fourth year.

The studies vary considerably in the sizes of their samples and the length of their data collection periods. What they share, however, is that they all involve regular interviews with the same individuals from a national sample of households. Data collected cover such issues as employment, income, household structure, housing, health and social and political values. Many of them were also specifically designed to be general research resources, collected by a research team who designed the study to fit their own research agendas but with the needs of the wider research community in mind. This means that, for most of them, documentation issues had to be considered early on in the design process. A generalised discussion of the production of documentation of these panels will serve to illustrate the key elements of information required to assist the user of household panel data and will serve to describe the ideal sets of procedures for the collection and organisation of that information in the form of documentation.

In the initial planning stages of the survey, the collection, retention and organisation of information required for the documentation must be a major concern. The design team must be aware not only that this was good research practice, but also that longitudinal panel studies require such special considerations. Decisions taken need to be recorded, as *aides-mémoire* for future waves, as justification to both funders and future users and to inform future users. There are often a number of pilot studies carried out on early versions of the questionnaire, and the links between these and the final version of the questionnaire for the first wave, as well as records of the reasons for inclusion of certain questions and the deletion of others, should also be meticulously recorded.

Table 8.3 provides an overview of the types of high-level information which most current panel dataset producers have considered essential for collection and presentation in household panel survey documentation. These information elements are present in different order,

Table 8.3 Information elements in panel documentation

Introduction and research study descriptions Statement on confidentiality and ethics statement	This information can be linked to bibliographic metadata systems
Survey design information	This includes information on questionnaires, overview of survey topics, sample design, research rationale of study and individual variables and so on
Survey context information	This includes fieldwork details (timetable, fieldwork and interviewing procedures, following rules and panel tracking procedures)
Advice on usage and data linkage	This includes an indication of analysis potential, health warning and linkages possible, again at question/variable as well as section level
Sampling error, weighting and imputation information	Procedures/algorithms used, coding scheme of imputation flags and so on
Data processing and coding information	Description of procedures, techniques and coding frames used
Publication and analyses details	References to all publications relevant to, or based upon, analysis of the data
Descriptive information	Notes on data structures, Notes on terms/concepts used Contextual information Technical information on database structure and design principles Information on user database construction Notes on derived variable construction Detail of derivation/sources, plus statistical procedures used in their construction

formats and level of detail depending on the orientation of the data producers. Information presented at variable level is outlined in Table 8.4.

If the design and implementation plan for the documentation is in place during the early stages of the panel, it will be possible to collect and preserve all of this information on a systematic basis. All members of the research team should be made aware of the need for information collection and preservation, and therefore feed the data to a central documentation point or file. Forward planning of this kind can do a great deal to overcome the perhaps natural reluctance of researchers

Table 8.4 Information elements at variable level in panel documentation

Question text and number
Questionnaire page number
Record name (if relevant)
Variable name
Variable label
Frequency tables
Value labels
Secondary derived variables
Index terms per variable
Index terms per section
Routing information
Links between waves
Links between pilot and mainstage (at Q and V level)
Question indices/scales
Question source/link

to spend time documenting their activities. Carrying out a panel study has been likened to walking on a treadmill. At any given time, panel team members must deal with at least three waves of data – one wave being planned, one in the field and one being cleaned, processed and analysed. In these circumstances, it is particularly helpful if the collection of documentary information can be organised and routinised at an early stage before the relevant staff become too concerned with other issues.

The information included in the documentation comes from a wide variety of sources within the team – the research design, survey management and fieldwork teams, the computing staff and database managers, the analysts and secondary users. To hold and manipulate the information, the BHPS team, for example, established an automated system designed to collect, store and manage this information. Such a database has a number of initial tasks. It is required to: (i) collect information of a variety of types and from a variety of sources and in a variety of different formats at differing times; (ii) produce an information database documenting the creation of the survey database, its design, data collection, data processing and user database construction for in-house use; (iii) both track a continuing panel through varying situations and incorporate new members of the panel; (iv) document and chart links between pilot and mainstage surveys; (v) document and chart the links to other surveys; (vi) document both continuing (repeated annually and intermittently) and new questions; (vii) output full information for printed and/or machine readable documentation for the data; (viii) allow the retrieval of all documents related to the study; and (ix) provide the database on which complex online searches can be made. Information is output from this system and reformatted as the multi-volume *British Household Panel Study User Manual* (Taylor *et al.*, 1999).

Distributing panel data

This brings us then to one of the thorniest problems to which we alluded earlier. Panel datasets increase in size each year, as new waves of data are released. Significant retrospective changes are made to data released in previous waves. The size of the printed documentation also increases with the release of each wave, and earlier releases of the documentation also become redundant and flawed. Most of the household panels distribute their documentation in a variety of formats – printed, on diskette and on CD ROM.

The development of the Internet as a primary source of information for researchers has led to significant research concentration on the most effective means for presentation of such information in a user-friendly and flexible manner. The documentation for many household panel datasets is now available for searching on-line.[8] Based on the increasing research on metadata standards and delivery formats, data and documentation can be linked in innovative and flexible ways. Interactive multilevel searches on index terms are already possible, offering a significant boon to users of such complex datasets. Another imaginative project utilising the new Internet tools to provide the information data users will require is the UK Centre for Applied Social Surveys' (CASS) Survey Question Bank, which offers on-line access to full original format questionnaires from major British surveys, full free text retrieval and retrieval via a number of topic indexes. Expansion to include more theoretical and explanatory aspects of the surveys whose questionnaires are included will add greatly to its effectiveness (Guy, 1999). The ultimate aim of all of this activity is that everyone from the novice to the expert should be able to navigate in the documentation system, locate and retrieve data from it and connect the retrieved information to the microdatabase, independently, on a desktop machine.

Much work is currently under way on delivery systems for linked data and documentation. One of the more successful of these for social science data is the NESSTAR (Networked Social Science Tools and Resources) project, which aims to develop a common interface on the Internet to the data holdings of a large number of producers and disseminators of statistical information world-wide. By means of NESSTAR, users will be able to locate data sources across national boundaries, browse detailed metadata about these data, analyse and visualise the data online and download the appropriate subsets of data in one of a number of formats for local use.[9] At least one household panel dataset, the BHPS, will be entered within the framework of this system within the coming year (2000–1). Other projects are under way which aim to tackle some of the other hindrances to full use of panel data. These include the LIMBER (Language Independent Metadata Browsing of European Resources) project, which will create a system which allows cross-national browsing of survey metadata across different sites by translation of definitions and of code values and so on.[10] These systems can only, however, be as effective and efficient as the comprehensiveness and quality of the information provided by the data producer.

Conclusion

Given both the complexity and the richness of panel data, the provision of user-friendly documentation that is both comprehensive and easy to use is clearly an issue of great importance. The success or failure of an expensive data resource can depend on its quality. Only those who are fully aware of both the difficulties and the virtues of the dataset can carry out research analysis of high scientific value.

David (1991: 94–6) has posited a series of issues, on the basis of which a documentation system can be judged.

   i Completeness. (Can the secondary user do the same things as the original data collector?)
  ii Verification. (Can the user compute the same estimates that appear in published sources?)
 iii Understanding design (Can the user understand the design and execution of data collection?)
  iv Error. (Can the user understand the logical inconsistencies which have been checked and detected? Can the user identify changed, revised, edited and recoded data, as well as data that are known to be wrong but are not corrected?)
   v Evaluation. (Can the user share the data collectors' evaluations of the validity of the data, e.g. bias, mean square error, and so on?)
  vi Ambiguity. (Can the user unambiguously interpret the survey responses? Are truncated or randomly altered data adequately described? Are algorithms supplied?)
 vii Portability. (Can users move the data to their local computer?)

This sets rather stringent standards for documentation standards which a distressingly large amount of current documentation fails to meet. For panel data, these standards must be regarded as minimal. Documentation gives meaning and context to the data. Without it, the data are, at best, meaningless, and, at worst, subject to serious misinterpretation.

Notes

1 For full minutes of the Workshops, see the following URLs:

http: //hosted.ukoln.ac.uk/ec/metadata;
http: //www2.echo.lu/libraries/en/metadat2.html;
http: //www.echo.lu/libraries/en/metadat/metadata3.html.

2 See URL: http: //purl.org.dc.
3 For full papers, see URL: http//www.unece.org.
4 See Documentation Standards Working Group (1996). For more information on these *Guidelines,* contact the author (marcia@essex.ac.uk).
5 This can be found on the World Wide Web at the following URL: http: //www.icpsr.umich.edu/ICPSR/Archive/Deposit/dpm.html.
6 See URL: http: //www.umich.ed/DDI.
7 For a description of XML, see, among other publications, Curral (1999).
8 The URLs for some major household panels with on-line documentation are:

British Household Panel Study
http: //www.iser.essex.ac.uk/centres/BHPS

German Socio-economic Panel Study
http: //www.diw-berlin.de/soep/

Panel Study of Income Dynamics
http: //www.isr.umich.edu/src/psid/

Panel Comparability Study
http: //www.ci.rech.lu/paco/

Belgian Household Panel Study
http: //psw-www.uia.ac.be/psbh/

Hungarian Household Panel
http://rs2.tarki.hu/90/panel/MHP.html/

Luxembourg Household Panel
http://www.ceps.lu/psell/pselpres.htm

9 For a full description, see URL: http: //www.nesstar.org/.
10 For a full description, see the project description at URL: http: //venus.cis.rl.ac.uk/limber.

Part III

Panel data analyses

9 Dynamics of poverty and determinants of poverty transitions

Results from the Dutch socioeconomic panel

Ruud J. A. Muffels

Introduction

As we saw in Part I, panels are excellently suited for causal modelling of individual and household behaviour. Keeping track of individuals and households during the life cycle enables researchers to study in depth the occurrence and duration of life events and the underlying causal mechanisms. The modelling can be carried out more accurately if information is available over a longer time period. In the case of socioeconomic panels such as the PSID (Panel Survey of Income Dynamics) in the USA, the SOEP (Sozial-Ökonomisch Panel) in Germany, the British Household Panel Study (BHPS) in Britain and the Dutch SEP (Sociaal-Ekonomisch Panel), a number of topics have been dealt with or are under study. The potential for panel research is high and what particularly has been learned from the experiences with American panel studies is that panels provide datasets of high quality permitting advanced methodological and substantive research. Since the start of the Dutch panel in 1984, a number of issues have been addressed in publications of both The Netherlands Central Bureau of Statistics and Tilburg University (see Berghman *et al.*, 1988, 1990). Among these are labour market mobility, job search modelling, income dynamics, demographic changes and household formation (marriage, divorce and separation, birth, death, children leaving home, migration, etc.), consumption and saving behaviour, dynamic analysis of indebtedness, sociocultural changes (changes in attitudes), housing mobility, transition and duration analyses of social welfare and social security programmes (social assistance, unemployment, disability) and research on the social and economic position of various social groups such as the poor, the disabled, the unemployed and the elderly.

This chapter focuses on income poverty in The Netherlands in the second half of the 1980s. The SEP datasets of October 1985 to October

1988 are used for analyses. Although the study of poverty is only one of the many subjects which can be explored in panel surveys, the aim of this chapter is to give a clear picture of the kind of information that a panel study is able to provide. Cross-sectional data on poverty (Muffels *et al.*, 1990) provides information on the distribution of income poverty in 1 year and on aggregate changes in income poverty for specific groups between years. Multivariate relationships on the determinants of poverty may be examined by using regression techniques, but they provide rather weak causal information about the relationship between the occurrence of life events and poverty. Moreover, cross-sectional data cannot provide information on the timing and duration of poverty spells because the dependent variable 'poverty status' is a *latent* construct which does not allow retrospective questioning. Only panel or cohort data can therefore provide information on the timing and duration of poverty spells. This implies that panels may provide much richer information on issues such as the permanent nature of poverty, changes in poverty status of individuals and households over time and about the events related to entry into and escape from income poverty.

The definition and calculation of three poverty lines

First, in this analysis, the proportions of individuals and households are calculated whose disposable incomes are below the level of the so-called National Social Minimum Income (Muffels *et al.*, 1990), below the level of the so-called European Statistical Minimum Income poverty line (O'Higgins and Jenkins, 1989) or below the level of the Subjective Poverty Line (Goedhart *et al.*, 1977).

National Social Minimum Income (NSMI)

Although no official poverty line exists in The Netherlands, the level of the lowest social security benefits in the Social Assistance Act might be considered to represent a certain minimum income level required for households to live in security of subsistence. This minimum income level will be referred to as the National Social Minimum Income (NSMI). The calculation of the poverty line for every type of household in the sample is based on the benefit levels of the General Social Assistance Act, the Incidental Benefit Act (a benefit scheme for households living entirely from a single minimum income), the Family Allowances Act and the Study Grants Act (see Muffels *et al.*, 1990). Each household's disposable income has been compared with the level of the NSMI corresponding to that type of household. If disposable income is below the NSMI, a household is considered to be poor. Households may indeed have an income below the safety net of the 'social minimum' because of a reduction in the level of benefits (sanction regulations, payment of credit commitments, capital income ceilings) or because of non-take up of benefits (underconsumption of social security benefits that the household is entitled to but, for whatever reason, does not want or dare to claim). Under-reporting of income could of course be a reason too, although only information is used from households reporting on the whole list of twenty-seven income components on which information is collected in the SEP questionnaire (Kapteyn and Melenberg, 1990).

Subjective Poverty Line (SPL)

Whereas the NSMI standard is to a certain extent based on a kind of social or political consensus, or at any rate on the views of experts (politicians) on the minimum income level that is supposed to be required to live in security of subsistence, the SPL is based on views of the households themselves. In the survey, a question is asked about the absolute minimum income a household needs in order just to make ends meet. This question is called the Minimum Income Question (MIQ). There are various versions of the SPL, depending on the model specification used. The model is theoretically based on the preference formation theory. The model used here is the model which assumes a close relationship between the answers on the MIQ and family composition (cost/need factors), current household income (influences of habit formation) and reference group characteristics (reference group influences). The poverty line is set where the actual household income equals the minimum income reported with the MIQ. Again, each household's income is compared with the level of the SPL for that household. If disposable household income is below the SPL, a household is considered to be poor (Goedhart *et al.*, 1977).

European Statistical Minimum Income (ESMI)

The poverty line which has been used in research commissioned by the European Community (Second Poverty Programme) to measure the extent of poverty in Europe is based on the idea of setting the poverty line at a level which corresponds to a certain fraction of median standardised household income in the country. The line to be used in this study is based on work by O'Higgins and Jenkins (1989). Standardisation of household income means correcting for differences in welfare due to differences in household composition. These differences can be expressed in a so-called equivalence scale for various household types. Various equivalence scales are distinguished in the literature. The equivalence scale proposed by O'Higgins and Jenkins (1989) starts from the poverty line for a single person. This equivalence scale then supposes that compared with the single person standard (which is set at 50% of the median income of the standardised income distribution) for each additional adult in the household a 70% increase in household income is needed to keep the household at the same welfare level. For each additional child, a 50% increase in household income is assumed to be needed. Again, if the household disposable income falls below this poverty line, the household is considered to be poor. In what follows, this poverty line will be referred to as the European Statistical Minimum Income (ESMI) standard.

Data and operationalisation

The analyses carried out in the study are based on the SEP datasets for individuals. The datasets of 1985–8 are matched through the personal identification number. To be able to calculate the incidence of poverty at an individual level the household income and the poverty line at household level are assigned to every person in the household. If the household lives in poverty, it is assumed that each person in the household lives in poverty. This assumption implies that the household is considered to be the consumption unit and not individuals within households. In welfare economic terms, this meets the assumption of a 'joint utility function'. The same procedure is followed for other variables at household level such as the socioeconomic status of the head of household, the marital status of the head, the age, education level, number of children and so on. From the perspective of analysing the dynamics of poverty or change in general, it is very important to take into account changes in household composition because family composition often changes fundamentally over the years for various reasons, such as birth and death, children leaving home, divorce or separation and marriage or remarriage. Thus, limiting the analysis of poverty dynamics to the household level appears inappropriate. Therefore, the analyses need to be shifted from the household to the individual level. Dynamic analyses of poverty can then be carried out at individual level, taking into account household characteristics. This approach is followed in the sections of this chapter on poverty dynamics. For a more detailed operationalisation of all variables used in the analysis, the reader is referred to Dirven and Berghman (1991).

Trend analysis 1985–8

Panel data may be analysed as if they represent a series of repeated cross-sections. Analysing the panel as a series of cross-sections enables us to carry out trend analyses which give further insight into the occurrence and magnitude of changes in poverty risks over time at the level of population categories.

As far as the overall picture is concerned, it appeared that a slight decrease in the incidence of poverty between 1985 and 1988 occurred according to the NSMI and ESMI poverty standards, whereas the SPL revealed a slightly upward trend in the incidence of poverty. Applying a loglinear approach as implemented in the SPSS-Loglinear routine, the results indicate that, except for the SPL, the trends turn out to be insignificant. The increasing trend for the SPL, which became manifest in 1987, may indicate that the reform of the Dutch Social Security system, as of 1 January 1987, did result in increasing feelings of subsistence insecurity. The poverty gaps turn out to be very stable over time, as Table 9.1 shows.

Using data from 1986 to 1988, an analysis of aggregate change has been performed at the level of (sub)groups (Dirven and Berghman, 1991). For a number of background characteristics, the hypothesis tested was that of the non-existence of a linear trend across the years. It appears that when applying the NSMI poverty line for a number of characteristics, such as age, socioeconomic status, main source of income, property income and type of household, the hypothesis of no trend has to be rejected. Although for the whole population stability seems to be more common than change, when broken down into population characteristics, the general conclusion was that the mobility flows appear to be quite large (Dirven and Berghman, 1991). Research on repeated surveys or trend research may therefore give a good insight into the aggregate change of poverty statuses at the level of social groups or categories. It permits us to test whether and what kind of trend exists across subsequent years. However, because the level of analysis is on groups, the potential for analysing structural changes related to changes in composition is much less than in the case of panel research. Structural changes related to changes in positions have to be assessed at the individual level.

The analysis of income and poverty mobility

The use of panel data may be particularly valuable when studying income changes or income mobility patterns at the individual level. A variety of methods have been proposed in the literature to study income

Table 9.1 Poverty ratios and poverty gaps for three income poverty lines, 1985–8

	1985		1986		1987		1988	
	% Households	% Persons	% Households	% Persons	% Households	% Persons	% Households	% Persons
Poverty standards								
SPL	14.7	10.1	16.3	11.5	18.4	12.8	18.6	12.3
NSMI	8.7	7.3	7.5	6.6	8.0	8.0	7.9	6.2
ESMI	8.5	11.1	8.2	10.5	8.5	8.5	7.5	9.4
Average poverty gaps (%)								
SPL	21	23	24	26	24	25	24	25
NSMI	19	31	26	28	27	29	26	26
ESMI	21	20	26	24	26	23	27	24

mobility patterns. In Table 9.2, a very simple technique is used which may give a preliminary insight into the magnitude of changes and into the nature of poverty over time. Is poverty a temporary phenomenon which is almost randomly distributed over the population? Or is poverty an issue which is concentrated within a small persistent group of people in society having very low incomes? Evidence is presented on upward mobility (moving out of poverty), downward mobility (moving into poverty) and persistent poverty (staying poor). The flows into and out of poverty between 1985 and 1988 are given for those persons who participated in the panel in both years. This was the case for about 77.3% of all persons who reported an income and participated in 1985.

In Table 9.2, information is given on the transitory and permanent character of income poverty. Persistent insecurity is highest for the SPL standard. Approximately 47% of the insecure in 1985 were still living in insecurity of subsistence in 1988. According to the EC standard, the percentage is somewhat lower, 41.3%, but the lowest estimate is derived for the NSMI standard. Only 18% of all persons insecure in 1985 were still insecure in 1988. It appears that the stability of income poverty standards is highest in case of the SPL and the ESMI and lowest in the case of the NSMI.

This is confirmed by the evidence in the last column of Table 9.2. It gives the cross-product or odds ratio, which represents a measure of association between income security in 1985 and in 1988. The higher the ratio, the higher the relative *stability* of the poverty standard. The odds ratio is the ratio of the odds for the non-poor compared with the poor and the odds for the poor compared with the non-poor. In the case of a two by two cross-tabulation, the odds ratio is given by:

$$(f11*f22)/(f21*f12)$$

where f represents the frequency of observations and the numbers refer to the cell locations.

In percentages of the insecure and secure populations upward mobility seems to be much higher than downward mobility. Upward mobility is highest for the NSMI standard. More than 80% of the NSMI insecure move out of subsistence insecurity in the years between 1985 and 1988, whereas according to the subjective standard only 53% of all persons were capable of escaping from subsistence insecurity. These percentages are much higher than the percentages linked with movements *into* subsistence insecurity. Only 4% of those living in security of subsistence according to the NSMI standard appear to move into poverty in the years between 1985 and 1988. This may probably give

Table 9.2 Upward and downward mobility and persistent subsistence insecurity between 1985 and 1988

Poverty standards	Poor 1985 (%)	Poor 1988 (%)	Upward mobility all (%)	Insecure (%)	Downward mobility all (%)	Secure (%)	Persistent insecurity all (%)	Insecure (%)	Relative mobility (odds ratio)
SPL	9.6	11.1	5.1	53.2	6.6	7.3	4.5	46.8	11.1
NSMI	6.7	5.1	5.4	82.0	3.9	4.2	1.2	18.0	5.0
ESMI	9.9	8.4	5.8	58.7	4.3	4.8	4.1	41.3	13.9

Notes

Secure, security of subsistence.

Insecure, insecurity of subsistence.

% all, as a percentage of all persons.

% poor in 1985, upward mobility + persistent insecurity.

% poor in 1988, downward mobility + persistent insecurity.

rise to the assessment that in the late 1980s the Dutch situation is more accurately delineated as a situation of 'permanent wealth' than as a situation of 'permanent poverty'. One needs to be cautious, however, in drawing strong inferences on the basis of these findings alone as the transition probabilities estimated in this classic mobility table may be biased because of measurement error (see Chapter 6; van der Pol, 1989; Hagenaars, 1990).

To test whether changes in poverty status are the result of measurement errors, a stationary discrete time-latent Markov model with correction for measurement error is estimated (van der Pol, 1989).[1] The method is developed for frequency data. The program uses the information of the contingency table on poverty status (income insecurity/income security) measured over the 4 years of observation (1985 to 1988). The model with latent variables applied here assumes that year-to-year income changes may be disentangled into a latent part, which is assumed to be time invariant, and a random part. If no real change occurs over time and thus all change has to be attributed to measurement error, the one latent class model should fit the data. In that case, people are supposed to have remained in their initial latent state (in poverty or not in poverty) without any real movement from one state to another. If the one latent chain does not fit the data, various models with increasing numbers of latent classes may then be estimated to discover which model best fits the data. The model implicitly treats all change that is not captured in the various latent classes as random or measurement error. The model has been defined for the relevant four waves of the Dutch panel dataset. A so-called first-order stationary latent Markov model is assumed which can be given by:

$$\theta_{sijkl}^{y^{1234}} = \pi_s^y \delta_{si}^{y^1} \tau_{sij}^{y^{12}} \tau_{sjk}^{y^{23}} \tau_{skl}^{y^{34}}$$

Restrictions

i   Stationarity:

$$\tau_{sij}^{y^{12}} = \tau_{sjk}^{y^{23}} = \tau_{skl}^{y^{34}}$$

ii   Mover–stayer model:

$$\tau_{sij}^{y^{tt+1}} = 1 \forall i = j; \quad \tau_{sij}^{y^{tt+1}} = 0 \forall i \ne j$$

where y denotes the latent variable. The θs denote the proportions of the population belonging to latent class s and being in state i,j,k,l, where the i,j,k,l have the values 1 if the person is 'in poverty' and 0 if the person is not 'in poverty' at time points 1, 2, 3 and 4 respectively. The θs are assumed to be the product of the πs, which equal the proportions of the population in latent class s, δs, the initial proportion of people at time point 1 in state i of latent class s, and the τs, the transition probabilities of the population within each class s moving between the two states of that class over subsequent years. The problem is to find an estimator $\hat{\theta}$ which comes closest to the observed θ. Estimation is based on maximum likelihood procedures.

Because of the large number of parameters to be estimated, the model can only be identified if restrictions are made on the parameter set. It is assumed that the process is first-order Markovian and *stationary*. The transition from a state of income poverty to income security or vice versa is assumed to depend only on the state currently occupied and not on the duration of the spell in the initial state. The Markov process is assumed to be without memory, for which reason only the τ^{t+1} are included in the model and the τ^{t+2} are left out. The latter assumption is obviously a very strong one because there is much evidence that the issue of duration dependency is important with respect to poverty (see Bane and Ellwood, 1986). A further restriction is made with a view to the assessment of *persistent poverty*. It is presumed that a so-called mover–stayer model would be particularly suited to capture the issue of persistent poverty since in such a model one class is fixed as a stayer class which either represents the persistent poor or the persistent rich. Hence, the mover–stayer assumption reflects the case of two or more classes in which one class is fixed as a stayer class with unity transition probabilities for $i = j$ and zero transition probabilities for $i \neq j$. The proportion of poor people belonging to the latent stayer class may then provide population-wide estimates of persistent poverty. The proportion of the population in the latent stayer class multiplied by the initial proportion who were poor in that class gives the model-based estimates of the incidence of *persistent poverty* in society.

The assumptions underlying this model are rather heroic because the model does not take account of the existence of 'duration dependency' and all income changes which are not captured in the latent classes are treated as random measurement error. This means that incidental income shocks over time which represent real changes in income are treated as measurement error in so far as they are not captured in the latent classes. The last feature of the latent class model also implies that the extent to which manifest (real) changes must be attributed to measurement error is overstated. The issue raised here is that part of the error term has to do with serially correlated measurement errors which are known to be significant in time series on reported incomes. The reason for its presence must be found in the tendency of incidental income shocks to persist over time. If the model had been corrected for this autoregressive component of the random error term, it is most likely that a larger part of the reported (manifest) changes would have turned out to be real changes instead of changes attributed to measurement error. Income mobility could then have been even higher than the model predicts. However, the last statement holds only when the estimated latent classes are not capable of properly capturing the changes in initial incomes. The estimation results are given in Table 9.3.

It emerges from Table 9.3 that, during the observation period of 4 years, some 11% of the population belongs to a latent class of '*movers*', either moving from the poor to the non-poor or from the non-poor to the poor. Almost 41% of this class appear to be initially poor. About 48% belong to a class of so-called '*mobile stayers*', either staying non-poor in the 4-year period or becoming poor in at least 1 of the 4 years. The model also shows that 41% of the population belong to a latent class of '*stayers*', either staying rich or poor during the observation period. About 96% of this group were initially rich and only 4% were initially poor.

The model-based estimate of persistent poverty is about 1.7% of the population (0.04×0.41). This percentage is lower than the percentage of persistent poor in Table 9.2 (4.1%) because the model-based estimate reflects the number of persons who stayed poor during the whole period, whereas in Table 9.2 it reflects the number of people still poor in 1988 compared with 1985, including therewith the people moving out of poverty temporarily in the years between. To examine the impact of measurement error on the reported changes, the latent transition probabilities have to be compared with the manifest ones. As the model fit appears to be quite good, and the observed matrix is therefore very well reproduced by the model, the correction for measurement error appears to have only a small effect on the observed transition probabilities.

Duration of poverty

From the cross-section analysis it becomes apparent that, in each of the 4 years, some 6–7% of the population had to rely on an income below the social minimum income level (NSMI standard). Yet, the panel analysis shows that as much as 14.5% of the population was in poverty

Table 9.3 Estimation results of a latent mixed Markov model on poverty transitions (ESMI standard) with three latent chains, of which one chain is fixed as a stayer chain

| | Proportions in class s, π_s^y | Initial proportions, δ_{si}^{y1} | Transition probabilities, τ_s^y | | | |
| | | | One year | | Three year[a] | |
			1 Insecure	2 Secure	1 Insecure	2 Secure
Chain 1	0.11 (0.076)					
Insecure		0.41 (0.14)	0.67 (0.15)	0.32 (0.19)	0.59	0.41
Secure		0.59 (0.14)	0.46 (0.20)	0.54 (0.20)	0.58	0.42
Chain 2	0.48 (0.61)					
Insecure		0.06 (0.12)	0.17 (0.20)	0.83 (0.20)	0.05	0.95
Secure		0.94 (0.12)	0.05 (0.09)	0.96 (0.09)	0.05	0.95
Chain 3	0.41 (0.67)					
Insecure		0.04 (0.068)	1.00 (fix)	0.00 (fix)	1.00	0.00
Secure		0.97 (0.068)	0.00 (fix)	1.00 (fix)	0.00	1.00

Notes

Annual information on four waves of the SEP panel, 1985–8 (N = 6,206; standard errors between parentheses).

Fit indices:

df = 6

Likelihood ratio = 3.55

Probability level = 0.74

Pearson χ^2 = 3.53

Probability level = 0.74

a The programme used for estimation of the model does not give the standard errors for the 3-year transition probabilities.

during 1 of the 4 years under observation. A similar finding is found for those living in subjective poverty (SPL). The annual figures show that 10–13% of the population had an income below the subjective subsistence level, whereas approximately 21% of the population lived below the subjective minimum in at least 1 year. For the European Standard (ESMI) the percentages are 9–11% and 19.4% respectively. In all cases, it appears that about *twice* as many people were at risk during the 4-year period than in any particular year. Table 9.4 presents further information on the evolution of poverty over time.

Despite the large proportions of people at risk of income insecurity across time, in general *stability* seems to be more common than change. According to the NSMI standard, more than 85% of the population remained in security of subsistence during the whole period. According to the subjective standard, the percentage is slightly lower, 79%. Table 9.4 also shows that a very high fraction of the poor remained poor for a single year. About 60% by the SPL, and as high as 75% by the NSMI standard, appeared to be in income insecurity for a single year. These figures suggest that income mobility is extremely high, particularly in the case of the NSMI standard. Apparently, poverty and insecurity of subsistence are permanent situations for only a minority of the population. Permanent poverty does not present itself from these figures as a major issue for policy-makers, although the outcomes differ somewhat across the various poverty lines. However, it will be shown that this general conclusion underestimates the issue of permanent poverty.

Table 9.4 Evolution of poverty between 1985 and 1988

Duration	SPL (%)	NSMI (%)	ESMI (%)
Percentage not in poverty in any year	78.8	85.5	79.6
Percentage in poverty in at least 1 year	21.2	14.5	19.4
Of which in poverty during			
1 year	59.7	74.6	63.5
2 years	23.4	20.8	21.0
3 years	11.7	3.9	12.5
4 years	5.1	0.7	3.0
Number of poor	3,483	2,379	3,184
Total	16,405 (100)	16,411 (100)	16,431 (100)

The method applied here follows Duncan (1984) but has one major drawback: *censoring* is not taken into account. For the poor, it is not known at the start of the observation period in 1985 how long they had been poor in the past (left censoring); and for the poor at the end of the period, it is not known how long they will remain poor in the future (right censoring). To solve this problem, it is necessary to switch to a spell approach (see Chapter 11; Bane and Ellwood, 1983, 1986). A poverty spell is assumed to start if in year $t - 1$ someone is non-poor but moves into poverty between $t - 1$ and t.

Because it is not known at what exact time someone became poor in the intermediate period, only discrete time models can be applied. If the respondent is observed for more than 2 years, *multiple spells* of poverty may occur. The classic approach for dealing with these spell data is the standard discrete time *'life table'* approach. More advanced continuous models for analysing mobility are event history analysis, survival analysis techniques, duration models and failure time models (see Kalbfleisch and Prentice, 1980). As the 4-year observation period was rather short, it was not feasible to apply continuous time duration models, and, instead, the *'life table'* approach was been applied.

In Table 9.5, the life table estimates for the various poverty lines are given. The information is again at the individual level. The standard errors of the survival estimates (exit rates) are not depicted but appear to be small (on average between 2% and 3%). Again, the high mobility among the poor becomes apparent. Mobility is particularly high in the first year of a spell beginning. Almost 50% of all spells, according to the NSMI standard, terminate in the first year after a spell beginning. For the ESMI and SPL standards, the percentages appear to be much lower, but still show that spells tend to end in the first year after beginning. If the spell lasts longer than 1 year, exit probabilities fall quickly, particularly according to the NSMI standard. In case of the NSMI standard, the exit rate falls in the second year to 16%. These findings confirm our earlier conclusion that a large number of spells appear to be spells of short duration, although the outcomes again differ quite markedly across the various poverty lines. Compared with the evidence in Table 9.4, the correction for *'right censoring'* turns out to lead to higher (cumulative) survival rates. According to the NSMI standard, after 3 years 58% of all spells were terminated; 42% of all persons experiencing a spell remain poor during the whole observation period. According to the SPL and ESMI standards, the percentages of persons remaining poor during the observation period are higher (52% and 50% respectively). Again, the conclusion should be that the ESMI standard and the SPL standard appear to be more stable than the NSMI standard. All in all, it might be concluded that the outcomes on the mobility flows

Table 9.5 Duration of poverty spells according to three income poverty lines, 1986–8

Spells in years	SPL				NSMI				ESMI			
	Nx	Tx	Qx	Cum Px	Nx	Tx	Qx	Cum Px	Nx	Tx	Qx	Cum Px
1	1378	350	0.34	0.66	1006	371	0.49	0.51	1330	332	0.32	0.68
2	329	46	0.20	0.52	129	13	0.16	0.42	399	78	0.26	0.50
3	74	0	0.20	0.52	17	0	0.16	0.42	123	0	0.26	0.50
$\alpha =$	0.79 (0.08)				1.15 (0.19)				0.78 (0.03)			

Notes

Nx = number of observations at beginning of spell.
Tx = number of terminations of spells.
Qx = exit rate.
Cum Px = cumulative survival rate.
α = indicator for duration dependency.
Standard errors of χ in parentheses.

into and out of poverty appear to set the various poverty line definitions quite apart from each other.

In Table 9.5, information is also included on the occurrence of '*duration dependency*'. The existence of duration dependency is very important from a scientific as well as a policy perspective because if 'duration dependency' occurs the probability of escaping poverty rises or falls with longer durations of poverty spells. In the case of 'negative duration dependency', the probability of escaping from poverty falls with increasing spell durations, and in the case of 'positive duration dependency' the probability of escaping from subsistence insecurity rises.

If it is assumed that the duration of poverty spells has a Weibull distribution, the occurrence of 'duration dependency' may be investigated. In the case of Weibull, the survival function is given by:

$$S(t) = \exp(-t^\alpha) \text{ and } \ln[-\ln S(t)] = \alpha.\ln t$$

If the log minus log of the survival estimates is plotted against the log of time, a straight line will be found if the duration process indeed proves to be Weibull. In such a case, α can be estimated with ordinary least squares (OLS) regression. Since the data are grouped because of the occurrence of multiple spells and spells with identical duration, the time variable representing the duration of the spells has to be weighted with the frequency of the spells. In the case of negative duration dependency, the indicator α will be less than 1 and in the case of positive duration dependency α will be greater than 1. The plot indeed indicates that the process is Weibull as a straight line was found. In Table 9.5, the αs for the various poverty standards and the corresponding standard errors are given. Negative duration dependency is present with the SPL and the ESMI poverty lines, which implies that the probability of escaping from subsistence insecurity *falls* with longer durations of poverty spells. The α difference from 1 is significant because it exceeds the two times standard error interval. The reverse holds for the NSMI standard, for which α proves to be greater than 1, but this difference is not significant because it falls within the two times interval of the standard error estimates. From Heckman and Singer (1982), it is well known that the duration effect may be overestimated because of the effect of '*unobserved heterogeneity*'. If the exit rate or hazard appears to be related to population group characteristics, part of the duration dependency effect has less to do with the autonomous time effect than with unobserved differences between these groups. If unobserved heterogeneity is indeed present, the magnitude of the negative duration effect will most probably be lower. This implies that the likelihood of moving out of poverty may still fall with rising duration but less because of an autonomous time effect than because of differences in unobserved personal (for example 'human capital') characteristics.

The evidence across the 3-year period suggests that the issue of 'persistent poverty' is of high relevance for current socioeconomic policies. The percentage of the poor population that remains poor during the observation period is quite high, some 40–50%, although it differs across the poverty lines. The proportion of 'persistent poor' would presumably be even higher if information over more years had been available. In the seminal article by Bane and Ellwood (1986), based on information from the PSID, it became clear that, over a period of 15 years, the bulk of the person–years of poverty is accounted for by the long-term poor. However, the assessment of Bane and Ellwood with regard to the length of welfare spells is not undisputed; Blank (1989) found shorter spells of welfare use and less evidence for duration dependency.

The determinants of spell beginnings and spell endings

Bane and Ellwood (1986) attempted to relate the beginnings and endings of spells to the occurrence of life events such as the birth of a child, a marriage or divorce, a decline in the head's or the wife's earnings, a fall in transfer income, a rise in the poverty level, etc. It appears that spell durations differ depending on the causes of a spell beginning or a spell ending. Spells that begin because of the birth of a child appeared to be the longest of all.

Because in the Dutch panel data used here information on the poverty status of persons and households is available for a limited period of time (4 years), Bane and Ellwood's approach (presuming the existence of large datasets covering a long period of time) is not applicable without a considerable loss of accuracy and reliability in the estimates of the density distributions for the completed spells of poverty. Hence, a different approach is adopted. The analyses will be focused on the determinants of transitions into and out of poverty by means of estimation of logistic models. To acquire as many poverty spells as possible on which to base the analyses, three pairs-of-years datasets were pooled, for 1985–6, 1986–7 and 1987–8.

The empirical model

From a scientific viewpoint, a very interesting question which still needs to be answered is what are the determinants that condition mobility into and out of income insecurity. Therefore, logistic models have been estimated with the transitions into and out of poverty between year t and $t + 1$ as dependent variables (see Maddala, 1983; McFadden, 1984). In the models to be presented here, the poverty line used is the National Minimum Income Standard (NSMI). In analysing the impact of possible determinants, three kinds of variables indicating the type of changes that condition exit from and entry into poverty are accounted for: changes in household formation [childbirth, divorce/separation, (re)marriage], changes in employment status (a change in employment status of the head of household, gaining or losing a job of at least 1 hour per week, the number of employed in the household at time $t + 1$) and changes in the poverty line level for the household as a result of changes in family composition (number of children, number of adults, change in number of adults, change in number of children).

Following this, a variable is implemented indicating the 'residual income' level of the household in terms of having neither an income from labour nor from social security benefit schemes. Second, a variable is added indicating the income shortfall of the insecure and the income surplus of the secure at time t. This variable is called the *NSMI ratio* and is defined as the log of the ratio of household income and the NSMI income standard level. It is considered to be an indicator of the *extent* of deprivation and acquired wealth (see also Duncan *et al.*, 1991). Furthermore, some background variables, such as the education level of the head of household, socioeconomic status, marital status, sex and age category of the head, all measured at time t, are implemented in the model formulation. Finally, three time variables for each transition period (1985–6, 1986–7, 1987–8) are implemented of which only the time variable for 1987–8 turns out to be significant.

Estimation results

The estimation results are presented in Table 9.6. It should be noted that, except for the job gain and job loss variables, all variables are measured at the household level. This implies in most cases that the information for the head of the household is assigned to all household members. The exponent values in the last column represent the conditional probabilities for a transition into or out of poverty according to the NSMI poverty standard. Values below 1 indicate a proportionally lower probability of passage into or out of poverty compared with the reference category (indicated with X), and values above 1 indicate a proportionally higher probability.

All variables related to *changes in employment status* of the household, such as the number of employed at $t + 1$, the change in employment status of the head of household between t and $t + 1$ and the gain or loss of a job of any person in the household between t and $t + 1$, appear to be very significant indicators of transitions into and out of income poverty or subsistence insecurity. The probability of moving out of subsistence insecurity is almost three times higher for persons in households of which the head found a job between t and $t + 1$ than for persons in households where no change took place in the employment status of the head. The probability of moving into poverty is twice as high for persons in households of which the head became unemployed.

Changes in household formation, through (re)marriage or separation (divorce or death of the partner), turn out to have much smaller effects than changes in labour market status. The effect of (re)marriage on movements out of poverty turns out not to be significant, although the exponent value indicates that (re)marriage has a large positive effect on the probability of escaping from subsistence insecurity. On the other hand, the effect of separation on transitions into subsistence insecurity appears to be quite strong too. Compared with a married couple, both persons belonging to a divorced or widowed household and single persons have a higher probability of entering poverty. *Changes in household composition* because of childbirth or of children leaving home have a marginal impact on the probabilities of escaping from poverty.

Finally, the results in Table 9.6 show that with respect to the *demographic and socioeconomic characteristics* of the household, particularly the age, the education level and the socioeconomic status of the head of household, there is a strong impact on the probabilities of escaping from insecurity or moving into it. The probability of escaping from income insecurity increases and the probability of moving into it falls strongly with increasing age and higher education. The risk of moving out of insecurity appears to be much lower for heads of households receiving a social assistance benefit and the risk of moving into income insecurity turns out to be much higher for persons living in households of which the head has no profession (students), or receives an unemployment, disability or social assistance benefit. Finally, the effect of sex has an unanticipated negative sign. Persons living in female-headed households (at time t) have a higher chance of moving out of subsistence insecurity than persons living in male-headed households. The effect of belonging to a household of which the head is divorced or widowed turns out to be insignificant with regard to transitions out of insecurity.

Table 9.6 Estimation results of a logistic regression model for transitions into and out of poverty, 1985–8, according to the NSMI standard

Valuation in equation	Out of poverty			Into poverty		
	Parameter estimate	*Significance level*[a]	*Exponent level*	*Parameter estimate*	*Significance level*	*Exponent level*
Log NSMI ratio	0.2	3.6	1.3	-0.2	-2.5	0.8
Residential income	0.1	10.3	1.1	-0.1	-13.0	0.9
Socioeconomic status						
Employed	X			X		
Unemployed	0.6	3.4	1.8	0.7	7.6	2.4
Retired	0.7	2.8	2.0	0.2	1.4	1.2
Social assistance	-0.4	1.5	0.7	0.9	4.9	2.4
No profession	-0.8	5.7	0.4	1.3	11.5	3.7
Education level						
Primary/secondary low education	X			X		
Secondary higher	0.3	2.3	1.3	-0.1	-1.4	0.9
Tertiary	0.7	3.1	2.0	-0.5	-3.5	0.7
University	1.3	3.9	3.7	-0.4	-1.4	0.8
Age class (years)						
< 34	X			X		
35–44	0.5	3.0	1.6	0.0	0.3	1.0
45–54	0.4	2.4	1.5	0.3	3.4	1.4
55–64	0.7	4.4	2.1	-0.3	-2.8	0.7
65–74	1.0	3.7	2.7	-0.1	-0.6	0.9
≥ 75	1.0	3.3	2.7	-0.1	-0.8	0.9
	-0.5	-3.4	0.6	-0.1	-0.6	0.9

	b	t	exp(b)	b	t	exp(b)
Sex (1 = male)	X			X		
Marital status						
Married	X			X		
Divorced/widow(er)	0.0	0.1	1.0	0.2	1.7	1.2
Unmarried	0.1	0.4	1.1	0.4	4.1	1.7
Number of adults	−0.2	−1.3	0.8	0.3	2.9	1.4
Number of children	0.1	0.7	1.1	0.4	4.4	1.5
Dummy change n children	−0.1	−0.3	0.9	0.1	1.4	1.1
(1 = > 0)	−0.2	−1.3	0.8	0.8	8.6	2.2
Dummy change n adult (1 = > 0)	0.8	1.5	2.2	n.s	n.s.	n.s.
(Re)Marriage separated/divorce	n.s.	n.s.	n.s.	0.4	2.2	1.5
Job gain	0.9	3.6	2.6	0.1	0.7	1.1
Job loss	−0.5	−1.3	0.6	0.6	4.8	1.9
Number of employed at (+) $t + 1$	0.6	10.1	1.9	−1.1	24.4	0.3
Change employment status						
No change	X			X		
Become employed	1.5	5.9	4.7	−0.7	−3.1	0.5
Become unemployed	−0.6	−2.1	0.6	1.1	8.7	3.0
Time						
1985–6	n.s.	n.s.	n.s.	n.s.	n.s.	n.s.
1986–7	0.0	0.4	1.0	n.s.	n.s.	n.s.
1987–8	−0.6	−6.2	0.5	0.1	1.0	1.1
Constant	−1.2	4.6	0.3	−1.0	−2.1	0.4

Note

All persons ≥15 years.

Log likelihood	−1.371	−5.296
Pseudo R^2 =	0.21	0.16
N =	2,626	30,284
$N_{success}$ =	1,653	1,614

a Significant if t-ratio ≥ 2. X = reference category. n.s., Not significant.

However, the model findings for transitions into poverty show that persons living in single households, or in households with a divorced or widowed head, have a higher chance of moving *into* insecurity than persons living in a nuclear family. The exponent values show that persons living in single households have a 70% higher probability of moving into poverty and that divorced and widowed households have a 20% higher probability of moving into poverty than those living in a nuclear family.

From these findings, one may conclude that the risks of falling into insecurity and the chances of escaping from subsistence insecurity appear to be quite unevenly spread among the population. There is high mobility into and out of poverty, but this is concentrated within particular social categories: the low educated, the unemployed, the disabled, the divorced and the widowed. The conclusion must be that for a high proportion of those living just below or just above the income poverty thresholds the changes in poverty status are due particularly to changes in employment and household formation statuses.

Conclusion

The results of the trend analysis of poverty show that the incidence of poverty remains rather stable over the 4-year period 1985–8. Also, the poverty gaps are quite stable over time. Yet, if the panel evidence on poverty is examined, it becomes clear that, whichever poverty line is taken, about *twice* as many people are at risk during the 4-year period (1985–8) than in any particular year. Thus, income mobility appears to be quite high.

This is confirmed by the results of the mobility and duration analyses of *income poverty*. These show that mobility into and out of income poverty is quite high over the years. At the same time, it emerges from the duration analysis that permanent income poverty is quite high too. In the 4 years under observation, about 40–50% of those who became poor in the first year of a spell remained poor during the whole observation period, and so obviously they failed to escape from income insecurity. The outcomes differ across the various poverty lines. The European Standard (ESMI) appears to be the most stable poverty line, whereas the NSMI standard turns out to produce the lowest permanency rates. Those who succeeded in escaping from income insecurity seem to have moved out particularly in the first year of a poverty spell. For those not escaping poverty in the first year, the probability of leaving poverty falls very quickly in subsequent years. As is shown by Sawhill (1988), core determinants of the increased occurrence of persistent poverty in the 1970s and 1980s seem to have been the structural changes in labour market conditions (for example structural unemployment) and family composition (increasing numbers of single households and one-parent households through changing marriage/remarriage and divorce/separation patterns). There is evidence that compared with the US similar causes are responsible for the occurrence of permanent poverty in The Netherlands in the 1980s (Duncan *et al.*, 1993a; Muffels, 1993). Hence, the mobility analyses carried out on the Dutch panel provide evidence on the issue of the 'permanent' and 'transitory' nature of poverty, something which cannot be obtained from cross-section analyses. The design of most panels, like the Dutch panel, permits the study of behaviour at the individual as well as the household level, which also means that the interrelations of individual and family well-being can be examined.

The elaboration of new techniques to analyse panels in the last two decades has contributed considerably to the enrichment of research practices, not least with respect to poverty research. In particular, the elaboration of discrete response and discrete time models such as log linear models or discrete choice models, event history, survival and failure time models allows inferences to be made on the poverty issue using the dynamic information included in socioeconomic panels. All in all, one might say that with the creation of panels an extremely rich and flexible analytical device is elaborated for studying individual and household behaviour. The higher efforts in terms of costs and time to analyse panel data seems to be justified by the results that can uniquely be obtained from panel analyses.

Note

1 Various models are estimated with PANMARK, a program developed by van der Pol (1989).

10 Low-income dynamics in 1990s Britain[1]

Sarah Jarvis and Stephen P. Jenkins

Introduction

In this chapter, we analyse the dynamics of low income in 1990s Britain using data from the first four waves of the British Household Panel Survey (BHPS).[2] Our research provides a longitudinal complement to the Department of Social Security's *Households Below Average Income* reports which are largely based on cross-section data. It also provides the first UK comparison with the pioneering work in the USA of Bane and Ellwood (1986), Huff Stevens (1994, 1995), Duncan *et al.* (1984, 1993a) using other national panel datasets, especially the PSID.

We document the size of the 'persistent poverty' problem and amount of low-income turnover. Low-income exit and re-entry rates are also calculated. In addition, we describe the characteristics of the people who were persistently poor, those making transitions out of low income and those making transitions into low income. For the last two groups, we also investigate how these income changes are related to changes in household employment and demographic composition over the same period. All the patterns that we describe are robust to the choice between two definitions of what the low income cut-off is.

We show that there is much turnover in the low-income population. Although there is a small group of people who are persistently poor, it is the relatively large number of low-income escapers and low-income entrants from one year to the next which is more striking. Almost one-third of our sample experienced low income at least once during the 4-year period. Simulations using estimated income exit and re-entry rates demonstrate the importance of repeated low-income spells (rather than single spells) for explaining how often people experience low income over a given time period. Thus low-income churning was a significant phenomenon in 1990s Britain.

Employment-related events such as getting a job are found to be associated with making transitions out of low income. For transitions into low income, job loss together with demographic events affecting household composition are important. The group with low income at all four interviews mostly included single pensioners and families with children headed by a couple or lone parent not in work.

Data and definitions

Our research is based on data from waves 1–4 of the BHPS. The first wave was designed as a nationally representative sample of the population of Great Britain living in private households in 1991. Households composing the first wave (interviews in Autumn 1991) were selected by an equal probability sampling mechanism using a design standard for British household social surveys. The achieved sample comprised about 5,500 households, which corresponded to a response rate of about 65% of effective sample size. At wave 1, over 90% of eligible adults, approximately 10,000 individuals, provided full interviews. Original sample respondents have been followed and reinterviewed at approximately 1-year intervals subsequently. The wave-on-wave response rate was about 88% for wave 1 to wave 2, and over 90% thereafter.[3]

We worked with the subsample of 7,910 persons (adults and children) present in each of the four waves and who belonged to complete respondent households. The first restriction arose from the desire to examine income sequences over all four waves; the second yielded the sample for whom we could derive our preferred income measure.[4] To account for differential non-response at wave 1, and subsequent differential attrition, all statistics presented below are based on data weighted using the BHPS wave 4 longitudinal enumerated individual weights.

Our income measure, net income, has the same definition as the HBAI 'before housing costs' measure used by the Department of Social Security (DSS) (see for example Department of Social Security, 1995). In short, net income is the sum across all household members of cash income from all sources (income from employment and self-employment, investments and savings, private and occupational pensions and other market income plus cash social security and social assistance receipts) minus direct taxes (income tax, employee National Insurance contributions, local taxes such as the community charge and the council tax), with the result deflated using the relevant McClements equivalence scale rate to account for differences in household size and composition. To compare real incomes, all incomes have been converted to January 1995 prices. The unit of analysis is the person; following standard practice, each person is attributed the net income of the household to which s/he belongs. The income receipt period is the month before the wave interview or most recent relevant period for each income component (except for employment earnings, which refer to 'usual earnings').[5] We have converted all sums to a consistent pounds per week basis. Because our income observations for each person refer to their incomes round about the time of an interview (i.e. some time during the last quarters of 1991, 1992, 1993 and 1994 for most respondents), we do not take account of the additional movements out of and into low income occurring outside the periods round the interview.

We side-step the vexed issue of what the appropriate definition of 'low income' is by using in parallel two definitions of the low-income cut-off:

i   half wave 1 mean income (a threshold which is fixed in real income terms);

ii the poorest quintile in each wave (a threshold which varies in real income terms).

The real income value of the first cut-off is some £127 per week for all four waves; the real income values of the second are £135, £139, £140 and £144 for waves 1–4 respectively. Half mean wave 1 income corresponds to the eighteenth percentile of the wave 1 distribution, but only the fourteenth percentile by wave 4.

There are empirical and conceptual advantages to using these two definitions in parallel. From a conceptual point of view, the dual usage strikes a balance between those who argue for a fixed real income cut-off, often on the grounds that the incidence of low income should necessarily decline as real income grows, and those who argue for a threshold which depends on the income distribution in question. Using the poorest quintile is an example of the latter approach (an alternative would be some fraction of the contemporary mean). From an empirical point of view, using the two thresholds allows sensitivity analysis of the conclusions drawn to variations in the generosity of the threshold: the quintile-based cut-off is higher than the absolute threshold (by some 6% at wave 1 and by about 13% at wave 4). The particular levels of the chosen thresholds are of course somewhat arbitrary as there is no clear-cut evidence of a sharp increase in poverty or deprivation at these specific values. However, half-the-average and quantile cut-offs do have the virtue of being commonly used in British empirical research on incomes; in particular, closely related definitions are used in the HBAI statistics from the DSS.[6] Finally, the cut-offs provide a sufficiently large number of cases in the low-income stayer, escaper and entrant subgroups to allow meaningful breakdowns by subsample characteristics.

Low-income dynamics

The extent of persistent poverty

Table 10.1 summarises the wave 1/wave 2/wave 3/wave 4 income sequence patterns for our longitudinal sample, in which an income has been recoded as L (low) if it is below the low-income cut-off for that year and as H (high) otherwise. The left-hand side of Table 10.1 shows the results for the case when the low-income cut-off is half wave 1 mean income; the right-hand side shows the case when it is the poorest quintile. For both cases, the table shows the relative incidence of each of the relevant sequences.

The first row of Table 10.1 helps to address the issue of how widespread the persistent poverty problem is. We find that 4.3% of the sample had an income below half wave 1 mean income at all four interviews (those with LLLL, row 1). This proportion is about seventy times larger than the proportion one would expect to find were the chances of having low income at each interview statistically independent (0.06%). If, instead, the low-income cut-off is the poorest quintile, the proportion of persistently poor rises to 7%, which is about forty-four times larger than the proportion were there statistical independence (0.16%). To put things another way, we find that of the group of people with incomes below half wave 1 mean income 52% still had low income when interviewed at wave 2. About one-third (34%) of the original wave 1 low-income group had low income at waves 1–3, and about one-quarter had low income at all four waves.

Whether these figures indicate that the incidence of persistent poverty is relatively high or not is difficult to judge and is likely to depend on whether one believes the cut-offs are meaningful or not in terms of individual deprivation. Nonetheless, we are struck by the sensitivity of the estimate of the proportion persistently poor to changing the low-income cut-off. Although the quintile cut-offs are only some 6–13% higher than half wave 1 income, the 'per cent poor for four waves' score is about 60% higher in the latter case. The lesson is that estimates of the incidence of persistent poverty can be sensitive to choice of low-income threshold, especially if they are located in a relatively crowded section of the income range, as in our case.

International comparisons provide another yardstick for judging whether our estimates of persistent poverty are large or small. As we

Table 10.1 Low-income sequence patterns for two low-income cut-offs

Income sequence	Low-income cut-off = half wave 1 mean		Low-income cut-off = poorest sample quintile	
	%	Cumulative %	%	Cumulative %
1 LLLL	4.3	4.3	7.0	7.0
2 LLLH	1.8	6.0	1.9	8.9
3 LLHL	1.2	7.2	1.2	10.1
4 LLHH	2.2	9.4	2.2	12.2
5 LHLL	1.2	10.6	1.4	13.6
6 LHLH	1.2	11.8	1.0	14.6
7 LHHL	0.7	12.5	1.2	15.8
8 LHHH	5.5	17.9	4.2	20.0
9 HLLL	1.4	19.3	2.5	22.5
10 HLLH	1.5	20.8	1.5	24.0
11 HLHL	0.9	21.6	0.9	24.9
12 HLHH	2.6	24.3	2.9	27.8
13 HHLL	1.8	26.0	2.2	30.0
14 HHLH	2.2	28.3	2.6	32.6
15 HHHL	3.0	31.3	3.6	36.2
16 HHHH	68.7	100.0	63.9	100.0
All	100.0		100.0	
Base n	7,910		7,910	

Note
The table summarises the income sequence wave 1 income/wave 2 income/wave 3 income/wave 4 income, with incomes recoded L if below the low-income cut-off and H if equal to the cut-off or higher.
Percentages calculated using BHPS longitudinal weights.

saw in Chapter 3, Duncan *et al.* (1993a) report estimates for six countries in Europe and North America of the percentage of families with children with incomes below 50% of median size-adjusted income in all 3 years of a 3-year period during the mid-1980s. For Germany and the Lorraine region of France, the percentages were about 1.5%, and for Luxembourg and The Netherlands the percentages were about 0.4%. They were much higher in Canada (11.9%) and in the USA (14.4%). Using estimates of the composition of the persistently poor population (presented later), we estimate that about 7% of persons in couple or lone parent families with children at wave 1 had an income below half the wave 1 mean at three consecutive interviews. Since half the mean is a more generous cut-off than half the median (£127 compared with £109 at wave 1), the 7% should be adjusted further downwards to enable comparison with the estimates by Duncan *et al.* (1993a). But even if this adjustment halved the proportion, the British estimate of persistent poverty among families with children would be larger than the European ones cited above. Drawing firmer cross-national conclusions requires closer attention to be given to the comparability of the income definitions and more up-to-date data. There may have been changes in persistent poverty rates between the mid-1980s and the 1990s.

How many people experience low income over a period of time versus at a point in time?

Although, on either definition of the low-income cut-off, a minority of the population had low income at every wave, many more had low income at one period or another. If we focus on the figures for the half wave 1 mean cut-off, we find that 5.6% had low income at three interviews, 8.1% had low income at two interviews (15.3% had two or more consecutive Ls) and 13.1% had low income at one interview in four. These statistics imply that during the 4-year period 9.8% of the sample had at least three low-income spells, 17.9% of the sample had at least two low-income spells and 31.3% of the sample had at least one low-income spell during the 4-year period. In other words, almost one-third of the sample is touched by low income at least once over a 4-year period, i.e. about twice the proportion with low income at one interview (which was 18% at wave 1 and 15% at wave 4).

If the poorest quintiles are the low-income cut-offs, the proportion touched by low income at least once is just over one-third (36%), which is 175% larger than the 20% proportion for a single wave.

We are struck by the extent of low-income turnover; so too are audiences to whom we have presented this research. The turnover is another manifestation of the Jarvis and Jenkins (1996) finding that there is much year-to-year income mobility for all income groups, albeit mostly short-range. It should also be remembered that our figures underestimate the proportion touched by low income throughout the 4-year period. Recall that low-income spells other than round about the time of the panel interviews are not examined here.

Low-income exit and re-entry rates

With four waves of the BHPS, we can begin to look at how low-income exit rates vary with the length of time that people have had a low income, and at how low-income re-entry rates vary with the length of time that people have been out of low income. In similar fashion to some of the analyses in the last chapter, these rates can be used to predict the length of time that people will spend in low income during a single continuous low-income spell and the number of times that they experience low income over a given number of years. The exit and re-entry rates which are relevant in this context are the ones which refer to the experience of a cohort of persons starting a low-income spell (and thence at risk of exit thereafter) and to the experience of persons finishing a low-income spell (and thence at risk of re-entry thereafter). The exit rates are not in general the same as the exit rates from the stock of low-income persons at a particular time; the stock contains a mixture of recent entrants and long-term stayers. An analogous argument applies to the re-entry rates.

To estimate exit rates, we use data for cohorts of persons beginning a low-income spell in the second or third wave (those with sequences HLXX and XHLX in Table 10.1), and to estimate re-entry rates we use data for cohorts of persons finishing a low-income spell in the first or second wave (those with sequences LHXX and XLHX). Low-income exit rates were calculated by dividing the number of persons ending a low-income spell after *d* waves with low income by the total number with low income for at least *d* waves. Low-income re-entry rates were calculated analogously. Our analysis is constrained by the small number of waves of data available; we can only estimate two exit and two re-entry rates.

Low-income exit and re-entry rate estimates

The low-income exit and re-entry rate estimates, for the two sets of low-income cut-offs, are displayed in Table 10.2. Also shown are the proportions of persons remaining on low income, or who re-enter low income, broken down by duration, corresponding to these estimates.

Table 10.2 Low-income exit and re-entry rates, by duration

Duration no. of interviews)	Low-income exit rate	Cohort still with low income (%)	Low income re-entry rate (%)	Cohort re-entered low income (%)
Low-income cut-off = half wave 1 mean income				
1	0.54	100	0.29	0
2	0.51	46	0.11	29
3		22		36
Low-income cut-off = poorest quintile				
1	0.50	100	0.30	0
2	0.38	50	0.23	30
3		32		47

Notes
Exit rates derived using data for persons beginning a low-income spell in the second or third wave (sequences HLXX and XHLX in Table 10.1). Re-entry rates derived using data for persons finishing a low-income spell in the first or second wave (sequences LHXX and XLHX in Table 10.1).

We find, using the half wave 1 mean cut-off, that the exit rate from low income after 1 year with low income is 0.54. The exit rate after two interviews reporting low income falls slightly to 0.51. The results imply that for a cohort starting a low-income spell just under one-half (46%) still have low income after 1 year, and about one-fifth (22%) still have low income after 2 years (i.e. after the third interview reporting low income). That is, almost four-fifths of the low-income entry cohort no longer have low income after 2 years.

The low-income re-entry rate 1 year out of low income (i.e. at the second interview) is 0.29, but after 2 years (at the third interview) the re-entry rate more than halves to 0.11. The rates imply that for a cohort of persons starting a spell out of low income 29% will start another low-income spell after 1 year, and more than one-third (36%) will have fallen below the threshold again after 2 years. Thus nearly two-thirds of the cohort will have incomes above the cut-off for at least 2 years (three interviews).

When the low-income cut-off is the poorest quintile, we find different magnitudes but similar patterns. The main difference is that exit rates are slightly lower and re-entry rates higher, which is not surprising since the real income levels characterising the low-income thresholds are slightly higher. A higher crossbar is harder to jump over than a lower one and easier to fall below. Another difference between the results for the different thresholds is that the low-income exit and re-entry probabilities do not decline as quickly in the poorest quintile cut-off case, again probably reflecting the crossbar effect. The differences in rates for the different low-income cut-offs have quite large implications. For the quintile thresholds, the proportion starting a low-income spell still with low income after 2 further years is about one-third (rather than one-fifth), and the proportion of low-income escapers starting a new low-income spell after 2 years is nearly one-half (rather than just over one-third).

Our estimated probabilities of exit and re-entry are higher than those found by Shaw *et al.* (1996) in their study of UK Income Support (IS) receipt during 1991–2. Their life table estimates show that the proportion of a cohort starting an IS spell and still claiming after 1 year is about 60%, and that about one-half are still claiming 2 years after the spell start (Shaw *et al.* 1996: Ch. 10). The proportion of former IS claimants who start another claim after 1 year of finishing the previous spell is estimated to be about 25%. The results are consistent with our results for low income because IS entitlement levels are less generous than the thresholds we are using – the crossbar is lower still (see footnote 6).

Our results can also be compared with estimates of US poverty exit and entry rates for 1971–81 made by Bane and Ellwood (1986) and for 1970–87 by Huff Stevens (1994, 1995) using Panel Study of Income Dynamics (PSID) data. Bane and Ellwood's classic study reported that the probability of exit from poverty after 1 year was 0.45, and after 2 years 0.29 (see Table 10.6; Bane and Ellwood, 1986), and Huff Stevens reports almost identical figures when eliminating some 1-year poverty spells as Bane and Ellwood did. When these adjustments are not made, Huff Stevens estimates the poverty exit rate after 1 year to be 0.53, and 0.36 after 2 years. She also reports poverty re-entry rates of 0.27 after 1 year out of poverty, and 0.16 after 2 years out of poverty (Table 10.1; Huff Stevens 1995). We are struck by the fact – differences between the US and British welfare states, and the periods covered, aside – that our estimates are not too far out of line from those of Huff Stevens.

It is important to take the exit and re-entry probability results together. The exit rates, if looked at on their own, might suggest that the majority of people falling into low income will spend only a couple of years in this situation. However, the path out of low income is not a one-way 'up' escalator; the re-entry estimates remind us that there is a not insignificant chance of finding oneself on the 'down' escalator to low income again within 2 years. This implies that low-income spell repetition is an important phenomenon in Britain and needs to be taken into account alongside the issue of single long-term low-income spells.

Accounting for multiple spells is important for predicting the number of low-income interviews over a given period

These remarks are emphasised by the results of a simulation exercise comparing single-spell and multiple-spell predictions of the number of interviews at which people will have low income during a fixed period with the actual number. The methodology follows that used by Huff Stevens (1995: Table 2), although we have data for a much shorter period (2 years rather than 10) and as a consequence our sample sizes are much smaller (hundreds rather than thousands). The single- and multiple-spell predictions have been derived using the exit and re-entry rates shown in Table 10.1, and the actual distribution of 'number of interviews with low income out of next three' is derived using data for all persons composing the low-income entry cohort at wave 2 (those with an income sequence HLXX in Table 10.1).[7]

The results are summarised in Table 10.3. The single-spell distribution estimates (column 1) suggest that about one-half of those starting a low-income spell will have low income for only 1 year, and

Table 10.3 Distribution of 'number of interviews with low income out of next three': single spells and multiple spells

Number of interviews with low income	Distribution of single spells	Distribution of 'number of interviews with low income out of next three'	
		Predicted	Actual
Low-income cut-off = half wave 1 mean income			
1	0.54	0.38	0.42
2	0.24	0.38	0.36
3	0.22[a]	0.23	0.22
Low-income cut-off = poorest quintile			
1	0.50	0.35	0.37
2	0.19	0.34	0.31
3	0.31[a]	0.31	0.32

Note
a Three or more interviews.
Columns 1 and 2 derived from Table 10.2 exit and re-entry rates. Column 3 derived from wave 2 low-income entry cohort (sequences HLXX in Table 10.1).

this fraction is much higher than actually occurred (column 3) or was predicted by the multiple-spell distribution estimates (column 2). These results underline our point that repeated low-income spells are an important feature of poverty dynamics in Britain.

Comparisons of the multiple-spell distribution estimates with the observed distributions provide a guide as to how well simple life table models predict observed distributions of the number of years with low income over a given period (more precisely, the number of interviews out of three with a low income). As it happens, they do fairly well, in the sense that the estimates are not too far apart. Nonetheless, it appears that the simulations underpredict the fraction experiencing low income at only one interview out of three and overpredict the fraction experiencing low income at two interviews.

These results are consistent with the findings of Huff Stevens (1994, 1995) (for the USA) that taking account of repeat spells provides much better predictions than does relying on single-spell estimates. She also reports that the former underpredict very short poverty spells. As Huff Stevens proceeds to demonstrate, better predictions of the time spent in poverty over a given period require substitution of the simple life table methods with poverty exit and re-entry models which allow rates to differ between people with different levels of education, age and other characteristics. Application of these more sophisticated modelling methods to British poverty dynamics will become more feasible as the number of waves of BHPS data increases.

Who are the persistently poor?

From a policy perspective, it is important to be able to distinguish the causes of long- and short-term poverty in order to tailor anti-poverty policy measures accordingly. Is long-term low income systematically associated with having some particular set of characteristics, or are the persistently poor simply a random subset of those who are poor at a particular point in time? If the latter case obtains, then there is no particular reason to develop a policy programme specially directed at long-term poverty alleviation separate from the 'standard' anti-poverty measures for the point-in-time poor population (Duncan *et al.*, 1984).

We begin to address these issues here by looking at the characteristics of low-income stayers, defined as those persons having low income at all four interviews. We compare breakdowns by sex, family type and family economic status for this group with the corresponding breakdowns of all the people who had low income at wave 1 (see Table 10.4). We shall discuss the results based on using half wave 1 mean

Table 10.4 Characteristics of low-income stayers, by person type, family type and family economic status; low-income cut-off = half wave 1 mean income

	Low-income stayers		Low income at wave 1 (%)	All at wave 1 (%)
	Wave 1 (%)	Wave 4 (%)		
Person type				
Male adult	20	22	27	36
Female adult	45	46	46	42
Dependent child	35	32	28	22
Family type				
Single pensioner	24	27	21	11
Couple pensioner	7	7	12	10
Couple and child(ren)	35	37	34	40
Couple, no child(ren)	4	2	8	21
Single and child(ren)	26	19	17	7
Single, no children	5	7	8	13
Family economic status				
1+ adults full-time self-employed	5	6	5	11
All adults employed full time	0	0	2	2
Couple: 1 full time, 1 part time	0	0	2	14
Couple: 1 full time, 1 not in work	3	7	8	13
Single or couple: 1+ part-time work	10	4	11	7
Head or spouse aged 60+ years	33	36	36	19
Head or spouse unemployed	25	22	18	5
Other (lone parent, disabled, etc.)	23	23	17	6
All	100	100	100	100
Base *n*	321	321	1,386	7,910

Notes

Low income defined as having income less than half wave 1 average income. Low-income stayers are those with low income at all four waves (income sequence LLLL in Table 10.1).

'Low income at wave 1' column refers to all persons with low income at wave 1.

'All at wave 1' column refers to all longitudinal sample members at wave 1.

Family type and family economic status definitions as in HBAI reports (Department of Social Security, 1995). Percentages calculated using BHPS longitudinal weights.

income as the low-income cut-off as the results for the other threshold definition are very similar (for details, see Jarvis and Jenkins, 1996).

The characteristics of low-income stayers

We find that, although many of the same types of people who are low-income stayers are the same as those who compose the wave 1 low-income population, there are some marked differences in the breakdowns. The wave 1 low-income population mostly consists of elderly persons (single adults and married couples) and non-working families with children (married couple and lone-parent families), and each of these subgroups is over-represented relative to their numbers in the wave 1 sample as a whole (Table 10.4, compare columns 4 and 5). In contrast, the breakdowns of the wave 1 characteristics of the low-income stayer group reveal that elderly persons and non-working families with children are heavily represented among this group too, but in a different mix from the wave 1 low-income population. In particular, there are noticeably more people belonging to lone parent families (26% compared with 17%) and to couple families with children in which neither the head nor the spouse is working (25% compared with 13%). As a result, there are more dependent children among the low-income stayers than among the wave 1 low-income group (35% compared with 28%). There are also more single pensioners (24% compared with 21%).

There are both similarities and differences between our findings and those of Duncan *et al.* (1984) based on US PSID data for 1969–78. The results are similar because we also find that the persistently poor differ from the short-term poor. However, the differences that we find are not as marked as those of Duncan *et al.* (1984), although this may simply reflect the different definitions and observation period (for example they define persistently poor as 8 or more years poor out of 10, and discuss the 1970s rather than the 1990s). Like us, Duncan *et al.* (1984) find an over-representation of families headed by a woman.

Table 10.4 also breaks down the low-income stayer population according to their characteristics in wave 4, and interestingly the distribution across subgroup categories is broadly similar to that found for wave 1. Not everyone remains in the same subgroup however. Over time, people's household contexts change: people marry, divorce, have children, children leave home, get jobs, lose jobs, etc. We calculate, for example, that 18% of the sample experienced a family type change between waves 1 and 4, and 32% experienced a change in their family's economic status. These results do not lead us to change our conclusions about which sort of people are most likely to be persistently poor as the wave 4 breakdowns are much the same as those for wave 1. However, we are struck by how much family context change was experienced even within the low-income stayer group, whose incomes did not fluctuate significantly over the period (by definition). We look at the relationship between economic and demographic flux and income changes in the next section.

Who moves out of low income? Who moves in?

We now turn from considering the characteristics of the low-income stayers to seek to identify those who escape from low income and those who enter it. We examine the characteristics and events associated with making a transition out of low income or making a transition into low income. Bane and Ellwood's (1986) study of US poverty spells during 1970–82 is the pioneering example of such research. In common with all such studies, we had to consider the issue of how to identify 'genuine' transitions separately from those simply representing measurement error or random year-to-year fluctuations. Following Duncan *et al.* (1993a), we defined a low-income escaper to be someone with an income below the low-income cut-off at wave t and an income at least 10% higher than the low-income cut-off at wave $t + 1$, where $t = 1, 2, 3$. Similarly, a low-income entrant has an income above the low-income cut-off at wave t and an income at least 10% lower than the low-income cut-off at wave $t + 1$. We then pooled all the transitions and examined the characteristics and events of those experiencing them.[8] Between one in six and one in seven of the sample made a transition out of low income over the four waves, and a similar fraction made a transition into low income (see Table 10.5).

In seeking to document the factors associated with transitions into and out of low income, our analysis has two dimensions. First, we describe those making transitions between waves t and $t + 1$ in terms of their characteristics at wave t. Second, we examine the associations between low-income exit and entry and contemporaneous economic and demographic changes in a person's family environment. More precisely, we compare the incidence among those who escape or who enter low income between waves t and $t + 1$, of various events occurring between waves t and $t + 1$, with the incidence among the sample as a whole. The events considered are changes in family type, number of adults and number of children in the household, family economic status and number of earners in the household. Results are broadly the same whichever low-income cut-off definition is used, and so we refer below

Table 10.5 Characteristics of low-income escapers and entrants at the wave before the transition; low-income cut-off = half wave 1 mean income

	Low-income escapers (%)	Low-income entrants (%)	Low income at wave 1 (%)	All at wave 1 (%)
Age (at wave 1 interview)				
Dependent child	24	30	28	22
Adult aged (years)				
< 30	16	18	14	18
30–39	10	13	10	15
40–54	12	11	8	18
≥ 55	37	29	40	28
Person type				
Male adult	34	32	27	36
Female adult	45	42	46	42
Dependent child	21	26	28	22
Family type				
Single pensioner	19	14	21	11
Couple pensioner	9	6	12	10
Couple and child(ren)	32	37	34	40
Couple, no child(ren)	12	13	8	21
Single and child(ren)	11	14	17	7
Single, no child(ren)	16	16	8	13
Family economic status				
1+ adults full-time self-employed	7	15	5	11
All adults employed full time	2	9	2	24
Couple: 1 full time, 1 part time	3	7	2	14
Couple: 1 full time, 1 not in work	9	9	8	13
Single or couple: 1+ part-time work	11	12	11	7
Head or spouse aged 60+ years	33	21	36	19
Head or spouse unemployed	17	11	18	5
Other (lone parent, disabled, etc.)	18	16	17	6
All (as % of total longitudinal sample)	100 (15)	100 (12)	100 (18)	100 (100)
Base *n*	1,132	897	1,386	7,910

Notes
A low-income escaper has an income below the low-income cut-off at wave *t* and an income at least 10% higher than the low-income cut-off at wave *t* + 1. A low-income entrant has an income above the low-income cut-off at wave *t* and an income at least 10% lower than the low-income cut-off at wave *t* + 1.
'Low income at wave 1' column refers to all persons with low income at wave 1.
'All at wave 1' column refers to all longitudinal sample members at wave 1.
Transitions pooled from *t* = 1, 2, 3.

to results for the low-income cut-off of half wave 1 average income (for the full set of results, see Jarvis and Jenkins, 1996).

The characteristics of low-income escapers and entrants

Table 10.5 displays the breakdowns by age at wave 1, pre-transition person type, family type and family economic status. By definition, low-income escapers are drawn from among the low-income population and entrants are drawn from among the non-poor, and so it is of interest to know how the characteristics of the mover and at-risk groups match up – are the movers a random selection of those at risk? Table 10.5 reveals that escapers are predominantly elderly people or belong to non-working families with children, i.e. precisely the same groups mostly commonly found among the low-income group as a whole (see the 'Low income at wave 1' column). However, some interesting differences stand out; note among the escapers the higher proportions of childless couples (and adults aged 40–54 years at wave 1) and childless single adults (and adults aged less than 30 years). We have checked whether these two groups were disproportionately located close to the low-income cut-off in the first place and it does not appear that this was, in fact, the case, suggesting that the results do not arise simply because childless people required smaller income changes to escape low income.[9] Remember that these childless groups form a minority of the escapers in any case.

When we look at the characteristics of the low-income entrants, we find that their profile is similar to that of the escapers. In other words, the entrants' group consists mainly of elderly people (about one-fifth is from pensioner families) or people from families with children (about one-third are couple families, about one-sixth lone parent families). Compared with the distribution for the sample as a whole at wave 1, there are disproportionately more unemployed or part-time couple and lone-parent families (and hence dependent children) and single pensioners. In part this is because these groups are more likely to have incomes relatively close to the income cut-off and have less far to 'fall' – this comment applies particularly to single pensioners and unemployed and part-time employed couple families.[10]

Economic and demographic events associated with low-income exits and entries

We now investigate the association between *changes* in people's household context and changes in income, comparing the incidence of events among low-income escapers and entrants with those of the sample as a whole (see Table 10.6).

We find that family economic status changed for about one-third of escapers and for more than 40% of entrants, which is much higher than the incidence among the sample as a whole (about one-quarter). The incidence of pure family type changes is less than the incidence of family economic status changes for all groups, but this is to be expected since changes in one's family economic status can come about via family type changes.[11] Looking at family type changes, there is above average incidence for entrants (14%) but, interestingly, not for escapers (about 10%). There is a similar pattern in the relative incidence of joint changes in family economic status and family type. They were experienced by 6% or fewer of the total sample, and by low-income escapers, but by about one-tenth of the entrants.[12]

The lower panels of Table 10.6, focusing on changes in the numbers of earners, adults and children in a person's household, provide greater detail and reveal some clear patterns. Looking at the changes in the number of earners first, we find that increases in the numbers of earners in the household are associated with transitions out of low income, whereas decreases in the number are associated with transitions into low income. The number of earners increased for 18% of escapers compared with 11–12% of the sample as a whole. For entrants, the contrast with the sample as a whole is even more distinct: the proportion with a decrease in the number of earners is more than twice the average sample incidence, i.e. 30% compared with 12–13%.

There are also some interesting associations between household composition change and low-income status change. Escapers appear to experience about average, or slightly above average, demographic stability: the percentage of the group with the same number of adults is much the same as for the whole sample, the percentage with the same number of dependent children is a little larger than for the total sample and there are slightly lower percentages experiencing either increases or decreases in numbers. There is a more distinctive picture for entrants. In particular, the number of adults in the household decreased for 14% of this group, twice the percentage for the total sample. Entrants also experienced (slightly) above average changes in the numbers of children in the household.

In sum, escapers appear to have above average incidence of increases in the numbers of earners, combined with roughly average changes in the number of adults and number of children. Increases in the numbers of earners may arise by an existing household member getting a job, by the arrival of a new partner who also works or both. Because the

Table 10.6 Percentages experiencing economic and demographic events: low-income escapers and entrants compared with whole sample; low-income cut-off = half wave 1 mean income

	Total sample			Low-income escapers (%)	Low-income entrants (%)
	W1–W2 (%)	W2–W3 (%)	W3–W4 (%)		
Family economic status changed	26	23	23	32	43
Family type changed	11	7	8	11	14
Both economic status and type changed	6	4	2	6	10
No. earners decreased[a]	13	13	12	15	30
No. earners same	75	76	77	67	56
No. earners increased	12	11	11	18	14
No. adults decreased[a]	7	7	5	6	14
No. adults same	82	88	87	85	79
No. adults increased	11	5	8	9	7
No. children decreased[a]	10	3	6	4	8
No. children same	86	93	90	91	85
No. children increased	4	4	5	4	6

Note
a Unit is the household. Low-income escapers and entrants defined as in Table 10.5.

incidence of household composition change is about average for this group, this suggests that getting a job plays a particularly important role in taking people out of low income. Stability in household composition may also have a benign influence. This story best fits the escapers who are in non-working families with children. For others, such as pensioners, it is less relevant. For this subgroup, it may simply be that transitory income fluctuations are much more important. These may be due to measurement errors rather than genuine transitory fluctuations (expected to be less important given the nature of most pensioners' income packages).

Our results about the correlates of transitions out of and into low income are not directly comparable with those of Bane and Ellwood (1986) for the USA and of the cross-national study by Duncan *et al.* (1993a) because we have not used such a detailed (and mutually exclusive) list of named economic and demographic events as they did.[13] However Duncan *et al.* (1993a) conclude that employment-related events were the most important events associated with transitions both into and out of poverty for their samples of families of children, and this finding is consistent with those that we report for this group. Duncan *et al.* and Bane and Ellwood also draw attention to the impact of demographic events (for example marriage/remarriage and divorce/separation) and report that such events were more important for entries into poverty than exits. This appears to be the case in our analysis as well.

Conclusion

This chapter has provided evidence about low-income dynamics using a large sample of British households interviewed annually during the early 1990s. From one year to the next there are significant numbers of both low-income escapers and low-income entrants. Over time, there is significant churning in the low-income population, and this is highlighted by our simulations of low-income experience over a period based on the low-income exit and re-entry rate estimates.

The results have implications for both welfare benefit and labour market policies. The large amount of low-income turnover means that the welfare benefit system has an important role providing short-term support: over 1 year, many more people are helped by the benefit system than would be revealed by focusing on the benefit caseload at a point in time (which disproportionately includes long-term stayers). Longer term help from the benefit system is also important of course, particularly for poor people beyond retirement age. Single pensioners form about one-quarter of the persistently poor group but they have limited opportunities to improve their incomes through paid work, or marrying someone with sufficient income. These opportunities, especially the former, are of course more relevant to those of working age. However, although we have shown that getting a job is associated with escaping low income, it should be remembered that we examined associations with short-term income changes. If the job gained were of only short duration then the low-income escape is also likely to be only temporary (as the turnover and spell repetition results remind us). Policies for permanent escapes need to increase the tenure and quality of labour market attachment.

Notes

1 This chapter was originally published in *Fiscal Studies* 18, 2, May 1997, pp. 123–43, and is reproduced by permission of the editors. Research for this chapter was financed by the Joseph Rowntree Foundation (JRF). The support of the Economic and Social Research Council and of the University of Essex is also gratefully acknowledged. We thank our ISER colleagues and our JRF project Advisory Group for helpful discussions and Gerry Redmond for the Council Tax imputations. The views expressed and conclusions drawn are those of the authors alone.

2 Jarvis and Jenkins (1995), Taylor *et al.* (1994) and Webb (1995) examined income dynamics using only two waves of BHPS data. Department of Social Security (1996) – which appeared after the more detailed version of this chapter (Jarvis and Jenkins, 1996) – also used four waves of BHPS income data, but with different definitions and analyses. Most other UK research has largely focused on specific income components rather than the more comprehensive measure of personal living standards, i.e. income itself. Earnings dynamics are analysed by, for example, Dickens (1996) and Ball and Marland (1996), and welfare benefit dynamics are analysed by, for example, Shaw *et al.* (1996).

3 For a detailed discussion of BHPS methodology, representativeness and weighting and imputation procedures, see Taylor (1994) and Taylor *et al.* (1999).

4 For some analyses, this criterion may impart some selection biases which are not fully offset by the use of the BHPS weights. (We return to this issue again later in the chapter.) We hope to develop methods for imputing income values for the remainder of the BHPS sample.

5 The derivation of the net income distributions requires much manipulation of the raw BHPS data. For detailed discussion of variable construction, and a demonstration of the validity of the derived distributions relative to a range of relevant HBAI benchmarks for waves 1 and 2, see Jarvis and Jenkins (1995). The Council tax imputations are explained by Redmond (1997). Our derived variables have been deposited with the Data Archive at the University of Essex.

6 Another reference point is social assistance benefit levels. These have remained fairly constant in real terms over this period and our half 1991

mean income cut-off is more generous than the entitlements for many people. For example, in October 1991, a childless married couple with no income of their own was eligible for Income Support of £62.25 per week, plus Housing Benefit covering housing costs. If housing costs were £25 per week, total social assistance entitlement would be £87.25. In equivalent net income terms (converted using the McClements equivalence scale and reflated to January 1995 prices), this is a figure of about £94 per week. People with social assistance entitlements near to our half wave 1 mean cut-off (£127 per week) would be those with above average housing costs.

7 Our thanks to Carol Propper for suggesting this exercise. The formulae used to generate the estimates are given in Jarvis and Jenkins (1996).

8 By construction, each person contributes a maximum of one transition out of low income and a maximum of one transition into low income. For the very small number of persons making two transitions in (or out), we use the later transition.

9 We compared the composition of the group with incomes between the cut-off and 10% less with the group with lower incomes. If any group among the escapers was notably disproportionately close to the cut-off, it was the elderly.

10 We compared the composition of the group with incomes between the cut-off and 10% above it with the group with higher incomes.

11 We should stress that our economic status variable refers to an individual's family context. Changes in this may occur even if the individual in question has not changed his or her own work pattern. They may also arise via changes in work status for other family members or by a change in family composition. (An example would be a married couple family at wave t with the husband working full time and the wife part time. If the woman is a lone parent at wave $t + 1$ but still working part time, her family economic status, according to our definition, will have changed.) The emphasis on family (or household) context is entirely appropriate because we are interested in household income.

12 The decline in the incidence of economic status and family type changes between waves 1 and 2 and waves 3 and 4 may arise for several reasons. One is that it may reflect a sample selection bias: we are working with a longitudinal sample from complete respondent households, and one might expect that economic and demographic change – especially the latter (for example divorce and separation) – is more common among households with incomplete responses, and that this effect will cumulate over time. That part of the impact of complete non-response (i.e. panel attrition) which is not fully accounted for by the longitudinal sample weights which we use would have a similar effect. The trend might also be genuine: there was a general recovery in the British economy after 1991 and with this may have come greater stability in family context.

13 This is the subject of current work. However, for some more detailed breakdowns of Table 10.6, by pre-transition family type and economic status, see Jarvis and Jenkins (1999). Jarvis and Jenkins (1997) provide detailed evidence about the income changes associated with marital splits.

11 A new approach to poverty dynamics[1]

Karl Ashworth, Martha S. Hill and Robert Walker

Introduction

As Duncan explained in Chapter 3, the arrival of long runs of panel data has radically altered the American perception of poverty (Duncan *et al.*, 1984; Hill, 1985; Bane and Ellwood, 1986; Ellwood, 1988; Ruggles, 1990). As we have seen in the last two chapters, rather than being conceptualised as a static state, with an immutable distinction between the poor and the not poor, poverty is recognised to be dynamic and to occur in finite spells with beginnings and ends. This has opened the way to thinking about the specific causes of poverty and the means by which spells of poverty might be brought to an early end.

However, the focus on spells has had a number of less desirable consequences. The spell has tended to replace the individual or household as the unit of analysis, making it possible to lose sight of the characteristics of people who are poor. Similarly, there has been a tendency to ignore repeated spells of poverty and therefore to see the poor dividing into those whose experience is transitory and others who are more or less permanently poor. This may miss an important dimension of some people's experience of what it is like to be poor. Another consequence has been to uncouple the measurement of poverty from the study of distributional questions relating to the incidence or prevalence of poverty (prevalence being the proportion of the population that experiences poverty over a given period). The focus on spells and their duration also seems to have been at the expense of work on the severity of poverty, i.e. the amount by which income falls short of needs as represented by the poverty standard.

Ironically, therefore, the rather static one-dimensional view of poverty once gleaned from cross-sectional data has been replaced, to a worrying degree, by a fascination with another unidimensional measure, duration. The task at hand is to begin the process of correcting this imbalance by more fully exploiting the richness of panel data to yield a more rounded understanding of the nature and distribution of poverty, taking the USA as an illustrative example. Particular attention is paid to the duration, severity and temporal patterning of poverty and to the cumulative shortfall in income to needs that can accrue over time.

Rationale

Spellbound approaches

The focus on poverty spells may be seen as a reaction to the problem of sample censorship encountered in existing longitudinal studies. Sample censorship occurs because some occurrences of the phenomena of interest, in this case periods of poverty, commence before the survey data begin whereas others end after the latest period of observation. Earlier work, promoted by Coe and his colleagues (for example, see Coe, 1976; Duncan *et al.*, 1984), which simply recorded the number of years in which individuals were poor within a given period, has been criticised for underestimating the proportion of people who spend a long time in poverty (Bane and Ellwood, 1986). If their longitudinal data had spanned the full lifetime of a cohort then there would have been no censorship problem. However, the data covered a considerably shorter time span for multiple cohorts, and one cannot assume that a spell of poverty that begins at the time of the last observation will last for only the equivalent of one observation period when it might, in fact, last a lifetime. What is more, the methodology now exists to estimate, by a process of simulation, the likely length of the truncated spell (Bane and Ellwood, 1986). Leaving this technical advance to one side, it remains true that the spell in question, whatever its ultimate length, only lasted for one observation period during the span of the survey and, hence, contributed only one unit to the total sum, or duration, of poverty experienced over that time.

In practice, neither approach can fully encapsulate the entire range of poverty sequences for both epistemological and technical reasons. They are, however, both useful in telling different parts of a related story. Figure 11.1 illustrates some of the issues. The figure plots the poverty careers of a number of fictitious individuals across the window of observation provided by a longitudinal survey. Individual A serves to represent the case already mentioned, for whom a spell of poverty begins just before the end of the observation period and continues beyond it. The Coe methodology would create a very distorted impression of the characteristics of this particular spell of poverty whereas, depending on the validity of the assumptions used in the modelling process, the Bane and Ellwood approach might accurately capture its form.

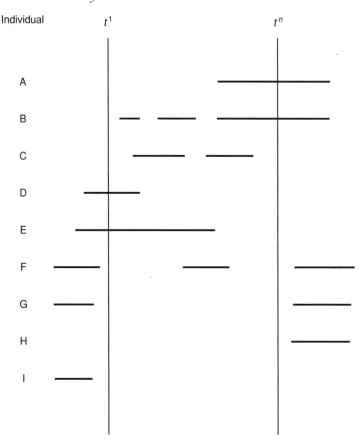

Key: ——————— A spell of poverty

Figure 11.1 Observing poverty spells

Individual B presents similar difficulties for the Coe approach in that one spell of poverty extends beyond the observation period. However, individual B also experiences two spells of poverty in the middle of the observation period, the length of which can be observed directly. This presents no problem for Coe, whereas under the basic Bane and Ellwood approach this set of spells would not be linked to a particular individual because the unit of observation is a spell not a person. The same is true for individual C, whose two experiences of poverty both fall within the observation period.

Individuals D and E present problems irrespective of the approach since both begin spells of poverty before the study begins that last into the observation period. Bane and Ellwood simply ignore these individuals, which means ignoring, especially in the case of individual E, a not inconsequential amount of poverty. The Coe approach entails truncating the spells, but at least the fact that these individuals experienced poverty is acknowledged.

People such as individual F, who experience a lot of poverty during their lives but only a short spell during the observation period, and individual G, who fall into poverty both before and after the observation period but not during it, also present problems for both approaches. Coe counts individual G as never being poor, which is true of the observation period if not an accurate representation of the person's lifetime experience. Bane and Ellwood's strategy essentially ignores those people who are not poor (individuals G, H and I). Doing so means that no estimates of the prevalence of poverty can be provided. Both strategies understate the lifetime poverty experience of individual F.

The experience of individuals G and H serves to highlight another feature of the basic spells methodology which is also shared by a refinement that seeks to take account of multiple spells of poverty (Ellwood, 1986). The basic model takes as its population spells that begin during the observation period. This is obviously a restricted population but no more arbitrary than Coe's use of the window of observation provided by a particular longitudinal survey. However, in the context of benefit receipt, the spells methodology has been used to model repeated spells of poverty (actually periods of benefit receipt) encountered after the observation period by those individuals who experienced a spell of poverty during the observation period (for example, see Ellwood, 1986; Burstein and Visher, 1989). This effectively expands the population of spells considered but not in an easily interpretable way because although individuals G and H might have experienced poverty in the period covered by the simulation these spells of poverty would not have been counted. It might be possible to derive probabilities of entry into poverty by inspection and thus to simulate F's experience, but it is not altogether clear how the resultant population of events would be meaningfully closed.

In sum, while the Coe approach cannot provide a reliable estimate of the proportion of the population which experiences long spells of poverty, or indeed the proportion that experiences any kind of poverty if the reference period exceeds the period of observation, it does give an accurate indication of the prevalence of poverty during the observation period. Clearly, the longer the observation period, the more complete spells of poverty will be directly observed and the less strong become the main criticisms of this approach. The Bane and Ellwood approach, on the other hand, with its focus on spells rather than individuals, gives no guide to the prevalence of poverty and, in its simplest form, reveals little about the existence of multiple spells.

Ignoring severity

It is significant that it proved unnecessary to mention the severity of poverty in the foregoing discussion of the two main approaches to the use of longitudinal data in studies of poverty. This reflects the fact that, with some notable exceptions (for example Hill, 1983), debate has scarcely advanced beyond a univariate conceptualisation of poverty and does not fully exploit the potential of panel data. If one takes the simplest generic formulation of poverty (P) measured over time, as proposed by Nicholson (1979):

$$P = CT$$

where C is the income deficit, the amount by which income falls short of the poverty standard, and T is the duration; most US studies have implicitly dealt with a specific case where C is taken to be 1. As a consequence, the very different experience that is represented by poverty of equal duration T but of substantially different severity C has gone unremarked.

The analysis

If it is important to address distributional issues and link a concern with severity to that of duration, what of the problem of spell censorship which has prevented work in this area in the past? The problem has been the relatively short and arbitrary nature of the observation period provided by existing surveys which has caused the incidence of spell censorship to be high and analytically troublesome. However, the Panel Study of Income Dynamics in the USA now offers over 30 years of data, so that the observation period is not short. Nor need it be arbitrary.

The lifetime is a natural time frame for the study of poverty. It is long and, equally important, it has personal and social meaning. However, life course analysis teaches us that there are periods of less than a lifetime which are equally meaningful. Rowntree (1901), as early as 1899, identified five stages in the life of a British labourer (characterised as contrasting periods of 'want and comparative plenty'):

childhood, early working adulthood, child rearing, working life after children have grown up and old age. Hindu culture (Sen, 1961) allows for four stages (asramas). O'Higgins *et al.* (1988) recognise ten stages whereas Duncan (1988) has defined ten life cycle categories defined solely in terms of age and sex. Others (for example Elder, 1985b) have argued for the existence of multiple interlocking trajectories (marriage, working life, parenthood and the like), each consisting of sequences of states and events. Setting the observation period to coincide with a life state means that any spell censorship that occurs coincides with a socially meaningful event or transition. As a consequence, it becomes reasonable to talk about the extent of poverty in childhood, working life or old age.

Such a formulation also allows the temporal patterning of spells to be examined. This is important for three principal reasons. First, a single long spell of poverty is likely to be experienced differently from a series of shorter spells of the same total duration. Adaptive responses may be different as may any long-term effects on personal well-being. Equally, the aetiology of the poverty is unlikely to be the same.

Second, different types of poverty are likely to require different policy responses and selective targeting. For example, the Government might want to bridge repeated short spells of poverty, perhaps by offering loans, but would probably think twice about such a strategy in relation to long spells (Ashworth *et al.*, 1992a).[2]

Third, there is a direct link between the patterning of poverty spells over time and the concentration of poverty within a population. Concentration will be highest, for a given aggregate of poverty, when individual spells of poverty are long and repeat spells are frequent. High concentration is consistent with the development of an underclass: the poor have no chance of escape and little in common with the wider community. Likewise, those who were not poor would have no direct experience of the problems faced by those in poverty.

Life stages are usually defined in one of two ways: chronological age (0–15 years, 16–30 years, etc.) or life experience (childhood, young single, young couples, parenthood, etc.) (Elder, 1985a,b,c). The former is technically easier and permits a time frame of equal duration to be imposed on the analysis which simplifies comparison of the prevalence of poverty at different life stages. However, it means that individuals at various experiential stages are brought together in the same analytical category, thus increasing within group variance and decreasing between group variance. This can hinder attempts both to examine the distribution and kinds of poverty associated with different life stages and to elucidate aetiological models.

The second strategy enables the timing and duration of the life stage to be treated as contingent factors that may be associated with both the type and the risk of poverty which is experienced. It also allows recognition of the fact that the life course does not follow the same predetermined sequence. The increase in divorce and remarriage, for example, means that many individuals repeat the stages of household formation and child rearing. On the other hand, the disadvantages of the life experience approach mirror the advantages that come from using chronological age. Since both approaches have certain strengths, there is a good case for further experimentation, although in this preliminary attempt chronological age is used for reasons of simplicity. The illustrative data presented in this chapter relate to childhood.[3]

Method

The data were taken from the Panel Study of Income Dynamics (PSID). Five waves of children were selected from the PSID datatape: those aged 1 year in 1969, 1970, 1971, 1972 or 1973. These five waves were then treated as a single cohort in order to maintain a sample size capable of producing robust statistics. Childhood was defined as the first 15 years of life. The sixteenth year and above were avoided because the chances of children splitting from the parental household increase dramatically after the fifteenth year of life (see Buck and Scott, 1993).

Cases where data were not available for all 15 years were dropped to avoid complications of missing data and subsequent imputations. The analyses were carried out on weighted data. This was to overcome the bias introduced by the original oversampling of low-income households and from any differential non-response. The weights used were those for the final year (age 15 years) of childhood for each wave composing the cohort.

Poverty was defined by an income to needs ratio of less than one. Income and needs were first adjusted to a 1987 US dollar value using the Consumer Price Index U-X1 weights. The PSID need measures were used in this study (but see below). They are based on the 'low-cost plan' for individual weekly food expenditure requirements, a budget that is 25% higher than the 'thrifty food plan' that forms the basis of official US poverty statistics. This latter budget is designed to meet nutritional requirements on a short-term emergency basis and is, arguably, overly parsimonious for children in long-term poverty. No adjustment was made to the needs for farmers to reflect their lower food costs. Income refers to total family income including transfers.

Over the period covered by the analysis (1968–87), the annual rate of poverty among children first fell from about 12% in 1968 to 11% in

1974 and then rose to over 15% in 1983, falling back to around 13% in 1987.

Results

Duration

Table 11.1 is quite familiar territory for those who have followed the developing debate on childhood poverty. It shows that 38% of children experience some poverty during their first 15 years (i.e. prevalence). The largest group experiencing poverty do so for a relatively short period (1–3 years), but one-fifth, representing 7% of all children, spend much the greater part of their childhood in families with insufficient resources to meet basic needs.

Although the figures may be familiar, it is hard to dismiss them as being unimportant. About 3.5 million children were born each year in the late 1960s, so that the 7% who were destined to spend most of their first years in poverty translates into 245,000 children. If the proportion were to hold constant for successive cohorts (and some have suggested that the situation has worsened), it would mean that in any year one could find about 3.7 million children with similarly depressing prospects.

Table 11.1 shows that the majority of those who are poor are not poor for long periods, with the result that the proportion of children who ever experience poverty exceeds the proportion poor in any one year by a factor of almost three (38% and 13.6% respectively). However, this is not to say that poverty is evenly distributed. If it were, given the total sum of poverty experienced by children in the cohort (expressed

Table 11.1 Prevalence and duration of poverty in childhood

	Years in poverty					
	0	*1–3*	*4–6*	*7–10*	*11–15*	*ALL*[a]
% of all children	62	18	8	5	7	99
% of children experiencing poverty	–	46	22	13	20	101
% of all childhood poverty[b]	0	14	20	19	48	101
Weighted sample	12,932	3,643	1,710	1,025	1,547	20,857
Unweighted sample	619	216	134	123	177	1,269

Notes
a All percentages are based on weighted sample.
b Childhood poverty defined as the total number of years of poverty experienced by all children in the cohort, i.e. child–years that were years of poverty.

218   *Panel data analyses*

in child–years), every single child could expect to spend 2 of their first 15 years in poverty.

The anatomy of this inequality is evident from the third row of Table 11.1, which shows how the total sum of poverty is divided. The 7% of children that are poor for more than 10 years account for 48% of all the child–years of poverty endured. This is an inevitable consequence of the great length of time for which they are poor. On the other hand, only 14% of the total sum of child–years of poverty is accounted for by the 46% of children who are poor for short periods.

This pattern of inequality is portrayed graphically in the Lorenz curves presented in Figure 11.2. The lower curve shows the proportion of total childhood poverty (i.e. years of poverty) which is borne by a given proportion of children. The diagonal represents the curve which would exist if poverty were distributed equally; the labelled axes define the curve which would describe the situation in which only one child was poor. The Gini coefficient is simply the ratio of the area between

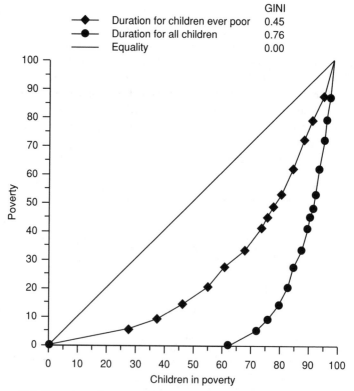

Figure 11.2 Duration of poverty (Lorenz curves)

Table 11.2 Patterns of poverty

	Pattern of poverty[a]					
	All children (%)	Children experiencing poverty (%)	All childhood poverty[c] (%)	Duration, means (SD)	Weighted sample	Unweighted sample
No poverty	62	–	–	0.0 (0.0)	12,932	619
Transient	10	27	5	1.0 (0.0)	2,162	113
Occasional	3	8	4	2.5 (0.8)	637	44
Recurrent	16	41	53	6.9 (2.9)	3,240	294
Persistent	5	14	12	4.7 (3.3)	1,102	90
Chronic	2	5	13	13.5 (0.7)	426	55
Permanent	2	5	13	15.0 (1.0)	358	54
ALL[b]	100	100	100	5.4 (4.4)	20,857	1,269

Notes
a See text for definition.
b All percentages are based on weighted sample.
c See Table 11.1 for definition.

the curve and the diagonal to the total area below the diagonal and it ranges from 0, equality, to 1, in which a single child is poor.

The lower curve confirms that the distribution of childhood poverty is far from equitable. Indeed, whereas, as already observed, no poverty at all is experienced by 62% of children, the 10% of children with the longest durations account for 54% of all childhood poverty. The inequality remains stark even when consideration is limited to the 38% of children who spend some time in poverty. The middle curve shows that 82% of the poverty is borne by the 50% of children with the longest durations and 20% by the 10% of children who have the longest durations of all.

Finally, to return again to the third row of Table 11.1, this can be interpreted in a way which answers another important question; namely, what proportion of the children who at any one time are poor will suffer long durations of poverty before they reach adulthood (Ellwood, 1987). The answer is that only 14% of the children that we find to be poor in 1 year will have experienced no more than 3 years poverty by the time they reach 16 years; 48% will have been poor for more than 10 years.

Patterns of poverty

Table 11.2 takes account of the frequency, duration and spacing of spells to define six patterns of poverty that might be argued, a priori, to constitute different experiences. The six patterns, or types, of poverty are defined as follows:

i Transient poverty: a single spell of poverty lasting a single year.

ii Occasional poverty: more than one spell of poverty but none lasting more than 1 year. In practice, the duration of relative prosperity always exceeds the duration of poverty in this cohort.

iii Recurrent poverty: repeated spells of poverty, some separated by more than a year and some exceeding a year in length.

iv Persistent poverty: a single spell of poverty lasting between 2 and 13 years.

v Chronic poverty: repeated spells of poverty never separated by more than a year of relative prosperity.

vi Permanent poverty: poverty lasting continuously for 15 years.

All six kinds of poverty were found in the cohort. By far the most common is recurrent poverty, which described the experience of 16% of children in the cohort, 41% of those who were ever poor and 53% of those in poverty at any given time. This finding underlines the inappropriateness of ignoring multiple spells of poverty, as has happened in the past, and draws attention to the instability which seems to characterise many peoples' lives (Duncan, 1988; Burkhauser and Duncan, no date). For the households in which these children reside – noting, though, that some children will move households – the experience is one of frustrated prospects, when spells of relative prosperity are followed by longish spells of poverty; circumstances in which plans are impossible or are as likely as not to come to nought.

Transient poverty, the second most common form, may be the least worrying from a policy viewpoint. First, it appears to be self-rectifying. Second, it accounts for a very small proportion of total poverty and of the children who are poor at any one time (5%). Occasional poverty, the other 'mild' form of poverty, in which relatively lengthy periods of comparative prosperity are interspersed with short bouts of poverty, is much less common and only accounts for 3.5% of total poverty.

Of the children who are poor, 14% experience a single spell of persistent poverty. This particular form of poverty accounts for a similar proportion of the total experienced in childhood (12%). In marked contrast, the 4% of children who are either permanently poor or suffer chronic poverty with little respite account for hugely disproportionate amounts of the total duration of poverty. As an inevitable corollary, they form substantial proportions of the children who are poor at any given time (13% in each case).

Duration remains central to this typology and is apparent in the fourth row of Table 11.2, which shows the average length of poverty associated with each poverty type. Durations for transient and permanent poverty are fixed. On average, children experiencing recurrent poverty spend more time in poverty than those who experience a single persistent spell.

Linking severity and duration

As previously stated, Nicholson (1979) and Atkinson (1984) have suggested that a truly satisfactory measure of poverty would need to combine lack of resources and duration. There is, Atkinson argued, 'some level of income deficiency which is serious enough even for short periods and a lesser extent of deprivation which becomes serious if it lasts long enough' (Atkinson, 1984: 15).

Nicholson's generic formulation of poverty measured over time was presented as $P = CT$. Adopting different terminology and notation, Ashworth *et al.* (1992a) provide a more specific definition of what they term absolute cumulative poverty, i.e. the income deficit summed over each accounting period covered by a study, which in this case is a year. Thus, absolute cumulative poverty is calculated by summing the difference between income and needs in each year that a child is poor.

This formulation, following Nicholson, makes no allowance for the fact that the same absolute shortfall in income will impose different financial constraints depending on the needs and size of the household unit. One response to this deficiency is to adjust the absolute measure by the equivalence scale implicit in the original measure of needs. Thus, to calculate equivalised cumulative poverty, needs in each year are first divided by an equivalising constant and, for each year that a child is in poverty, the difference between equivalised needs and income is summed. In the examples which follow, the equivalising constant represents the needs of a male and female couple aged 21–35 years, which equals $9,272.51 (1987 US dollars).

A more readily interpretable approach, which achieves the same effect, involves summing [1 − (income to needs ratio)] for years in poverty to yield the cumulative income deficiency ratio. A value of unity indicates that a shortfall in income equivalent to the needs for 1 year has been experienced over the period observed. It can be shown that equivalised cumulative poverty and the cumulative income deficiency ratio have identical distributions.

None of the above measures takes account of spells of relative prosperity experienced during the observation period. This can be achieved by cumulating each measure over the entire observation period rather than over episodes of poverty.

Thus, the absolute life stage income deficit is simply the sum of the difference between needs and income in each year. Similarly, the equivalised life stage deficit is the sum of the difference between equivalised needs and income over childhood. Again, the life stage income deficiency ratio sums the difference of income divided by needs subtracted from unity in each year. A final measure, life stage poverty, records instances in which equivalised income during the entire observation period falls short of needs, i.e. when the equivalised life stage income deficit is greater than zero.

The results of applying these various measures to the cohort of American children are presented in Table 11.3. Care should be taken in interpreting the maximum and minimum values which sometimes appear as outriders to the distributions. The first five measures relate only to children who experience some poverty; the prevalence of poverty among the group (as noted above) is 38%.

Comparing the first two columns shows that taking account of family size substantially reduces the apparent level of cumulative poverty. Because childhood poverty is more frequent in large families than in small ones, the equivalisation process also has the effect of slightly reducing the apparent inequality in the distribution of cumulative poverty (the Gini coefficient falls from 0.62 to 0.56). Even so, it is clear that poverty, measured as the cumulative shortfall in income, is far from equitably distributed even among those children who experience some poverty.

The cumulative income deficiency ratio highlights the pattern of inequality. The mean value of the ratio is 1.99, indicating a shortfall in income during periods of poverty which is very nearly equivalent to the income required to meet the needs of a family for a 2-year period. However, the distribution is very skewed and the median value is only 1.0; on the other hand, the corresponding value for the first quintile is 3.63.

The final three columns in Table 11.3 take account of the income received during periods of relative prosperity which, for all but 25% of children who suffer poverty, more than compensates for the shortfall in income experienced while in poverty. (It should be noted that no account is taken of the sequencing of periods of poverty and relative prosperity.) It can be calculated from Table 11.3 that, for the average child experiencing poverty, family income during childhood exceeds needs by about 64%. For children in the fifth decile, this value is in excess of 120%.

Table 11.3 Temporal measures for poverty for children in the USA

Quintiles	Absolute cumulative poverty ($)	Equivalised cumulative poverty ($)	Cumulative income deficiency ratio	Equivalised childhood income deficit ($)	Childhood income deficiency ratio	Childhood poverty ($)
Maximum	13	9	0.00	−1,262,014	−136.10	49
4th	3,499	2,904	0.33	−166,996	−18.01	15,112
3rd	9,501	6,484	0.70	−87,397	−9.43	34,029
2nd	21,468	13,880	1.50	−34,864	−3.76	44,319
1st	51,336	33,671	3.36	14,186	1.53	58,205
Minimum	285,917	112,205	12.10	112,205	12.10	112,205
Mean	32,732	18,472	1.99	−89,761	−9.68	39,931
Median	15,692	9,272	1.00	−62,148	−6.70	40,661
Prevalence	38	38	38	38	38	9

Source: Calculations from the Panel Study of Income Dynamics based on a cohort of children born between 1968 and 1972 and followed until aged 16 years. The poverty measure used is about 25% above the official US datum.

In the final column of Table 11.3, the accounting period is effectively set equal to childhood. The result is that the prevalence of poverty falls to 9.4%. The distribution is less skewed than for the other measures. The deficit for those in the fifth quintile roughly equates to the annual needs allowance for a two-parent/two-child household, whereas that for the first quintile is four times as great.

There are unresolved difficulties with the composite measures of poverty presented above. For example, it is self-evident that the consequences of a shortfall equivalent to annual needs that is concentrated in 1 year are likely to be more severe than the same shortfall spread over several years. However, all the measures treat a given shortfall in the income to needs ratio as equivalent irrespective of the length of time over which it occurs. A more fundamental criticism derives from the logic of arguments presented earlier. If poverty is no longer to be conceptualised as a single phenomenon but is to be differentiated according to temporal patterning (among other attributes) then it is inappropriate to conflate the different types by use of a single measure. Rather, attention would be better focused on establishing the incidence and distribution of the different kinds of poverty experience.

Temporal patterning and living standards

Finally, Table 11.4 links temporal patterning and severity and adds weight to the contention that the six patterns or types of poverty index different experiences. The first column reports the mean cumulative income deficiency ratio for each poverty type (medians reveal a similar pattern). Income averages about 70% of needs during spells of poverty irrespective of whether a child spends between 1 and 3, between 4 and 6 or between 7 and 10 years in poverty. There is also very little difference in the severity of poverty encountered by children experiencing transient, occasional, recurrent or persistent poverty (although, as comparison of the standard deviations indicates, experience is more varied among the first two types of poverty). However, it is evident that poverty among children who are permanently poor, or who suffer very brief spells of respite, is very severe even when account is taken of differences in household composition. For the former group, annual income amounts to only 46% of need and for the latter group it averages 59% during spells of poverty.

The second column in Table 11.4 takes account of the income received in years when income exceeded needs to give a measure of childhood living standards. As the duration of poverty increases, so the number of

Table 11.4 Severity of poverty[a]

	Income to needs ratio during poverty spells[b], mean (SD) ($)	Income to needs ratio during childhood[c], mean (SD) ($)
Duration (years)		
0	–	3.31 (1.60)
1–3	0.71 (0.23)	2.32 (1.13)
4–6	0.69 (0.15)	1.43 (0.37)
7–10	0.67 (0.14)	1.08 (0.18)
11–15	0.57 (0.13)	0.66 (1.60)
Experience		
Transient	0.71 (0.26)	2.63 (1.30)
Occasional	0.69 (0.21)	1.82 (0.49)
Recurrent	0.67 (0.15)	1.21 (0.45)
Persistent	0.70 (0.14)	1.66 (0.63)
Chronic	0.59 (0.09)	0.66 (0.08)
Permanent	0.46 (0.13)	0.46 (0.13)
Total	0.67 (0.20)	2.68 (1.63)

Notes

a Some of the distributions depart significantly from normal and the interpretation given in the text is informed by comparison of the full distributions.

b Average of ratios of income to needs for individual years in poverty.

c Ratio of income to needs for individual years averaged over the 15 years of childhood.

years in which to acquire income in excess of minimum needs falls. Not surprisingly, therefore, the income to needs ratio falls steadily with duration, with the turnaround point occurring between 8 and 9 years; children who are in poverty for any longer are entrenched in a childhood of penury.

The figures suggest that transient poverty is typically a one-off aberration from an accustomed way of life. Certainly, children who experience a single year of poverty generally do not spend the remainder of their childhood living on the margins of poverty. The ratio of income to needs for these children, when averaged over the 15 years of childhood, is 2.63 compared with 3.31 for children who are never poor. Indeed, one in six of them has an income to needs ratio that exceeds the average for children who are never poor.

In terms of childhood living standards, the position of children who encounter occasional short spells of poverty is similar to those who experience a single spell of persistent poverty. In both cases, the income deficits incurred during years of poverty are generally more than offset by income received in the more prosperous years. Nevertheless, taking childhood as a whole, income levels are not high. At first sight, the apparent similarity between these groups is a little surprising as 65%

of the first group are in poverty only twice and none of this group for more than 4 years, whereas 32% of the second group have spells lasting 5 or more years. What appears to be happening is that, for many children, the repeated spells of poverty simply represent small downward fluctuations in the financial circumstances of families living for long periods on very constrained budgets. The single spells of persistent poverty, on the other hand, frequently constitute major departures from normal living standards of the kind associated with relationship breakdown, redundancy and substantial loss of earning power occasioned by illness and disability (see Duncan, 1988).

Recurrent poverty appears qualitatively different again and is very homogeneous given the large size of the group. It is severe and lasting hardship and is experienced by 16% of all children. Only 30% of the children in this group live in families which, during their childhood years, have incomes which exceed needs by more than 30%. Moreover, for another 31% of children, income falls short of need; this proportion represents 2.6 million children, by far the largest group to spend their childhood beyond the margins of the affluent society.

If recurrent poverty is the most common experience of harsh poverty, the very worst experience is reserved for the 2% of children in permanent poverty. Family income falls short of needs by 54%, the equivalent of US$6,540 per annum for a two-person household. No child in this group resided with a family which had an income that averaged more than 70% of needs, and for 24% of children the income–needs ratio was less than 0.33. This is poverty of a Third World order.

Chronic poverty is also severe. During spells of poverty, the shortfall in family income averaged 43% and exceeded 50% for one child in seven. Moreover, income received during the years when the family was not poor was never sufficient to offset the long spells of poverty. However, it did locate many of the children in chronic poverty one rung up the ladder from those in permanent poverty. Over the 15 years of childhood, needs exceeded income by an average of 33%; this was true of just 5% of children in chronic poverty.

Discussion

The concept of poverty is incomplete if no account is taken of time. An innocent setting out for the first time to describe poverty would ask whether income falls short of needs and, if so, by how much and for how long. They would also ask who suffers poverty and whether those who do constitute a large or small fraction of the total population. The more astute observer might further ask whether the same shortfall in income always equates to the same level of economic welfare. Panel data enable account to be taken of time, but technical factors have meant that few studies have provided answers to all these very basic questions.

The approach proposed in this chapter goes some way to circumvent the problem of spell censorship, which has hitherto prevented a comprehensive study of the nature and distribution of poverty. This is achieved by setting the observation period equal to the duration of a social state (or life stage) so that any censorship coincides with a transition from one social state to another. As a consequence, the observation period can be treated as a complete entity and the duration of poverty measured directly rather than estimated. The distribution of poverty, defined to take account of duration, can also be plotted.

Although one major impediment to study may be overcome, it is inevitable that new ones – perhaps of a lesser order – become apparent. A life stage or social state can be defined in chronological, behavioural, social or psychological terms. Which is most appropriate will depend on the topic, context and what is technically feasible. Varying definitions are likely to generate different answers to what may ostensibly be the same question.

Perhaps of greater importance, viewed from the current vantage point, is the need to develop measures of poverty that do justice to the generic formulations proposed by Nicholson and Atkinson which simultaneously take account of severity and duration. None of the measures presented allows for the fact that a given shortfall of income concentrated over a short period is likely to have more detrimental consequences than the same shortfall spread over a longer period. Similarly, none takes account of the sequencing of periods of relative prosperity and want.

In this chapter, great importance has been attached to the sequencing, or patterning, of poverty over time. Indeed, it is argued, on largely a priori grounds, that poverty can be differentiated according to the number, duration and spacing of spells. These different kinds of poverty are characterised by varying levels of economic welfare, as measured over childhood. Elsewhere, it is shown that each type of poverty is associated with a distinct sociodemographic profile: particular kinds of poverty appear to be suffered by children in specific types of family living in particular localities (Ashworth *et al.*, 1992a). A next step is to evaluate the impact of the sequencing on economic welfare both within and between different patterns of poverty.

However, a warning is in order at this point. Just as the measured incidence of poverty is affected by the level at which the poverty threshold is pitched, so too is the prevalence of the different kinds of poverty defined above. Ashworth *et al.* (1992b) have shown that the prevalence of permanent poverty falls from 5% to 2% when the poverty threshold is lowered by 25%, whereas the incidence of occasional poverty increases from 8% to 10%.

Our recognition that poverty may need to be differentiated came from observing its distribution over time. The same conclusion is reached when one reflects on the implications of the way in which poverty is distributed within society. As already noted, high concentration provides conditions consistent with the development of an underclass. The poor would have no chance of escape and little in common with the wider community, whereas those who were not poor would have no personal experience of the problems faced by those in poverty.[4] Low concentration, given the same aggregate amount of poverty, would be consistent with situations where distributional justice of the kind proposed by Rawls (1973) prevailed and where the chances of experiencing poverty were more equally shared. Moderate concentration, again with the same fixed sum of poverty, implies something in between these two extremes with scope for people (and societies) to differ in terms of the constancy or recurrence of their poverty.

Moreover, the way in which poverty is distributed over time affects the distribution of poverty within a population, and vice versa. If most spells of poverty are long, prevalence – i.e. the proportion of people who experience poverty in any given period – will be low. Where spells are typically short, prevalence will be higher (given the same total sum of poverty). Just how high depends on the number of people who experience repeated spells.

Adding severity as a third distributional dimension not only makes it practical to ask how far the total sum of poverty, and the sum of misery that it represents, is concentrated on a few individuals but it may also generate the need to differentiate poverty further not just in degree but perhaps also in kind.

Conclusion

In sum, to the extent that the epithet 'a new approach' in the title of this chapter is justified, it is based on two developments. The first is to equate the observation period provided by a panel to the duration of a social state, with the result that problems of spell censorship are circumvented and distributional issues can once again be addressed. The second is to emphasise the distribution or patterning of poverty over time. The outcome is a recognition that the nature of poverty may be a function of its distribution and, moreover, that as a consequence there may not be one kind of poverty but many.

Notes

1 This chapter has appeared previously in the *Bulletin de Methodologie Sociologique*, March 1993, 38, and is reproduced with permission of the editors. We would like to thank Jean Yeung for her help in preparing the data used for the analyses in this study.

2 Targeting short-lived versus long-lived poverty for differential treatment can, however, be problematic, as Hill and Jenkins (1999) show with a numerical illustration based on British data.

3 Although the focus of this chapter is on childhood, it is hoped to extend the analyses in a number of ways. First, it is important to extend the analysis to later stages in the life course and also to follow successive cohorts through the various stages in the life course and to compare the different incidences of poverty under different social and economic conditions (Hutton and Walker, 1988). It should even prove possible to simulate a full lifetime. This could be done in two ways. First, hazard models could be used, allowing for time varying covariates, repeatedly to predict a new set of outcomes for the following year (as Ellwood and Kane, 1989, have done for the elderly). The second, more direct, approach would involve defining life cycle stages so as to overlap each other and then, by matching individuals at the intersections, to construct life histories as the aggregation of the life cycle stages of ostensibly similar people. Short panels, along with expectations that meaningful results are to be found by subdividing life stages into finer divisions, can lead to examining short pieces of lifetime. For example, having no more than 6 years of British panel data, and noting US findings showing early childhood as the most critical low-income time for children, prompted Hill and Jenkins (1999) to subdivide childhood into early, middle and late stages.

4 Poverty is of course unevenly distributed in space as well as time and this is important in any discussion of the underclass (Walker and Lawton, 1988; Walker and Huby, 1989; Adams and Duncan, 1990; Wilson, 1991). The term 'concentration' is used here as in its common usage. If 'concentration' referred to the distribution of the poverty gap (the total poverty population shortfall in income to needs) then the observations about the necessary conditions for the formation of an underclass would only hold if there was no, or a positive, relationship between duration and severity. Empirically, as Table 11.4 illustrates, there is a strong positive correlation between duration and severity.

12 Using panel data to analyse household and family dynamics

John Ermisch

Introduction

Analyses of family dynamics have primarily relied on retrospective marital, cohabitation and birth histories. Any recent issue of *Demography* or *Population Studies* provides examples. These data contain a sequence of dates of events and often some 'background' variables, many of which are measured at the end, rather than the beginning, of the history. The methods of event history (survival) analysis are applied to these data, with varying levels of model sophistication.

While these analyses provide, in many respects, reliable information, the nature of the data places limitations on the types of analysis which can be carried out, as Rose noted in Chapter 1. First, retrospective data are likely to suffer from recall errors, which is less of a problem with panel data, particularly if the interval between interviews is relatively small. The analysis of the young women's cohort of the American National Longitudinal Survey of Work Experience (NLS) by Peters (1988), which compares data from a retrospective marital history with data derived for the same people from panel information, indicates that there are systematic inconsistencies which seem to relate to factors that increase the difficulty of recall. Some information, such as the composition of the household of which one was a member, may be particularly unreliable when collected retrospectively. Household composition (for example co-residence with parents) may change often and the dates of change are often unrelated to legally recorded events such as marriages and births. Cohabitation histories may present similar recall problems. Statistical techniques for the analysis of transition data appear to be relatively robust to errors in dating events, but failure to recall events entirely is more problematic. This may not be so important for events such as births, marriages and divorces, but may be for events such as cohabitation beginnings and ends and leaving and returning to the parental home.

Panel data also have the advantage over retrospective data in terms of the explanatory variables available for models of family and household transitions. Those characteristics which vary over time, such as wages or other income, are difficult to collect in retrospective surveys, but are collected in panels. These characteristics may be important explanatory variables, but analyses based on retrospective histories would omit them. Only variables fixed over time, such as sex, race and, for some analyses, education, or 'community-level' variables, such as the regional unemployment rate, or time varying variables which can be constructed from other parts of the life histories, such as job status or age of youngest child, can be used as explanatory variables in analyses using retrospective data.

Thus, panel data reduce problems of recall and can provide a richer set of explanatory variables. This chapter illustrates the use of panel data for the analysis of family and household dynamics. Its empirical analysis is based on the first four waves of the British Household Panel Study (BHPS).

Methods

This chapter's analyses of family and household dynamics use a discrete time 'hazard model' approach, which incorporates 'competing risks' and amounts to a discrete time Markov model in most of the analyses. When estimates from these models are used in life table analysis, we can derive synthetic cohort measures, such as median age at first partnership. As is now shown, these methods are very simple to implement with standard software.

As a concrete example for defining and illustrating the methods, consider analysis of the entry to first partnership. At each wave of the data, people who have never been married and are not living with someone 'as a couple' are 'at risk' of entering a partnership, either a legal marriage or cohabitation without marriage. Let the number of such people of age a at wave t be N_{ta}. Between wave t and $t + 1, E_{tac}$ move into a cohabiting (c) union and E_{tam} move into a marriage (m). Let θ_{ac} and θ_{am} be the annual transition rates governing the dynamics of partnership, which we wish to estimate. Given the four waves of data which we have (i.e. three observations of wave-on-wave changes), the maximum likelihood (ML) estimates of θ_{ac} and θ_{am} are, respectively, $(\Sigma_t E_{tac})/(\Sigma_t N_{ta})$ and $(\Sigma_t E_{tam})/(\Sigma_t N_{ta})$, where the summations Σ_t run from 1 to 3; i.e. the ML estimators are the ratio of the total number of transitions to a particular destination to the total person–years at risk for such transitions. The partnership rate ('hazard') at age a is $\theta_a =$

$\theta_{ac} + \theta_{am}$, and we estimate it by summing the two estimated transition rates.

If these estimated age-specific rates primarily represent first entry into a partnership (as they undoubtedly do) and they were constant for a cohort then we can use life table methods to examine the patterns of entry to first partnership for a synthetic cohort.[1] These are illustrated below.

It is also easy to allow the transition rates θ_{ac} and θ_{am} to depend on explanatory variables, denoted by the vector $\mathbf{X_t}$. A natural way to model these rates is to assume a multinomial logit model, which permits us to take account of the 'competing risks' of cohabitation and marriage in a simple way. The transition rate to union type i is given by:

$$\theta_i = \exp(\beta_i \mathbf{X_t})/[1 + \exp(\beta_c \mathbf{X_t}) + \exp(\beta_m \mathbf{X_t})], i = a,c$$

where $\mathbf{X_t}$ is a vector of explanatory variables, including age; the β_i are vectors of parameters. The estimates of β_i show the effects of the explanatory variables on the logarithm of the odds of each type of union formation relative to remaining unpartnered $\{\ln[\theta_i/(1 - \theta_m - \theta_c)]\}$. Furthermore, the logarithm of the odds of cohabiting relative to marrying is given by:

$$\ln(\theta_c/\theta_m) = (\beta_c - \beta_m)\mathbf{X_t}$$

The parameters β_c and β_m are estimated by maximum likelihood using person–years as observations, i.e. it pools wave-on-wave partnering data for each person. Thus, in the BHPS 4-year panel, each person could contribute up to three observations. This pooling estimation approach does not allow for persistent differences in transition rates across people not captured by the observed variables in $\mathbf{X_t}$. If such 'unobserved heterogeneity' is important, this approach would produce biased estimates of the parameters. In this case, a 'fixed effects' estimation procedure could produce consistent estimates (for example see Chamberlain, 1980). We now implement these methods with information from the BHPS.

First partnerships

Table 12.1 shows the relevant data for partnership transitions among never married people. The first four waves of data contribute 4,787 person–years at risk of movement from the never married, unpartnered, state into a partnership, of which 6.9% contribute a partnering event.

Table 12.1 Partnership formation by the never married

	Number	%	Estimated transition rate(q_r)
Cohabitation	246	5.1	0.0514
Marriage	84	1.8	0.0175
No partnership	4,447	92.9	
Person–years at risk	4,787	100.0	

Source: British Household Panel Study, waves 1–4 (1991–4).

For example, the annual transition rate into cohabitation for this population, undifferentiated by age or sex, is computed as the number of cohabitation entries (246) divided by total person–years at risk (4787).[2] The estimated rates suggest that three-quarters of new partnerships formed by the never married are cohabitations.

It is, of course, well known that partnership formation rates vary with age and sex. The same methods are used to estimate age- and sex-specific transition rates for persons aged 16–34 years. Person–years at risk for the calculation of these rates fall with age, varying from 208 to 18, but they are always above 80 for persons aged 16–25 years, where we find most of the action in terms of events. Treating the estimated rates as *first* partnership rates and incorporating them into a life table, we obtain the patterns of first partnership formation shown in Figures 12.1 and 12.2. These show the cumulative proportions of a synthetic cohort who have had a first partnership by each age, distinguishing by type of partnership.

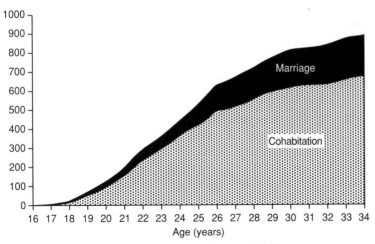

Figure 12.1 Cumulative proportions partnering, per 1,000: men

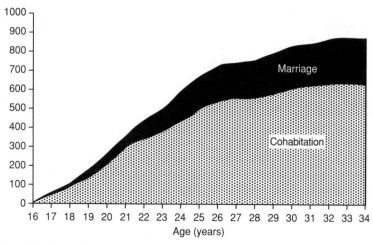

Figure 12.2 Cumulative proportions partnering, per 1,000: women

Comparison of Figures 12.1 and 12.2 indicates that, not surprisingly, women form partnerships earlier than men, and their first partnership is more likely to be a marriage than men's first partnership. Indeed, the estimated transition rates indicate that the median age at first partnership is about 24 years for women and 26 years for men. Among the nearly 90% in the synthetic cohorts who would have had a first partnership by the age of 35 years, 76% of men cohabited in their first partnership compared with 73% of women. These estimates can be compared with those made from the retrospective partnership histories collected at the second wave of the BHPS. The life table estimates by Ermisch (1995a) for women born since 1962 indicate that by the age of 26 years, 53% would have cohabited in their first partnership, 25% would have gone directly into marriage and 22% would not have partnered. The corresponding percentages for our synthetic cohort (represented by the panel data estimates of the transition rates) are 51%, 17% and 31%. The differences suggest continuation of the trends towards later partnership and away from direct marriage, although they may also partly reflect some potential biases in construction of the life tables leading to Figures 12.1 and 12.2.[3]

As noted, one of the main advantages of panel data is the availability of a richer set of explanatory variables for the transition rates of interest, particularly variables which vary over time and which are difficult to recall. To illustrate, the analysis considers the potential influences of a number of personal characteristics measured *in the previous year* on partnering the following year. These include the person's age, income, highest qualifications (up to that point), whether or not they were unemployed, whether or not they were a student and, finally, a fixed characteristic, such as the occupation of the father when the person was aged 14 years. Some experimentation with different variables and tests of their statistical significance suggested the model in Table 12.2.

It is immediately clear that men with some qualifications have a much larger chance of starting a cohabitation at any given age than those who have not obtained qualifications. Furthermore, the cohabitation entry rate increases with the level of qualification obtained. Being a student in the previous year more than halves the odds of entering a cohabiting union at any given age. Thus, better educated men appear to match up with partners faster after completing their education. This effect is masked in studies using retrospective data because highest qualification level is measured *at the end* of the history, thereby confusing the postponement of partnering while in education with the stimulating effect of men's education on partnering afterwards.

Other than age and student status, none of the explanatory variables considered had a significant impact on women's first partnering rates (results not shown). Thus, the later partnering of more educated women evident in most studies using retrospective data appears merely to reflect the lower partnership rates while in education, not a lower partnering rate after obtaining the qualifications.

None of the explanatory variables considered had a significant impact on men's age profile of direct movement into marriage. Men's age profile for the cohabitation transition rate increases up to the age of 27 years

Table 12.2 Multinomial logit model of first partnership, men aged 16–34 years; absolute value of ratio of coefficient to asymptotic standard error in parentheses

Observed proportions	Cohabitation 0.0575	Marriage 0.0178
Age_{t-1}	1.185 (4.55)	1.225 (2.60)
Age-squared$_{t-1}$	−0.0216 (4.21)	−0.0213 (2.33)
Student$_{t-1}$	−0.874 (2.22)	−0.977 (1.27)
Degree/teaching qualifications$_{t-1}$	2.543 (2.47)	0.348 (0.30)
A-level/other higher qualifications$_{t-1}$	2.347 (2.31)	1.578 (1.53)
Other qualifications$_{t-1}$	2.263 (2.22)	1.008 (0.96)
Constant	−20.31 (6.02)	−21.58 (3.58)

Note
$N = 2017$, $\chi^2 = 136.04$ (12 df).

and then declines, whereas the marriage rate profile does not reach its peak until 29 years.

Leaving the parental home and returning to it

When young people leave their parental home and whether and when they return to it are of interest in studying the transition from childhood to adulthood and household formation in the housing market. Yet relatively little is known about these processes. They are difficult to study with retrospective data because of recall problems, although Ermisch and Di Salvo (1995) have done so with a history of addresses for the 1958 birth cohort of Britons using the National Child Development Study. Panel data provide better opportunities for estimating these dynamic processes.

Whether young adults are living with one or both of their parents at each wave of the BHPS is obtained from the household 'enumeration grid' of the survey instrument. A move away from parents is recorded when at least one parent was in the panel member's household in the previous wave, but neither parent is now present in the household. Returns to the parental home are recorded in an analogous way.

Evidence of departure from or return to the parental household between waves 1 and 2, between waves 2 and 3 and between waves 3 and 4 is combined to calculate annual rates of departure and return by year of age in the same way as we calculated the partnership transition rates above. The annual rate of departure from the parental home is shown for three age groups in Figure 12.3.[4] It clearly increases with age. Women have a higher departure rate than men, and as a consequence they usually leave home sooner than men. Using the life table methods again, if these age-specific rates were constant for a cohort of women and primarily represented first departure from the parental home then just over half of them would have left home by the age of 21 years. The age at which half of men would have departed from their parents' home is about 22 years. Among members of the 1958 birth cohort, the median age of departure was almost 23 years for men and 20.75 years for women (Ermisch and Di Salvo, 1995). Thus, it appears that, although women's median leaving age has stayed about the same as that for the 1958 birth cohort, men's median leaving age has declined by about 1 year.

Whom young people go to live with when they leave their parents appears to have changed more. Three destinations are distinguished: (i) a student in full-time education; (ii) living with a partner (but not a student); and (iii) living alone or with others (but not a student nor in

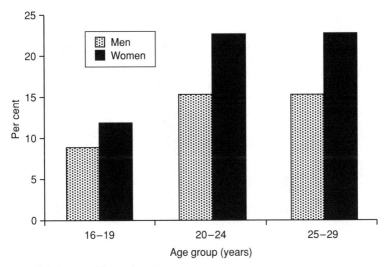

Figure 12.3 Parental home leaving rates

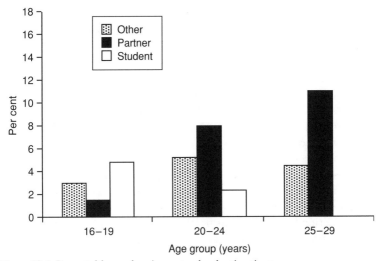

Figure 12.4 Parental home leaving rates by destination: men

a partnership). Treating these three destinations as competing risks, Figures 12.4 and 12.5 show estimates of these destination-specific leaving rates for men and women respectively. Later partnering (marriage or cohabitation) among men is readily apparent. While both sexes have relatively high rates of leaving home as students over the ages 16–19 years, men's partnership rate lies well below the rate for

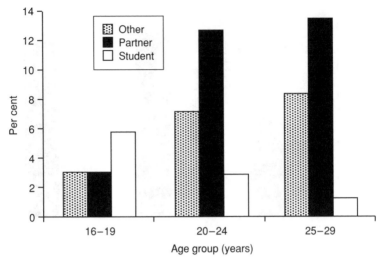

Figure 12.5 Parental home leaving rates by destination: women

other non-student departures over the ages 16–19 years, but this is not the case for women.

If we treat these age- and destination-specific departure rates as representing first departure (which will be true for the vast majority of cases) and as applying to a cohort, we can use life table methods to calculate the destination distribution of first departures from the parental home by the age of 30 years. This is shown in Table 12.3. Although the destination categories are not exactly the same as those used in Ermisch and Di Salvo (1995), they are close enough for Table 12.3 to suggest major changes in whom young people go to live with when they leave their parents. In the 1958 cohort, living with a partner was the destination for 60% of the women and about 55% of men, but the proportion leaving for this destination is now only about two-fifths (36% of men and 41% of women).

Table 12.3 Simulated leaving home patterns

Destination	Men (%)	Women (%)
Student	22.7	28.1
Partner	36.4	40.5
Other	28.1	27.8
Still with parents at age 30 years	12.8	3.6
Total	100.0	100.0

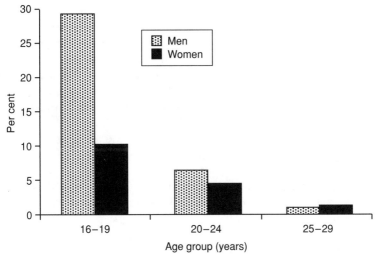

Figure 12.6 Annual rate of return to the parental home

Estimates of the rates of return to live with at least one parent by age and sex are shown in Figure 12.6. Although the estimates of return rates at young ages are not very precise because of the small samples, the return rate clearly declines with age, and for those below the age of 25 years it is higher for men than for women.

If the estimated age-specific return rates are assumed to apply to a cohort, then the proportion who are expected to return to their parents' home at least once can be calculated. If a person leaves home at the age of 21 years, these return rates suggest that 28% of men and 21% of women would return sometime before the age of 30 years. As this estimate may be biased upward because of non-ignorable attrition (see Ermisch, 1996), this is similar to the one-fifth of members of the 1958 cohort who returned to their parental home at least once.

Econometric models of home leaving and return

As noted at the outset of this chapter, one of the advantages of panel data is its facility for incorporating explanatory variables that change over time, particularly economic ones, which are difficult to measure retrospectively. An economic model of a young person's decision whether to live with their parents or not suggests that a higher income of the young adult is associated with a higher probability of living apart from parents, whereas higher parental income has the opposite effect (for example see Rosenzweig and Wolpin, 1993, 1994). Thus, we start by estimating a simple model of departure from the parental home during a year where the departure rate depends on the young person's own monthly income in the previous year, monthly family income other than their own in the previous year ('parental income'), whether or not they were a student in the previous year and whether or not they were unemployed in the previous year. Three types of departure are distinguished: leaving to live with a partner, leaving as a student and leaving to live alone or with others (but not a student).

Leaving home

A multinomial logit model is estimated in order to accommodate these three alternatives ('competing risks'). The probability of departure type i is given by:

$$P_i = \exp(\beta_i \mathbf{X})/[\Sigma_j \exp(\beta_j \mathbf{X})]$$

where the summation in the denominator runs from 0 to 3 (type 0 is remaining in residence with parents), $\mathbf{X}$ is a vector of explanatory variables, the β_i are vectors of parameters and $\beta_0 = 0$ (i.e. the reference type is remaining with parents). The estimates of β_i in Table 12.4 show the effects of the explanatory variables on the logarithm of the odds of each type of departure relative to remaining with parents $[\ln(P_i/P_0)]$.

The data are obtained from pooling wave-on-wave data on departure from the parental home from the first four waves of the BHPS. We focus on persons aged 16–29 years. This produces 2,642 person–year observations for those 'at risk' of leaving home in the following year (i.e. they reside with at least one parent), of which 6.2% leave to live with a partner in the following year, 3.7% depart to be a student, 4.5% go to live alone or with others and 85.6% remain at home.

The parameter estimates in Table 12.4 indicate that a higher income for the young adult (in the previous year) clearly increases the chances of leaving the parental home, with impact on leaving to live with a partner and on departing to live alone or with others being statistically significant. Higher parental income makes it less likely that the person leaves to live alone or with others, but raises the chances of leaving as a student. These results are consistent with the predictions of the economic theory. Controlling for income, unemployed young people are *more* likely to leave their parents in the following year to live alone or with others, perhaps for job search reasons. In addition, women are more likely to leave home than men, particularly to non-student destinations, thereby implying that they leave home earlier than men

Table 12.4   Multinomial logit models of annual departure from parental home; absolute value of ratio of coefficient to asymptotic standard error in parentheses

Observed proportions	Partner 0.062	Student 0.037	Alone /others 0.045
Own income$_{t-1}$/100	0.062 (3.17)	0.043 (1.13)	0.064 (2.77)
Parental income$_{t-1}$/100	0.007 (0.96)	0.027 (3.99)	−0.024 (2.49)
Unemployed$_{t-1}$	−0.108 (0.37)	0.070 (0.11)	0.906 (3.43)
Student$_{t-1}$	−2.348 (5.43)	1.962 (6.04)	−1.317 (3.50)
Female	0.617 (3.68)	0.279 (1.00)	0.501 (2.56)
Constant	−3.630 (10.53)	−5.274 (10.60)	−3.474 (8.63)

Note
$N = 2642$, $\chi^2 = 268.04$ (15 df).

Table 12.5   Multinomial logit models of annual departure from parental home; absolute value of ratio of coefficient to asymptotic standard error in parentheses

Observed proportions	Partner 0.062	Student 0.037	Alone /others 0.045
Own income$_{t-1}$/100	0.013 (0.57)	0.002 (0.05)	0.044 (1.79)
Parental income$_{t-1}$/100	0.011 (1.62)	0.029 (4.12)	−0.023 (2.35)
Unemployed$_{t-1}$	−0.211 (0.70)	−0.043 (0.07)	0.860 (3.24)
Student$_{t-1}$	−1.947 (4.41)	2.241 (6.29)	−1.190 (3.09)
Age$_{t-1}$	0.152 (5.92)	0.120 (2.73)	0.057 (1.88)
Female	0.539 (3.17)	0.215 (1.01)	0.483 (2.46)
Constant	−6.595 (10.42)	−7.611 (7.47)	−4.550 (6.29)

Note
$N = 2642$, $\chi^2 = 309.77$ (18 df).

if all else is equal. Being a student in the previous year clearly increases the chances of leaving home as a student and reduces the probability of leaving parents to other destinations, particularly to live with a partner.

It is implicit in the models of Table 12.4 that the age profiles of departure from the parental home shown in Figures 12.4 and 12.5 are generated solely by age profiles in own income, unemployment and student status. The models in Table 12.5 also include age as a regressor.

Own income now only has a significant positive effect on departing to live alone or with others, and there are positive age gradients for each type of departure. Unemployment continues to stimulate departure to live alone or with friends, controlling for own income. Effects of other variables are similar to those in Table 12.4, including a positive effect of parental income on leaving to be a student and a negative effect of parental income on departing to live alone or with others. Table 12.5 also suggests that higher parental income also encourages departures to live with a partner. Thus, it appears that factors other than income, unemployment and student status contribute to the age patterns in departure rates observed in Figures 12.3, 12.4 and 12.5.

Returning home

The effects of economic and other variables on the likelihood of returning to the parental home are obtained from estimation of a simple logit model. In our pooled data for those aged 16–29 years, there are 3,811 person–years 'at risk' to return home (i.e. they are not living with their parents), of which 3.2% are observed to return to their parental home in the following year. As we cannot obtain an estimate of parental income for many persons who are no longer residing with their parents, parental income is excluded from the model.[5] However, we include whether or not the person had a partner in the preceding year and whether they were unemployed during the current year as potential influences on the chances of returning to the parental home in addition to the other ones considered in the leaving model. The parameter estimates are shown in Table 12.6.

A spell of unemployment during the year increases the chances of returning to the parents' home. People with a partner are clearly less likely to return, and, all else equal, women are less likely to return. These effects are robust to the inclusion of age as a regressor in the model, but this is not the case for those associated with own income and student status.

In the model excluding age, higher own income reduces the probability of returning to live with parents, as we would expect from the economic theory, but this income effect virtually disappears when age is included as a regressor. Similarly, it appears from the model without age that being a student in the previous year substantially increases the chances of returning, but this is no longer the case in the model with age. Thus, the steep negative age gradient shown in Figure 12.6 remains after controlling for a number of variables which change with age, such as own income, student status and the presence of a partner. The inclusion of unemployment status *in the previous year* has little effect on the other coefficients (also when age is excluded), but it has a significant *negative* effect on returning home when controlling for other factors. This variable may serve as a control for other omitted factors, i.e. young people who did not return home in the previous year,

Table 12.6 Logit model of annual return to the parental home; absolute value of ratio of coefficient to asymptotic standard error in parentheses

Observed proportion	Return 0.032	Return 0.032	Return 0.032
Own income$_{t-1}$/100	–0.053 (2.38)	–0.001 (0.06)	–0.015 (0.63)
Student$_{t-1}$	0.715 (2.90)	0.170 (0.66)	–0.026 (0.10)
Unemployed during year	0.844 (3.75)	0.854 (3.74)	1.091 (4.45)
Unemployed$_{t-1}$			–0.802 (2.16)
Age		–0.265 (7.44)	–0.270 (7.50)
Female	–0.365 (1.83)	–0.381 (1.90)	–0.438 (2.15)
Partner$_{t-1}$	–1.344 (6.33)	–0.985 (4.44)	–0.996 (4.48)
Constant	–2.072 (4.84)	3.725 (4.32)	4.110 (4.69)

Note
$N = 3811$, $\chi^2 =$ 122.69 (5 df)   181.60 (6 df)   186.58 (7 df)

despite their unemployment, may be people with a lower return probability.

Duration of partnerships

Studies of marital disruption are now relatively common. Many have used retrospective data (for example, for Great Britain, Murphy 1985; Ermisch, 1991: Ch. 5; for the USA, Lillard *et al.*, 1995), but recent studies have estimated sophisticated models using panel data, particularly the Panel Study of Income Dynamics (PSID) (for example Lillard and Waite, 1993; Hoffman and Duncan, 1995). Willis and Michael (1994), Bumpass and Sweet (1989) and Wu and Balakrishnan (1995) estimate durations of North American cohabitations with retrospective data. This section presents some simple analyses of the durations of British cohabiting unions and marriages using the first four waves of the BHPS.

The economic approach to union formation and dissolution suggests two general causes for union dissolution (see Becker *et al.*, 1977). Search for a partner is costly and meetings occur randomly; thus, a union which is currently acceptable may become unacceptable if a person meets a partner who would be a superior match. Second, traits which influence the benefits of a union can change over time in an unpredictable manner; such 'surprises' can cause either partner to reconsider their original decisions. It is beyond the scope of this chapter to develop fully an empirical implementation of these ideas, but it does suggest certain variables which may affect union dissolution. For instance, people who form a union earlier in their life are likely to have searched for a shorter time and therefore are more likely to make a poor match. Thus, they should be more likely to dissolve the union in the future, and a negative relationship between age at first marriage and the probability of marital dissolution has usually been found. Also, variables which represent 'surprises', such as unexpectedly low income, may affect union dissolution.

Panel data often do not provide information about events of interest, such as partnerships, that occur before the first round of the panel survey.[6] Thus, we would not know the age at partnership for people who were in a partnership at the start of the panel. Restricting the sample to only those individuals who partnered after the start of the panel, for whom we know their partnership formation date, may appear to solve this problem, but such a restriction would bias the sample in favour of younger people and those with shorter partnership durations. In general, panels often suffer from inadequate information to account for the initial states in which panel members are observed, and this so-called 'left censoring' or 'initial conditions' problem can bias dynamic analyses because of non-random sample selection. As we saw in previous chapters, this problem can be remedied by collecting some salient life history information at the beginning of the panel, and the BHPS did in fact collect partnership (marital and non-marital), birth, employment and occupational histories. These had not, however, been fully integrated with the panel data at the time of writing, and so the analyses of union dissolution below use, where appropriate, age as a control variable to capture, in combination, effects of age at union formation, union duration and birth cohort effects.

Cohabiting unions

It was shown in Figures 12.1 and 12.2 that a large majority of British people now cohabit without legal marriage in their first partnership. How long do such unions last and how do they end?

These questions are addressed with the panel data by looking at two pieces of information in the BHPS: the reported *de facto* marital status, which includes 'living as a couple' (not married) as one of the states, and the personal identity number of the partner. The latter is particularly important for cohabiting unions because a person could be 'living as a couple' in two consecutive waves, but they could have changed partners between waves; indeed, eighteen such cases are found. Thus, people in cohabiting unions are defined as those not married but 'living as a couple', and their union is defined to end either if they are not 'living as a couple' unmarried in the next wave or they have changed partners. There are two ways such unions can end: either the person marries their partner or the union dissolves. The methods again compute transition rates by examining events relative to person–years at risk, and the data for never married women is shown in Table 12.7.

Over one-quarter of cohabiting unions end each year. If the estimated transition rates were constant over time, they suggest a median duration of about 26 months.[7] About three-fifths of the unions turn into marriages. Similar calculations were done by Ermisch (1995a) for never married women's first cohabiting unions using the BHPS partnership histories. These suggest a similar proportion turning into marriages, but a median duration of only 20 months. This difference suggests longer durations of cohabitations in the 1990s than earlier, which is consistent with data on the median duration of *incomplete* cohabitations (Haskey, 1995).

Although estimation of the effects of age at union formation and union duration on the risk of dissolution can usually be accomplished with retrospective data, panel data are required to study the effects of 'surprises'. For instance, one particularly adverse surprise may be to end up under such a financial strain that the couple is dependent on means-tested welfare benefits, the primary one of which in Great Britain is Income Support (IS). Table 12.8 shows that about one in nine cohabiting women are on IS, and these women are less likely to marry their partner and more likely to dissolve their union in the following

Table 12.7 Resolution of cohabiting unions, never married women

	Number	%	Estimated transition rate(θ_i)
Dissolved	65	10.6	0.1055
Marriage	104	16.9	0.1688
Remain cohabiting	447	72.6	
Person–years at risk	616	100.0	

Source: British Household Panel Study, waves 1–4 (1991–4).

Table 12.8 Departure from cohabiting unions by receipt of income support, women

Income support during previous year	Marry partner (%)	Dissolve union (%)	Total outflow rate (%)	Number
Yes	8.0	13.0	21.0	100
No	17.0	10.1	27.1	822
All	16.1	10.4	26.5	922

Note
Pearson $\chi^2 = 6.71$ (2 df); likelihood ratio chi-squared $= 6.56$ (2 df).

year than cohabiting women not on IS. On balance, the women on IS remain cohabiting longer.

Of course, this simple difference in departure rates from cohabitation could reflect the impacts of income, the presence of children and age, all of which may be correlated with receipt of IS. Estimates of the parameters of a multinomial logit model in Table 12.9 indicate that, in the multivariate context, receipt of IS continues to have a large negative impact on the chances of marrying one's partner, which is statistically significant even after controlling for the other variables in Table 12.9; indeed, other than age, the coefficients of these other variables are not significantly different from zero. While IS receipt does not affect the union dissolution rate, more of the unions of IS recipients are likely to dissolve eventually because fewer are turned into marriage.

Marriages

As with cohabiting unions, two pieces of information in the BHPS, the reported *de facto* marital status and the personal identity number of the partner, are used to define a marital dissolution (divorce or separation). Those at risk of dissolving their marriage are those who are married *and* have a spouse present. Dissolution during the following year is defined to happen if one of the following occurs: (i) they report themselves as divorced or separated in the next wave; (ii) they report themselves as 'living as a couple' with a different partner; or (iii) they report being married, but a spouse is not present. Those who are widowed are treated as a separate category. Among married women aged under 55 years with a spouse present, 2.1% separate or divorce in the following year, which suggests that one-third of marriages would dissolve in 20 years if this rate were constant throughout the duration of the marriage.

Table 12.9 Multinomial logit model of cohabitation resolution, women aged under 55 years; absolute value of ratio of coefficient to asymptotic standard error in parentheses

Observed proportions	Marriage 0.169	Dissolve union 0.0908
Age$_{t-1}$	−0.0357 (2.94)	−0.0403 (2.42)
Income support$_{t-1}$	−0.844 (2.12)	0.065 (0.18)
Household income$_{t-1}$/100	0.0106 (1.31)	−0.0123 (0.96)
Child present$_{t-1}$	−0.115 (0.41)	−0.222 (0.62)
Constant	−0.551 (1.47)	−0.685 (1.38)

Note
$N = 848$, $\chi^2 = 25.44$(8 df).

Keeping with the notion that dependence on means-tested welfare benefits may be a particularly adverse 'surprise' in a marriage, Table 12.10 shows that receipt of IS is associated with a more than tripling of the marital dissolution rate. Again, we explore whether this association is robust to controls for other variables, particularly the presence and number of children, own and household income and age.

Table 12.11 shows that receipt of IS continues to more than double the odds of dissolving one's marriage, even after controlling for these other variables. Other than age, none of these is statistically significant. Although not well determined, the other coefficients suggest, not implausibly, that women with more income of their own and with more children are more likely to dissolve their marriage, whereas higher amounts of income other than their own and the presence of a child reduce the chances of dissolution.

While the impact of IS receipt on union dissolution is intriguing, these results represent the mere beginning of analysis of union

Table 12.10 Marital dissolution by receipt of income support, women, aged under 55 years

Income support during previous year	Dissolving marriage (%)	Number
Yes	7.3	124
No	1.9	5,467
All	2.1	5,591

Notes
Pearson $\chi^2 = 17.03$ (2 df).
Likelihood ratio $\chi^2 = 10.53$ (2 df).

Table 12.11 Logit model of marital dissolution, women aged under 55 years; absolute value of ratio of coefficient to asymptotic standard error in parentheses

Observed proportion	Dissolve 0.0206	
Age_{t-1}	–0.0721	(4.81)
Income support$_{t-1}$	0.874	(2.31)
Household income$_{t-1}$/100	–0.009	(0.92)
Own income$_{t-1}$/100	0.020	(1.00)
Child present$_{t-1}$	–0.341	(1.05)
Number of children$_{t-1}$	0.186	(1.54)
Constant	–1.254	(2.59)

Note
$N = 5591$, $\chi^2 = 57.10$ (6 df).

dissolution in Great Britain using panel data, which is necessary to capture the impacts of 'surprises' as well as 'poor matches' on dissolution decisions. Receipt of IS could just be an indication of other unmeasured attributes of a couple which are also correlated with dissolution risk. For instance, partners exhibiting less commitment to each other may also be less committed in their jobs, and therefore are more likely to be unemployed and receive IS. It could also reflect aspects of the social milieu in which people on IS live.

Conclusion

Panel data provide the opportunity to obtain contemporary information about processes of family and household change which are not readily measured in official statistics, such as parental home leaving and return and cohabitation. It also provides an opportunity to model the causes and consequences of family and household dynamics using a rich set of socioeconomic variables. For instance, Ermisch and Di Salvo (1996) show that a partnership break generates considerable change in housing tenure, including moves back to the parental home.

Notes

1 The BHPS collected partnership (marital and non-marital) histories in the second wave of the panel which, in conjunction with the panel data, would allow us to determine which people have never been in a partnership. These had not, however, been fully integrated with the panel data at the time of writing.

2 The panel data clearly would miss cohabitations which started and ended between two annual waves of the panel, thereby tending to understate cohabitation transitions.

3 The differences could reflect the assumption in constructing the life table that the panel data estimates of the transition rates are *first* partnership rates. Use of the life history data collected in wave 2 in conjunction with earlier waves of the panel for each person would allow estimation of the rates exclusively for those who have never had a partnership. Understatement of the cohabitation transition rate could also be responsible for the larger proportion estimated to be never partnered at age 26 years.

4 About 14% of men and women aged 16–29 years who were living with at least one parent are not present in the panel study in the next wave. The wave-on-wave attrition rate for persons aged 16–29 years who are not co-residing with their parents is about 13%. There is reason to believe that attrition may be higher for those who leave their parents' home than for those who remain. Similarly, among those living apart from their parents, attrition may be lower for those who return to their parents. This potential differential attrition has not been taken into account in the estimation of

the departure and return rates (i.e. movers' and stayers' rates of attrition are assumed to be the same). Although ignoring it may bias downward (upward) the estimates of the departure (return) rates, the *Appendix* in Ermisch (1996) shows that this bias is likely to be small with the data that are being analysed here.

5 To identify parents and their incomes, young people must be observed co-residing with their parents at least once in the panel.

6 For instance, neither the US PSID nor Canada's Survey of Labour and Income Dynamics collected life history information at the start of the panel.

7 With constant transition rates, the median duration of cohabitation is given by $ln(0.5)/ln(1 - \theta_m - \theta_d)$, where θ_m and θ_d are the annual marriage and dissolution transition rates respectively.

13 Using panel surveys to study migration and residential mobility

Nicholas Buck

Introduction

The study of migration poses, in particularly acute form, the issues raised by Rose in Chapter 1 concerning the relationship between microprocesses at the individual level and macroprocesses and structures at the societal level. The understanding of this relationship is at the core of the sociological enterprise (Coleman, 1990) and is critical in many other social science contexts. The problem is to understand, first, how structural factors influence individual behaviour, second, the influence of past events in the individual's life course on current behaviour and, third, how structures are modified by the accumulation of individual behaviours. The study of migration has precisely had this three-sided character. First, it has involved a study of the factors which lead to residential mobility, including both social and economic situation, and the characteristics of areas. These factors may be understood either as leading to the formation of preferences with regard to mobility or as structuring opportunities for mobility or constraints on mobility. Second, it has involved the study of the role of migration in the life course, either in terms of life course factors which promote or retard migration or in terms of the consequences of migration for life chances. Third, it has involved the study of the role of migration in changing the structure of localities. As migration is almost always socially selective, both in and out migration are liable to lead to significant changes in the social and economic structure of places. Important examples have been the selective pattern of migration from inner city areas.

This chapter aims to show how panel studies may contribute to some parts of the migration research agenda outlined above, by presenting some evidence from the British Household Panel Study (BHPS). This sheds new light on the processes of migration[1] in Great Britain in the early 1990s. The design of a household panel study makes it particularly valuable as a vehicle for studying the processes by which people move house and the way in which this relates to household formation, given that it tracks individuals' moves between locations over time.

Moreover, the study of migration is inherently longitudinal – it requires information about the situation of individuals before and after moves, or, at the minimum, information that a migration event has occurred within a defined time period. There is clearly a range of possible data collection methods which might be used to study mobility and migration. The role of panel studies in migration research may best be illuminated through a brief discussion of the range of data sources which may be used to analyse migration behaviour. We may identify five main types of individual- and household-level data which may contribute to the study of migration: large general population censuses and surveys, special purpose retrospective migration surveys, record linkage methods, population registers and panel surveys. As indicated above, because longitudinal information is required for the study of migration, and is problematic to collect, each type of information has its limitations as well as strengths.

General population cross-sectional sample surveys and censuses with retrospective data

The Population Census and the Labour Force Survey (LFS) are two prime examples of this type of data for the UK, and they have been particularly important across the range of migration research. The Census contains retrospective information about location, but about nothing else. This means that inferences about the process of migration is limited to the effects of area of origin, distance of move, age, sex and, to a more limited degree, household structure. The LFS contains rather more retrospective information about labour market status, allowing rather more inference about labour migration. However, the large sample size of the LFS and the complete coverage of the Census does make them well suited to understanding the role of spatial factors in migration, e.g. for analysing how inflows and outflows may be related to differences in local economic conditions or local housing markets or how they may contribute to population recomposition. The General Household Survey (GHS) has on some occasions collected rather fuller information than the LFS, including retrospective tenure information and moving intentions. Its smaller sample size places some limits on the ability to study subgroups.

Migration surveys

There have been a limited number of special purpose surveys which have been used to explore migration. There are two main types. The first attempts to identify recent migrants or potential migrants and attempts to capture information about motivations or other events associated with migration. The second collects full retrospective histories of residential mobility (usually combined with histories of demographic and labour market behaviour). The need to find a sample of movers makes the first form of survey relatively expensive to mount, and thus restricts sample size. In consequence, relatively few large-scale examples exist. One is reported in Johnson *et al.* (1974). The ability to focus on migration processes in depth makes such surveys a potentially valuable tool, particularly for the study of migration motivations and to differentiate migrant streams. General population residential mobility histories are rather rare (the recent Working Lives Survey sponsored by the UK Employment Department is an example). Some idea of the potential may be gained from the National Child Development Study, a cohort study of those born in 1958. Analysis of the migration histories is reported in Ermisch and Di Salvo (1995a). Both these types of survey rely on retrospective data, which is subject to questions of reliability and also potentially to problems of *post hoc* rationalisation.

Record linkage

Migrants may be identified by matching administrative or census records across time. A major example in the UK is the Census Longitudinal Study, which has matched a 1% sample of individuals among the 1971, 1981 and 1991 censuses. This has been particularly important in understanding how migration, and especially long-distance migration, relates to changes over the life course, for example career development (Savage *et al.*, 1992), as well as giving some information on the sequences of multiple moves. The main limitation is the absence of information about events over much of the period between censuses.

Population registers

In a number of European countries, population registers have provided the basis for migration research. Where these combine a substantial level of social and economic data on households with location information, as in Sweden, their potential is enormous. The only major information gaps in such a data resource would be on subjective motivations, and parallel labour market events. Unfortunately, nothing similar exists in the UK. The National Health Service Central Register provides the nearest approximation, and although it provides some information on gross flows between areas it is of little use in microbehavioural research.

Household panel surveys

As we have seen, panel surveys involve repeated interviews with a sample of individuals (including all members of each household containing a sample member), at intervals, usually of 1 year. Where the design involves the following of individuals as they move, as in the BHPS, this allows the collection of information before and after migration about household and economic situation, and at least potentially about preferences and motivations towards migration. As noted in previous chapters, the important distinction with the first two categories above is that information is collected both prospectively and retrospectively. We have data collected before any potential move, and information that a move has taken place. As Ermisch noted in the previous chapter, this is a significant improvement over retrospective surveys because a much wider range of prior information will be available, and with much higher data quality. For causal modelling of migration, it is important to have information about circumstances before the migration occurred. For some information, retrospective data collection is possible, but risks of memory failures, or contamination by subsequent events, mean that panel data collected at the time will be of much higher quality. Some data simply cannot be reliably collected in a retrospective fashion, such as prior preferences to move. Panel studies also have significant advantages in relating migration directly to processes of household formation and dissolution as household composition before and after moves is known. The design will also permit collection of data on repeat migration. There are, however, limitations. The first is that it is rarely practical to have the very large sample sizes which would be necessary to explore the geography of migration in detail. Second, panel attrition is a potential problem, especially as migrants are more likely to be lost through non-contact than other sample members.

Thus, while panel studies clearly cannot replace other data collection methods, they have an important additional contribution. The importance of true longitudinal data on migration was highlighted by Coleman and Salt (1992: 399–400):

The focus in most surveys on cross-section data restricts the use to be made of the information collected. It is difficult to put the move into some kind of temporal sequence despite the emphasis in much of the literature on life cycle and career paths, which imply a distinct time element. What is required is more longitudinal data which will allow migration to be placed in the context of a series of events. The general lack of longitudinal data is a major vacuum in understanding British migration yet the importance of this approach is apparent when we see that previous migration history is closely related to subsequent movement: those who have moved once are more likely to move again.

As we will see later, there are a number of aspects of migration which can be illuminated through panel data. This chapter focuses on microbehavioural aspects of the migration process – how migration relates to other life events and to household formation processes as well as how it is rationalised, in terms both of *a priori* preferences and in terms of *a posteriori* explanations. In doing this, the chapter addresses a number of the priority areas for migration research which an Institute of British Geographers working party identified. In summarising this report, Champion (1992) drew attention to a number of priority research themes. Of particular relevance to this chapter are the role of housing tenure in migration, as against other sociodemographic factors, the relationship between housing factors and labour mobility and the association between migration and household change. A number of the other priority areas could clearly also be addressed with panel data, including the migration behaviour of two-income and dual-career households, the impacts of labour market characteristics on migration and, more generally, the need to place migration within a life course perspective. These are however beyond the scope of this chapter.

The British Household Panel Study (BHPS)

In this chapter, we present some introductory analyses of the migration processes and patterns revealed by the first four waves of the BHPS. We focus mainly on five areas: (i) the level of mobility identified by the BHPS, including levels of repeat migration; (ii) the distances moved, and the reasons given for movement; (iii) how this mobility is associated with household composition change and the processes of household formation and dissolution; (iv) the nature of migration preferences and the degree to which they are realised; and (v) the factors which are associated with mobility. In this final section, we fit some hazard models for migration over the first three waves of the panel and identify characteristics and life events which make migration more or less likely. In addition, these models contrast the factors associated with long- and short-distance mobility. These models also allow us to derive some estimates of the predicted duration up to migration depending on individual and household characteristics. Before discussing these findings, we briefly describe the structure and design of the BHPS.

Some early results based on the first two waves of the panel study were presented in Buck *et al.* (1994) and this contained a more complete description of the panel than is possible here. In particular, some evidence on migration between the first two waves was presented. This mainly focused on the relationship between tenure change, household change and migration. This is developed rather more here, as is a discussion of the association between movement preferences and subsequent movement.

Fieldwork for the panel study began in the Autumn of 1991, with an achieved sample of 5,512 households, containing 13,840 individuals, both adults and children; 9,912 adults provided complete interviews. It is the migration behaviour of this sample over the following 3 years which we discuss in this chapter. As indicated above, we attempted to follow all movers who remained within Great Britain. Between each wave, there was a limited amount of attrition, through refusal or non-contact, as well as loss to the sample of those who died or moved out of scope. Between waves 1 and 2, attrition amounted to 13% of the original sample, between waves 2 and 3 it amounted to 10% and between waves 3 and 4 attrition amounted to 5%. As indicated above, attrition through non-contact is rather higher for migrants, with 28% of movers between waves 1 and 2 being lost. However, in the majority of cases, it was possible to identify that a move had taken place and to identify the destination area, even if no follow-up interviews were carried out. These cases are thus not entirely lost to analysis, and they also make it possible to estimate how far attrition may be biasing results. The panel study covers a range of domains, including income, labour market behaviour, health, values, household organisation and housing consumption. It also included a question on preference for moving, including reasons and retrospective reasons for mobility among those who had moved. These other data can clearly be used as explanatory factors in models which seek to understand the processes of migration.

Of the 13,840 individuals contained in respondent households at wave 1, we know at least whether or not they have moved for all but seventy-nine (these are largely cases in which the wave 2 interviewer could gain no information about who was resident in an apparently non-mover household). Of the remainder, ninety-nine had died and eighty-two were known either to have moved abroad or into an institution where they could not be followed. Of the remaining 13,580, 1,432 (10.5%) had made some other move. The 1991 Census found that 9.4% of the resident population reported a move in the last year. However, of these, only 8.3% reported a move within Great Britain, which is the retrospective measure similar to the prospective measure in the BHPS. There are a number of possible reasons for this discrepancy, over and above sampling error in the BHPS. The first would be potential biases in the original BHPS sample compared with the Census. However, the main known sources of bias (for example low response rates in inner city areas and among younger single people) are unlikely to bias migration estimates upwards – rather, the reverse. The second is possible under-reporting in the Census, which is possible since respondents had to volunteer the information and correctly estimate the date of the previous move. Third, the reference period in the BHPS is somewhat longer than 1 year because from wave 2 the fieldwork period was extended, in part to trace movers. This could quite plausibly have added one percentage point to the mover rate. Fourth, it is possible that some of the untraced movers were in fact moves abroad or into an institution, and thus not included in the similar Census figure. Finally, the reference period is different, with the Census covering the period April 1990 to April 1991, and the BHPS covering the period Autumn 1991 to Autumn 1992. Together, these factors appear sufficient to explain any discrepancy.

With four waves of the panel, we can also compare moves over a 1-year period with moves over a 3-year period and also examine the probabilities of making multiple moves. The annual movement rates are shown in Table 13.1. The movement rates between waves 2 and 3 and between waves 3 and 4 are broadly similar to the rates in the first year. We might then expect to find that around 30% had moved over the whole period. In fact, we find about 24.5% had moved at least once. Clearly then some individuals are making multiple moves. With the panel, we can look at the conditional probability of moving, given a move in the previous year. This is shown in the second column of Table 13.1. Thus, of those who moved between wave 1 and wave 2 (and were

Table 13.1 Percentage moved house by previous wave mover status

Moved at wave	All (%)	Mover previous wave (%)	Non-mover previous wave (%)	Mover at two previous waves (%)
2	10.5			
3	10.2	25.3	8.8	
4	10.4	27.8	8.7	37.2

enumerated at wave 2), about 25% made another move between wave 2 and wave 3. They were thus three times as likely to make a move as those who had not moved in the first year. Of those who moved in both of the first 2 years (and were enumerated at wave 3), around 37% moved between wave 3 and wave 4. The panel thus clearly confirms the suggestion of Coleman and Salt (1992), quoted above, that migration behaviour is related to previous migration history. What is not fully resolved, and requires further analysis, is the degree to which what we observe here is a genuine causal association between moves in the sequence or whether it represents a division of the population into individuals more or less prone to mobility.

Migration distances and motivations

The panel can also be used to analyse distance of move, provided the address at the end of the move is known. In the results reported here, we focus on the first move made during the first 3 years of the panel; 3,248 movers are identified by this criterion. Of these, 88.4% had an identified destination. Moves are mainly short distance; 66.4% were within a local authority district,[2] 19.9% were beyond local authority boundaries, but within standard regions, and 13.7% were inter-regional moves. This last figure is similar to the Census share of 12.7%.

The study also asked a set of retrospective questions about the reasons for moving. In Table 13.2, these reasons are related to the distance moved. The sample is restricted to adults who were interviewed after the move. Multiple reasons could be given, so that the percentages in the final column sum to more than 100%. Considering this column first, housing-related reasons are clearly the most substantial, especially when involuntary housing reasons, such as evictions and repossessions, are

Table 13.2 Reason for move by distance

Reason for move	Within LA district (%)	Between LA district within region (%)	Between region (%)	All moves (%)
Job related	21.8	36.5	41.6	16.3 (293)
Partnership	70.2	23.9	6.0	15.8 (285)
Other family	57.1	23.4	19.6	10.2 (184)
Education	12.1	29.3	58.6	6.4 (116)
Eviction	71.3	21.7	7.0	6.4 (115)
Housing	81.3	13.7	5.0	37.7 (678)
Area	68.0	22.7	9.3	10.8 (194)
Other	75.9	15.2	8.9	8.8 (158)
All moves	63.4	21.2	15.4	100.0 (1,799)

included. Job-related moves make up around one-sixth of the total. This is not dissimilar from the share of job moves found in earlier studies (see Coleman and Salt, 1992: 420). The formation and dissolution of partnerships accounts for almost the same proportion, and other family formation behaviour for around 10%. Around the same proportion gave reasons related to area preference.

There are marked differences in the distance moved by reason given. Housing-related moves are predominantly local. Partnership-related moves are also more local than average, as, surprisingly, are area-related moves – suggesting that it is local neighbourhood characteristics which are prompting the move. At the other extreme are job-related moves and education-related moves, which as expected are substantially more likely than average to be inter-regional.

Buck (1994) reported on the basis of two waves of data that local authority tenants were rather more likely to move than mortgage holders. There has been substantial research on the association between tenure and migration, mainly focused on the question of whether the housing system contributes to labour immobility (for example Hughes and McCormick, 1981, 1985). The main focus here has been on long-distance (i.e. inter-regional) migration. This research has found that council tenants have much lower probabilities of making inter-regional moves, but rather higher probabilities of making local moves. This is repeated in the BHPS data, at least as a simple cross-tabulation. Table 13.3 shows that there are marked differences in the distance moved by tenure group. While public sector tenants (here including housing associations) have higher mobility than owner occupiers with a mortgage, their probability of making a non-local move, and especially an inter-regional move, are very much lower. Renters in the private sector are, as expected, much more mobile than other tenures. It appears likely that the higher local migration of council tenants is

Table 13.3   Distance moved up to wave 4 by tenure at wave 1; percentage of all enumerated at wave 1

	Within LA district (%)	Between LA district within region (%)	Between region (%)	Unknown destination (%)	All moves (%)
Owned outright	6.1	2.8	1.5	1.2	11.6
Owned with mortgage	12.2	3.8	3.6	1.7	21.3
Public rented	17.8	3.3	1.0	4.9	27.1
Private rented	29.8	11.3	6.0	6.2	53.9

related to their lower mobility costs compared with owners. However, it is also likely to vary with the state of the housing market. The early 1990s were clearly a period of very low turnover among owner occupiers, and we would expect to find a narrowing of the differential at a time of greater housing market activity. Some evidence for this may be found in a comparison with retrospective data from the LFS. In 1992, 10.6% of public sector tenants had moved in the last year compared with 7.7% of those owning with a mortgage. However in 1987, whereas 9.0% of public sector tenants had moved, 10.9% of owners with a mortgage had done so. This confirms large cyclical fluctuations, although of course it takes no account of tenure change, and thus is likely to understate somewhat the mobility of council tenants. Of course, tenure mobility can also be studied using panel data, and some results are reported in Buck (1994).

Household composition change

Household composition is almost by definition likely to be related to residential mobility. Births and deaths are the only sources of change which are not directly dependent on mobility. One striking finding of the BHPS has been the extent of household composition change. Buck *et al.* (1994) showed that 14% of households experienced some form of composition change over a single year. We should therefore expect to find a substantial proportion of migration events associated with household composition change.

The added dimension from panel information in this area may be gauged from a comparison of Census data with the BHPS data. As indicated above, the overall level of mobility found in the BHPS is broadly similar. The Census divides individuals moving within Great Britain into two categories, those in 'wholly moving households' (i.e. cases where all members of the Census household had moved from the same address – strictly the same postcode – within the last year) and others where household members were in different addresses a year before. Around 69% of individuals are so defined as belonging to wholly moving households, with the remainder coming from multiple addresses. In the panel study, we can measure not only whether all members of a wave 2 household came from the same wave 1 household but also whether all members of a wave 1 household have moved to the same wave 2 household. This is shown in Table 13.4. This is restricted to individuals who moved and were enumerated at both waves. The total of the first column of the table shows the Census concept of the wholly moving household (i.e. with no one joining since wave 1, and the share

Table 13.4 Prospective and retrospective household composition change and migration

Whether separated from wave 1 household members	Whether joined by new household members at Wave 2		
	No (%)	Yes (%)	Total (%)
No	48.2	13.5	61.7
Yes	20.5	17.8	38.3
Total	68.7	31.3	100.0 ($n = 1,058$)

of all movers is similar to the Census result). However, the total for the first row shows that only 62% of individuals moved together with all the individuals who they were sharing a household with at wave 1. The top left-hand cell shows that less than half of individuals who moved were unaffected by some form of composition change.

The potential range of household composition change events which may be associated with migration is clearly very large, and here we only examine a subset of them. One complication in this analysis is that we are more likely to have information about separations rather than joins because the separation associated with a non-respondent departer is known, but any subsequent joins that may have taken place will be unknown. Table 13.5 shows the distance of move of migrations associated with different types of household change. Because some types of household change are more associated with non-response than others, the distribution of move types should be treated with some caution (for example children leaving home to join with a partner may be over-represented compared with children leaving home to other destin-ations). Taking this into account, it is still clear that children leaving the parental home, and the formation and dissolution of partnerships, do make up well over half of the migrations associated with composition change, but there remain significant numbers of other types of change, including returns of children who had previously left, and other miscellaneous movements, mainly involving unrelated people or more distant relatives. [The category 'childbirth' refers to situations where there has been a birth as well as a move by the parent(s)]. Moves involving household composition change are likely to take place over a longer distance than those involving no change. Moves involving adult children either leaving or returning to the parental home are particularly likely to be long distance, except where children leave home to form a partnership. There is some evidence that moves involving separations are more likely to be long distance than moves involving joining a household.

Table 13.5 Household composition change and distance of move

	Within LA district (%)	Between LA district within region (%)	Between region (%)	All moves (%)
No change	71.4	17.8	10.8	53.7
Partnership split	65.4	21.6	13.1	6.0
Child leaving home to partner	68.9	23.6	7.4	5.8
Child leaving home other	51.6	21.3	27.1	12.1
Partnership formation	55.1	36.0	9.0	3.5
Return to parent	57.5	22.5	20.0	3.1
Child birth	70.7	24.0	5.3	2.9
Other joins	68.9	23.3	7.8	3.5
Other separations	70.7	15.3	14.0	9.4
All moves	67.3	19.7	13.0	100.0
Number	1,727	505	333	2,565

Moving preferences

At each wave, we ask about preferences for moving. The question wording is 'If you could choose, would you stay here in your present home or would you prefer to move somewhere else?' It is important to note that this is a preference question, rather than asking about intentions or whether active steps are being taken to move. It is quite possible that respondents believe that they are not able to move, but may have some preference for doing so. We find in fact a very high level of moving preferences (41% at wave 1) compared with the level of those who typically say they are seriously considering moving (15% of a GHS 1983 sample used by Gordon and Molho, 1995). We must therefore expect only a relatively small proportion of these preferences to be realised over the short term given that only around 10% move each year. However, not surprisingly, as Buck (1994) showed, there was a clear association between an initial preference for moving and being able to make a move. Thus, 17% of those wanting to move did so compared with 6% of those who preferred to stay. One implication of this is that significant numbers (around 40%) of movers had expressed a preference to stay in the previous year. It is of course likely that the preferences of some portion of this group changed at some point between the survey and their move. On the other hand, it is likely that some moves remained involuntary. These will include evictions and repossessions, but also some job moves and some moves relating to family events. It is also possible that the move reflected the preference of some other household member than the household reference person who was interviewed.

This last point raises the issue of the interaction between preferences and mover behaviour within the household. The analysis in this chapter does not take this fully into account. Clearly, it would be possible to do so with a more complex analysis. The present analysis treats all individual respondents as independent.[3] However, some insight into the potential for intrahousehold analysis is shown by an examination of couple households. These could clearly express agreement in a preference to stay or in a preference to move or a disagreement as to preferences. This can then be compared with actual mover behaviour over the subsequent 3 years. Where there was agreement to stay, 7.3% of couples moved together (i.e. not including splits). Where one party preferred to move, but not the other, 14.6% moved. It made little difference whether it was the husband who wanted to move (14.2% moved) or the wife (15.1% moved). Where the couple agreed in wanting to move, 31.5% moved.

While the preference indicator is not directly associated with a very high probability of moving, it does have considerable predictive power and can contribute to an analysis of factors associated with mobility. This is because mobility may be conditioned both by the opportunities which people have (and which may vary systematically within the population) and by their preferences. If these preferences also vary systematically then we may have difficulty in interpreting variations in mobility as systematic variations in opportunities for mobility without taking the preferences into account. Difficulties remain, in part because preferences may be formed in response to beliefs about available opportunities (so-called adaptive preference formation – see Elster, 1983) and also because the distribution of current preferences may reflect variations in past opportunities. Thus, if a group has lower than average chances for mobility, those who want to move will take longer than average to find an acceptable opportunity. A cross-sectional survey will find more in this group wanting to move than in a group with higher mobility opportunities. These two complications limit the degree to which we can genuinely separate out preferences, but this chapter makes some preliminary attempts to take preferences into account in exploring mobility behaviour.

We pursue this in the next section in the context of models of the impact on migration behaviour of a number of social and demographic factors. Before doing this, however, we here explore the factors associated with mobility preferences. Table 13.6 shows the results of a logistic regression model for expressing a preference for movement at wave 1. The coefficients therefore show the effect of a unit change in the variable on the log of the odds of preferring to move rather than stay compared with the control group. Thus, the coefficient of 0.3392 for public sector tenure implies that, as 0.3392 exponentiated is 1.4038, a resident of this tenure will be around 40% more likely to wish to move than a resident of the omitted tenure owners.

In the model shown in Table 13.6, the age categories are based on the age at moving to the address rather than on the age at interview. The sample is restricted to those who moved to their wave 1 address after reaching the age of 16 years and before the age of 50 years. The

Table 13.6 Logistic regression on preferring to move house

Intercept	−0.9112
Age 16–19	0.3656*
Age 20–24	0.5022***
Age 25–29	0.3421**
Age 30–34	0.3405**
Age 35–39	0.2224
Age 40–44	−0.0876
Female	−0.0834
Public sector rented	0.3392***
Private rented	0.0447
Income decile	0.0143
Cohabiting	0.3292***
Single	−0.1134
Divorced or separated	0.1529
Widowed	0.1843
Persons per room	0.5554***
Number of children	−0.1136***
Service class	0.1971
Intermediate class	0.1734
Working class	0.0382
Own account worker	0.1231
Unemployed	0.2572*
Student	0.0500
Degree	−0.0305
Middle level qualifications	0.1203
Lower qualifications	0.0548
Duration at address (years)	−0.0260***
−2 Log likelihood	429.753
N events	7,347

Note
*$P < 0.05$; **$P < 0.01$; ***$P < 0.001$.

aim of this restriction, which is carried through to the models of migration behaviour in the next section, is to focus on migration processes in the working age population and to exclude, as far as possible, initial departures from the parental home and moves following retirement migration. The other covariates used include sex (female rather than male), tenure (where owning is the excluded category), marital status (with married the excluded category), housing density, income (transformed to a decile scale), numbers of children, employment status and class of current employment combined[4] (with inactive the excluded category) and highest qualifications[5] (with no qualifications the excluded category). The model also includes a variable for duration in years at the address.[6]

The duration effect is strong and negative, with around a 2.6% decline in the probability of expressing a preference for moving with each year at the address, reflecting growing inertia as individuals became settled. There are substantial life stage effects, with much stronger preferences for leaving an address where the respondent started living in the age range 16–34 years compared with later years. Preferences are strongest where the respondent moved to the address in their early twenties, suggesting pressures related to the early stages of family formation rather than, for example, those associated with the high mobility typically found in the teens. As indicated above, those in public sector housing are more likely to want to move. As we shall see later, tenants in private rented housing are highly mobile, but this is not reflected in strong preferences for mobility. There is a strong association with housing density (persons per room) in the expected direction. On the other hand, there is a negative association with numbers of children, perhaps reflecting the higher perceived disruption costs associated with moving children. There is no association with income or with qualification levels. Those in service class (professional and managerial) jobs were more likely to prefer to move than those in the working class, although the difference is not significant. The unemployed also expressed stronger preferences for movement.

We thus have some evidence here for a higher preference for mobility among those in worse housing situations, as measured by density, among those in what is widely seen as the least favoured housing tenure (public sector renting) and among those in a disadvantaged labour market position. This is additional to the preferences related to life cycle stage as indicated by the age effects (and also to some degree the positive association with cohabitation). This association with disadvantage would suggest that the preference measure is identifying dissatisfaction with unsatisfactory conditions. In the next section, we explore how far these mobility preferences can be realised, and how far there is any evidence of systematic constraints on mobility.

Correlates of migration in the BHPS

In this final section, we explore the association between prior characteristics, as revealed in the panel study interviews, with the probability of subsequent migration. To make full use of the information about the timing of moves, we create event history data from the panel records. This uses not only the information from the separate waves but also information on the date at which the move took place. This gives much fuller information on the time of move, and thus how rapidly different groups in the population are able to move. We use here a discrete time event history formulation (see Allison, 1982). This converts the data into person–month records for each observed month after the start of the panel. The dependent variable is a dummy variable coded 1 if a move took place in the month. The results will be very close to those from a continuous time event history analysis in which we are attempting to model the hazard of moving (i.e. the conditional probability of moving in the current period given that the respondent has not moved up to that point). Cases are censored if they become non-response, but are included up to the point at which they cease to respond. Although the respondents had been resident at their wave 1 address for varying amounts of time, we did know the date at which they started to live at the address, so they were not strictly speaking left censored. Jenkins (1995) discusses the treatment of data in this form, and shows that an analysis based on data for the observation period can still give unbiased estimates, provided the time of entry into the state is known. His example treats a somewhat more complex case involving a stock sample, which implied higher selection probabilities for those with a longer duration. In the present case, the sample is one of the whole population – since all the resident household population must have an address of residence and should give an unbiased distribution of periods of residence at addresses.

The results of analysis of the whole sample are shown in the first column of Table 13.7. This uses essentially the same set of variables as Table 13.6. However, some of the variables in the model are treated as time varying covariates. The most important of these is the log of the number of months since moving to the address. This allows us to capture the duration dependence of the hazard of moving. In this formulation, the model approximates to a Weibull formulation which allows a monotonically increasing or decreasing hazard. In addition to this, a

Table 13.7 Discrete time hazard model for moving home

	All	*Intraregional*	*Inter-regional*
Intercept	–5.0457	–5.0660	–7.9162
Log time (months)	–0.3381***	–0.3530***	–0.2335**
Age 16–19	0.7395***	0.6497***	1.3256**
Age 20–24	0.5802***	0.5476***	0.8408*
Age 25–29	0.2535*	0.2268	0.4599
Age 30–34	0.0562	–0.0200	0.5717
Age 35–39	0.0286	–0.0412	0.4967
Age 40–44	–0.1270	–0.1900	0.3224
Female	–0.0605	–0.0888	0.1018
Public sector rented	0.5179***	0.5900***	–0.1567
Private rented	1.2116***	1.2745***	0.7554***
Income decile	0.0871***	0.0746***	0.1632***
Cohabiting	0.4523***	0.5209**	–0.1876
Single	0.3879***	0.3858***	0.3644
Divorced or separated	0.6132***	0.6686***	–0.0017
Widowed	–0.1232	–0.1352	0.1547
Persons per room	0.5536***	0.5678***	0.3555
Number of children	0.0230	0.0329	–0.0647
Service class	–0.1394	–0.1566	0.0341
Intermediate class	–0.2099*	–0.1818	–0.3571
Working class	–0.2839**	–0.2829**	–0.2336
Own account worker	–0.0464	–0.0738	–0.1851
Unemployed	0.0959	0.0544	0.3563
Student	0.1303	–0.2092	1.5481***
Degree	0.1957	0.1958	0.0956
Middle level qualifications	0.2514**	0.2813**	0.0384
Lower qualifications	0.1364	0.1711	–0.1284
–2 Log likelihood	1,445.246	1,311.201	223.185
N events	1,520	1,312	208

Note
*$P < 0.05$; **$P < 0.01$; ***$P < 0.001$.

number of characteristics measured at each panel wave are included in the model. These include household income, marital status, housing tenure, housing density, number of children, level of highest qualification and social class of current job or whether unemployed or a student if not in a job. As in Table 13.6, age is included as a set of dummy variables representing the age at which the respondent started living at the address.

The models are again fitted as logistic regressions, but the interpretation of coefficients is slightly different. Here, it represents the effect of the characteristic on the log odds of the conditional probability of moving in a month, given that the respondent has not moved up to that point. We find a relatively high negative duration dependency (i.e. the longer individuals have lived at an address, the less likely they are to leave it). Clearly, duration will interact with age, and some large part of the falling probability of migration with age found in many data sources will be captured here by the duration variable. Having taken this into account, there is a significantly higher probability of migration from addresses entered below the age of 30 years. The effect is strongest for addresses entered under 20 years of age. These age effects reflect the rapid turnover characteristic of younger adults at this stage of the life cycle. Above 30 years, there are no significant age effects when age is measured as here.

As in the model for preferences, there is no significant sex difference in the probability of moving. The tenure differences in mobility shown in Table 13.3 are reflected here in the multivariate analysis, with significantly higher mobility associated with public sector renting compared with ownership, and still higher levels associated with private renting. There is a significant positive income effect. Those single, cohabiting or divorced and separated are all more mobile than the excluded category, which is those who are married. There is a powerful housing density effect. Those in intermediate and working-class jobs are significantly less mobile than the excluded category (the economically inactive). While the unemployed are somewhat more mobile, the difference is not significant. In general, those with educational qualifications are somewhat more mobile than those without, although the effect is only statistically significant for those with middle level qualifications but not degrees.

It is possible to use the results from this model to estimate the distribution of completed durations at addresses for respondents with different characteristics. Table 13.8 shows some estimated median durations for a limited range of characteristic sets. It gives some indication of the implications of the model coefficients. Thus, taking the first row, a married man with median income, a working-class job and no qualifications who started living in council accommodation aged between 20 and 24 years would expect a median duration of 51 months. By contrast, a similar man in owner-occupied housing would expect a median duration of 111 months. A similar aged man with a higher paying service class job and with a degree would expect a median duration of 45 months. The examples in the table show very clearly the declining mobility with increasing age, but they also show, controlling for this, that lower income families in council housing have similar mobility rates to higher income owner occupiers. It is lower income owner

Table 13.8 Estimated median durations at address

Age (years) at moving in (married unless otherwise indicated)	Tenure	Class	Income decile	Highest qualification	Median duration at address (months)
20–24	Public	Working	5	None	50.9
20–24	Owned	Working	5	None	111.4
20–24	Owned	Service	8	Degree	44.9
20–24	Public	Unemployed	3	None	37.3
25–29	Public	Working	5	None	83.4
25–29	Owned	Working	5	None	182.5
25–29	Owned	Intermediate	7	Middle	85.8
25–29	Owned	Service	9	Degree	64.5
35–39	Owned	Service	10	Degree	79.4
35–39	Owned	Working	5	None	256.3
35–39	Public	Working	5	None	117.2
16–19 (single)	Private	Student	3	Middle	3.7
20–24 (single)	Private	Intermediate	5	Middle	6.1
25–29 (single)	Private	Service	7	Degree	7.5
25–29 (single)	Owned	Service	7	Degree	46.7

occupiers who have very low mobility rates. To some degree at least, this must reflect the situation of the British housing market in the early 1990s, in which there was both very low overall mobility and a relatively large number of lower income purchasers who may have been trapped by falling house prices. The very short durations for single people in private rented accommodation implied by the model are also notable.

Returning to Table 13.7, the final two columns contrast intraregional with inter-regional mobility.[7] In this model, the two are considered as competing risks (i.e. the respondent is no longer at risk of making an inter-regional move from the original address after they have made an intraregional move). The intraregional model is very similar to the all moves model, reflecting the high proportion of all moves that are intraregional. The model for inter-regional moves is however rather different. The age profile is much steeper, and students show up as the only employment status or class group who are significantly more likely to migrate. The coefficient for inter-regional movement by the unemployed is larger than for local moves, but remains non-significant. The housing density effect is attenuated. However, the most important differences relate to income and tenure. The positive effect for public sector renting disappears, as we might have expected on the basis of Table 13.3. On the other hand, we do not find the strong negative effect which Hughes and McCormick (1981) found in data from the early 1970s. Their findings would lead us to expect a negative coefficient around six times as large. The 3-year BHPS data contain at least as many movers as their GHS sample, so it is unlikely that the difference is due to inadequate sample size. Other possibilities are a change in housing market functioning or, alternatively, that the data used here are better able to control for other differences. One indication that the latter is the case is given by the income decile variable. This is extremely significant and is around twice the size of the coefficient for intraregional moves. Income is clearly one of the types of data which are far more reliably collected in a panel study than in a retrospective study, so that useable income information before the move is unlikely to be available without panel data.

If we contrast the findings in Table 13.7 with the factors which explained preferences to move, discussed in the previous section, then we find that the disadvantaging factors which were associated with a preference for mobility (density, unemployment and public sector housing) are all positively associated with actual mobility. We cannot therefore tell whether the higher mobility of these groups represents stronger preferences or greater opportunities (or indeed greater levels of involuntary mobility). We do also find positive associations between mobility and indicators of higher social and economic status (for example income, qualifications and the negative association with working-class jobs). There is then a relatively complex social structuring to mobility, and clearly some social structure to the mobility; so we can only answer in a limited way the question of the nature of social and economic constraints on mobility.

Table 13.9 attempts to take this analysis further. Here, we carry out separate analyses of those who expressed a preference for movement (labelled movers) and those who did not (labelled stayers). The difference in the mobility probabilities are reflected in differences in the intercept terms, with those preferring to move much more likely to do so than those who expressed a preference to stay. In this model, the preference is expressed at wave 1, and the individuals are observed for up to 3 years. Thus, one interpretation of the 'stayers' who moved is that some change in their circumstances occurred which led them to consider moving. We thus might expect to find strong associations here with people in life cycle stages most subject to change. Indeed, we do find much stronger associations among the 'stayers' with age, with non-married individuals and with private renting than we do among the whole sample. By contrast, most class and education effects are weaker, as is the association with public sector housing. Clearly, we could take

Table 13.9   Discrete time hazard model for moving home – separating those preferring to move and those preferring to stay at wave 1

	Movers	*Stayers*
Intercept	–4.5904	–5.3931
Log time (months)	–0.2789***	–0.3617***
–2 Log likelihood	636.355	685.845
Age 16–19	0.4897***	0.8398***
Age 20–24	0.3682*	0.6309***
Age 25–29	–0.0093	0.4945**
Age 30–34	–0.1808	0.2005
Age 35–39	–0.0090	–0.0818
Age 40–44	–0.2365	0.0833
Female	0.0114	–0.1376
Public sector rented	0.4863***	0.3204*
Private rented	1.1141***	1.3100***
Income decile	0.0762***	0.0862***
Cohabiting	0.2683**	0.7050**
Single	0.2672*	0.6442***
Divorced or separated	0.3204	0.8934***
Widowed	–0.1344	–0.0973
Persons per room	0.5415***	0.5399***
Number of children	–0.0223	0.0860
Service class	–0.1730	–0.2534
Intermediate class	–0.2251	–0.4006*
Working class	–0.3809**	–0.2647
Own account worker	–0.1104	–0.0100
Unemployed	0.0592	0.1529
Student	0.0491	0.1832
Degree	0.3479*	0.0117
Middle level qualifications	0.2652*	0.1752
Lower qualifications	0.1606	0.0894
N events	947	557

Note
*$P < 0.05$; **$P < 0.01$; ***$P < 0.001$.

this further by exploring how preferences respond to changes in circumstances and how quickly a change in preferences converts into a move. This would probably require rather more waves of panel data.

Considering now those who expressed a preference to move, then some of the same considerations apply – a change in circumstances could lead to a switch in preferences, so that we cannot entirely exclude the possibility that non-movement reflects changed preferences. However, it is more reasonable to interpret the coefficients as indicating how readily a preference may be realised for different subgroups, and thus as giving some indication of how far opportunities for mobility are unequally distributed. We have no direct information here on whether preference was for local or inter-regional movement. Thus, we cannot yet use these data to explore the nature of constraints on long-distance migration, which as we saw above raised particular issues in relation to council tenants. Indeed, we see in Table 13.9 that mobility among this group is substantially above that for owners, even when we control for the higher level of initial preference. Similarly, higher housing density is more likely to be associated with mobility, even after controlling for preferences. The association with unemployment is non-significant after controlling for preferences. However, we do also find a substantial structuring of the mobility opportunities in terms of income, class and education. Those with higher qualifications and those with higher income are more likely to be able to realise mobility preferences, and those with a working-class job are substantially less likely to realise such a preference.

Conclusion

This chapter has presented new evidence on the processes of migration in Great Britain in the 1990s and of a kind which can only readily be derived from panel data. In doing so, it has introduced some of the ways in which panel data can be used in this study. It has argued that panel data are critical to developing our understanding of migration, across a range of areas. These include the motivations for migration, how it relates to other life events, including family formation and job change. Inevitably, this chapter only introduces the potential range of work in this area, and many further possible developments remain. These include the incorporation of information about other household members, the inclusion of more detailed information about *changes* in family and work circumstances into models of migration, the exploration of regional effects and the incorporation of information about changes in preferences over time. These research possibilities open out still further as the number of waves of panel data increase.

Notes

1 In this chapter, the term migration refers to any move in place of usual residence, regardless of distance. The term is qualified to distinguish short- from long-distance movements.
2 For these purposes, there was some grouping of smaller local authority districts to meet a population threshold of 120,000. For this reason, rather more moves are counted as local than in the Census, which finds 61.8% of

moves are within local authority areas.

3 Parallel analyses to those in the present and following section were undertaken restricted to 'heads of household' and these produced essentially similar results.

4 The class classification is based on the Erikson, Goldthorpe and Portocarrero schema (see Erikson and Goldthorpe, 1992). 'Service class' includes both lower and higher service classes. Intermediate includes routine non-manual workers, foremen technicians and skilled manual workers. Working class includes personal service workers, semi- and unskilled manual workers and agricultural workers. Own account workers outside the service class are separately identified.

5 Middle level qualifications include A levels and non-degree further education qualifications. Lower level qualifications include O levels, GCSEs and equivalents.

6 A squared term for duration was also included to capture non-linearities, but this was non-significant. Gordon and Molho (1995) would lead us to expect a non-linear relationship, and it may be that further work using different functional forms would uncover such a relationship. Other models were fitted to explore interactions between age and duration, but these revealed only slight differences in the youngest and oldest age ranges.

7 In Table 13.7, the Greater London area is treated as separate from the rest of the south-east region. This is for comparability with earlier results, especially Hughes and McCormick (1981). The two areas were combined in Tables 13.3 and 13.5.

Bibliography

Abelson, R.P., Loftus, E.F. and Greenwald, A. (1992) 'Attempts to improve the accuracy of self-reports of voting' in J. Tanur (ed.) *Questions About Questions: Inquiries into the Cognitive Bases of Surveys*, pp. 138–52. New York: Russell Sage.

Abercrombie, N. and Warde, A. (eds) (1992) *Social Change in Contemporary Britain*. Cambridge: Polity.

Abowd, J.M. and Zellner, A. (1985) 'Estimating gross labour force flows', *Journal of Business and Economic Statistics* 3, 254–83.

Adams K. and Duncan, G.J. (1990) *Closing the Gap: Metro–Nonmetro Differences in Long Term Poverty Among Blacks*. Ann Arbor: Institute for Survey Research, University of Michigan.

Alessie, R.E., Van Elderen, E.M. and Kapteyn, A. (1990) *Inkomens van Ouderen 1984–87*. Tilburg: The Netherlands Economic Institute, Tilburg University.

Allison, P.D. (1982) 'Discrete time methods for the analysis of event histories' in S. Leinhardt (ed.) *Sociological Methodology*, pp. 61–97. San Francisco: Jossey-Bass.

——(1984) *Event History Analysis: Regression for Longitudinal Event Data*. Beverly Hills: Sage.

—— (1994) 'Using panel data to estimate the effects of events', *Sociological Methods and Research* 23, 2, 174–99.

Altonji, J.G. (1986) 'Intertemporal substitution in labor supply: evidence from micro data', *Journal of Political Economy* 94, 3, 176–215.

——(1994) 'The use of the panel study of income dynamics for research on intergenerational transfers'. Paper prepared for PSID Board of Overseers Meeting. Ann Arbor: Institute for Survey Research, University of Michigan.

Anderson, M., Bechhofer, F and Gershuny J. (eds) (1994) *The Social and Political Economy of the Household*. Oxford: Oxford University Press.

Ashworth K. and Walker, R. (1991) *Reflections on the Role of Time in the Definition and Measurement of Poverty*. Loughborough: Loughborough University of Technology, Centre for Research in Social Policy. Working paper 154.

Ashworth K., Hill, M. and Walker, R. (1991) *The Severity and Duration of Childhood Poverty in the USA*. Loughborough: Loughborough University of Technology, Centre for Research in Social Policy. Working paper 144.

——(1992a) *Patterns of Childhood Poverty: New Challenges for Policy*. Loughborough: Loughborough University of Technology, Centre for Research in Social Policy. Working paper 169.

——(1992b) *Economic Disadvantage During Childhood*. Loughborough: Loughborough University of Technology, Centre for Research in Social Policy. Working paper 170.

Atkinson, A. (1984) *The Economics of Inequality*. Oxford: Oxford University Press.

Atwood, C.L. and Taube, A. (1976) 'Estimating mean time to reach a milestone, using retrospective data', *Biometrics* 32, 159–72.

Badham, R. (1984) 'The sociology of industrial and post-industrial societies', *Current Sociology* 32, 1–141.

Bailar, B. (1975) 'The effects of rotation group bias on estimates from panel surveys', *Journal of the American Statistical Association* 70, 23–30.

——(1984) 'The quality of survey data', *Proceedings of the Survey Research Section: American Statistical Association* pp. 45–53.

——(1989) 'Information needs, surveys, and measurement errors' in D. Kasprzyk, G.J. Duncan, G. Kalton and M.P. Singh (eds) *Panel Surveys*, pp. 1–24. New York: John Wiley.

Bailar, B., Bailey, L. and Corbey, C. (1978) 'Comparison of some adjustment and weighting procedures for survey data' in N. Krishnan Namboodiri (ed.) *Survey Sampling and Measurement*, pp. 175–98. New York: Academic Press.

Ball, J. and Marland, M. (1996) *Male Earnings Mobility in the Lifetime Labour Market Database*. London: Department of Social Security, Analytical Services Division. Working paper 1.

Ball, M., Gray, F. and McDowell, L. (1989) *The Transformation of Britain: Contemporary Social and Economic Change*. London: Fontana Press.

Baltes, P.B. (1968) 'Longitudinal and cross sectional sequences in the study of age and generation effects', *Human Development* 11, 145–71.

Bane, M.J. and Ellwood, D.T. (1983) *The Dynamics of Dependence: Routes to Self-sufficiency*. Report prepared for Office of Income Security Policy. Washington: US Department of Health and Human Services.

——(1986) 'Slipping in and out of poverty: the dynamics of spells', *Journal of Human Resources* 21, 1–23.

——(1989) 'One fifth of the nation's children: why are they poor?', *Nature* 245, 1047–53.

Barnes, R. (1980) 'Non-response on household surveys' in *Survey Methodology Bulletin*, vol. 11, pp. 34–41. London: Social Survey Division, Office of Population Censuses and Surveys.

——(1987) 'The use of lotteries and other forms of financial incentive in SSD' in *Survey Methodology Bulletin*, vol. 20, pp. 39–42. London: Social Survey Division, Office of Population Censuses and Surveys.

——(1991) 'Non-response on government household surveys' in *Survey Methodology Bulletin*, vol. 28, pp. 34–44. London: Social Survey Division, Office of Population Censuses and Surveys.

Barreiros, L. (1995) 'The European community household panel: its design, scientific and policy purposes', *Innovation: The European Journal of Social Sciences* 8, 41–52.

Bartholomew, D.J. (1987) *Latent Variable Models And Factor Analysis*. London: Edward Arnold.

Becker, G., Landes, E. and Michael, R. (1977) 'An economic analysis of marital instability', *Journal of Political Economy* 85, 1141–87.

Becketti, S., Gould, W., Lillard, L., and Welch, F. (1988) 'The PSID after 14 years: an evaluation', *Journal of Labor Economics* 6, 472–92.

Beedham, H. (1999) 'The Royal Statistical Society Working Group on Archiving Data Standards for Documenting Data for Preservation and Secondary Analysis' in R. Banks, C. Christie, J. Currall, J. Francis, P. Harris, B. Lee, J. Martin, C. Payne and A. Westlake (eds) *Leading Survey and Statistical Computing into the New Millennium: Proceedings of the Third ASC International Conference*, pp. 483–91. Chesham: Association for Survey Computing.

Bell, D. (1960) *The End of Ideology*. Glencoe, NY: Free Press.

Berghman, J., Muffels, R, de Vries, A. and Vriens, M. (1988) *Armoede, Bestaansonzekerheid en Relatieve Deprivatie*. Tilburg: Department of Social Security Studies, Tilburg University.

Berghman, J., Dirven, H., ter Huurne, A. and Muffels, R. (1990) *Report on the Dutch Feasibility Study on a European Community Household Panel (ECHP)*. Tilburg: Department of Social Security Studies, Tilburg University.

Beynon, H. (1992) 'The end of the industrial worker?' in N. Abercrombie and A. Warde (eds) *Social Change in Contemporary Britain*, pp. 167–83. Cambridge: Polity.

Binder, D.A. and Hidiroglou, M.A. (1988). 'Sampling in time' in P.R. Krishnaiah and C.R. Rao (eds) *Handbook of Statistics*, pp. 187–211. New York: North Holland.

Bird, E.J., Schwarze, J., Wagner, G. (1992) *The Changing Value of Human Capital in Eastern Europe: Lessons from the GDR*. Berlin: DIW. Discussion paper 55.

Blank, R.M. (1989) 'Analysing the length of welfare spells', *Journal of Public Economics* 39, 245–73.

Blossfeld, H.P., Hamerle, A. and Mayer, K.-U. (1989) *Event History Analysis*. Hillsdale, NJ: Lawrence Erlbaum Associates.

Blossfeld, H.P., Gianelli, G. and Mayer, K.-U. (1991) *Expansion of the Tertiary Sector and Social Inequality: is there a New Service Proletariat Emerging in the FRG?* Florence: EUI. Working paper SPS 91/8.

Bogestrom, B., Larsson, M. and Lyberg, L. (1983) 'Bibliography on nonresponse and related topics' in Panel on Incomplete Data (eds) *Incomplete Data in Sample Surveys*. Vol. 2. *Theory and Bibliographies*. New York: Academic Press.

Boruch, R.F. and Pearson, R.W. (1985) *The Comparative Evaluation of Longitudinal Surveys*. New York: Social Science Research Council.

—— (1988) 'Assessing the quality of longitudinal surveys', *Evaluation Review* 12, 3–58.

Bound, J. and Krueger, A.B. (1991) 'The extent of measurement error in longitudinal earnings data: do two wrongs make a right?', *Journal of Labor Economics* 9, 1–24.

Bound, J., Brown, C., Duncan, G.J. and Rodgers, W.L. (1990) 'Measurement error in cross-sectional and longitudinal labor market surveys: validation study experience' in J. Hartog, G. Ridder and J. Theeuwes (eds) *Panel Data and Labor Market Studies*, pp. 1–19. Amsterdam: North Holland.

Bowers, N. and Horvath, F.W. (1984) 'Keeping time: an analysis of errors in the measurement of unemployment duration', *Journal of Business and Economic Statistics* 2, 140–9.

Bradburn, N.M., Rips, L.J. and Shevell, S.K. (1987) 'Answering autobiographical questions', *Science* 236, 157–61.

Braverman, H. (1974) *Labor and Monopoly Capital*. New York: Monthly Review Press.

Breiman, L., Friedman, J.H., Olsen, R.A. and Stone C.J. (1993) *Classification and Regression Trees*. New York: Chapman and Hall.

Buck, N. (1994). 'Housing and residential mobility' in N. Buck, J. Gershuny, D. Rose and J. Scott (eds) *Changing Households: the British Household Panel Survey 1990–1992*, pp. 130–53. Colchester: ESRC Research Centre on Micro-social Change, University of Essex.

Buck, N. and Scott, J. (1993) 'She's leaving home: but why? An event history analysis of the leaving home process', *Journal of Marriage and the Family* 55, 863–74.

Buck, N., Gershuny, J., Rose, D. and Scott, J. (eds) (1994). *Changing Households: the British Household Panel Survey 1990–1992*. Colchester: ESRC Research Centre on Micro-social Change, University of Essex.

Buck, N., Ermisch, J. and Jenkins, S.P. (1996) *Choosing a Longitudinal Survey Design: the Issues*. Colchester: ESRC Research Centre on Micro-social Change, University of Essex. Occasional paper 96-1.

Bumpass, L.L. and Sweet, J.A. (1989) 'National estimates of cohabitation', *Demography* 26, 615–25.

Burgess, R.D. (1989). 'Major issues and implications of tracing survey respondents' in D. Kasprzyk, G.J. Duncan, G. Kalton and M.P. Singh (eds) *Panel Surveys*, pp. 52–74. New York: John Wiley.

Burkhauser, R. and Duncan, G.J. (no date) *Life Events, Public Policy and the Economic Vulnerability of Children and the Elderly*. Ann Arbor: Institute for Survey Research, University of Michigan.

Burkhauser, R., Duncan, G.J., Hauser, R. and Berntsen, R. (1991) 'Wife or frau, women do worse: a comparison of men and women in the United States and Germany after marital dissolution', *Demography* 28, 353–60.

Burstein, N.R. and Visher, M.G. (1989) *The Dynamics of Food Stamp Participation*. Report for the US Department of Agriculture, Food and Nutrition Service. Cambridge, MA: Abt Associates.

Call, V., Otto, L.B. and Spencer, K. (1982) *Tracking Respondents*. Lexington, MA: Heath.

Cantwell, P.J. and Ernst L.R. (1993). 'New developments in composite estimation for the current population survey' in *Proceedings: Symposium 92, Design and Analysis of Longitudinal Surveys*, pp. 121–30. Ottawa: Statistics Canada.

Capaldi, D. and Patterson, G. (1987) 'An approach to the problem of recruitment and retention rates for longitudinal research', *Behavioral Assessment* 9, 169–77.

Chamberlain, G. (1980) 'Analysis of covariance with qualitative data', *Review of Economic Studies* 47, 225–38.

——(1984) 'Panel data' in Z. Griliches and M.D. Intriligator (eds) *Handbook of Econometrics*, II, pp. 1247–318. Amsterdam: North Holland.

Champion, A (1992) 'Migration in Britain: research challenges and prospects' in A. Champion and A. Fielding (eds) *Migration Processes and Patterns*. Vol. 1. *Research Progress and Prospects*, pp. 215–26. London: Belhaven.

Chapman, D.W., Bailey, L. and Kasprzyk, D. (1986) 'Nonresponse adjustment procedures at the US Bureau of the Census', *Survey Methodology* 12, 161–80.

Chua, T.C. and Fuller, W.A. (1987) 'A model for multinomial response error applied to labour flows', *Journal of the American Statistical Association* 82, 46–51.

Citro, C.F. and Kalton, G. (1989) *Surveying the Nation's Scientists and Engineers*. Washington, DC: National Academy Press.

——(1993) *The Future of the Survey of Income and Program Participation*. Washington, DC: National Academy Press.

Clarke, L., Phibbs, M., Klepacz, A. and Grffiths, D. (1987) 'General household survey advance letter experiment' in *Survey Methodology Bulletin*, vol. 21, pp. 39–42. London: Social Survey Division, Office of Population Censuses and Surveys.

Clarridge, B.R., Sheehy, L.L. and Hauser, T.S. (1978) 'Tracing members of a panel: a 17 year follow up' in K.F. Schuessler (ed.) *Sociological Methodology*, pp. 389–437. San Francisco: Jossey-Bass.

Coe, R.D. (1976) 'Dependency and poverty in the short and long run' in G.J. Duncan and J.N. Morgan (eds) *Five Thousand American Families*, vol. 6, pp. 273–96. Ann Arbor: Institute for Social Research, University of Michigan.

Coleman, D. and Salt, J. (1992) *The British Population: Patterns, Trends and Processes*. Oxford: Oxford University Press.

Coleman, J.S. (1981) *Longitudinal Data Analysis*. New York: Basic Books.

——(1990) *Foundations of Social Theory*. Cambridge, MA: Belknap Harvard.

Corcoran, M., Gordon, R, Laren, D. and Solon, G. (1990) 'Effects of family and community background on economic status', *American Economic Review* 80, 362–6.

Corder, L.S. and Horvitz, D.G. (1989) 'Panel effects in the national medical care utilisation and expenditure survey' in D. Kasprzyk, G.J. Duncan, G. Kalton and M.P. Singh (eds) *Panel Surveys*, pp. 304–18. New York: John Wiley.

Courgeau, D. (1992) 'Impact of response errors on event history analysis', *Population: an English Selection* 4, 97–110.

Cox, D.R. and Oakes, D. (1984) *Analysis of Survival Data*. London: Chapman and Hall.

Crider, D.M., Willits, F.K., and Bealer, R.C (1971) 'Tracking respondents in longitudinal surveys', *Public Opinion Quarterly* 35, 613–20.

——(1973) 'Panel studies: some practical problems', *Sociological Methods and Research* 2, 3–19.

Crouchley, R. (ed.) (1987) *Longitudinal Data Analysis*. Aldershot: Avebury.

Currall, J. (1999) 'Everything you always wanted to know about xml, but...' in

R. Banks, C. Christie, J. Currall, J Francis, P. Harris, B. Lee, J. Martin, C. Payne and A. Westlake (eds) *Leading Survey and Statistical Computing into the New Millennium: Proceedings of the Third ASC International Conference*, pp. 459–470. Chesham: Association for Survey Computing.

Dahrendorf, R. (1987) 'The erosion of citizenship', *New Statesman* 12 June, 12–15.

Dale, A. and Davies, R. (1994) *Analyzing Social and Political Change*. London: Sage.

Danziger, S. and Stern, J. (1990) *The Causes and Consequences of Child Poverty in the United States*. Report prepared for the UNICEF Child Development Center. Ann Arbor: University of Michigan.

David, M. (1989) 'Managing panel data for scientific analysis: the role of relational data base management systems' in D. Kasprzyk, G.J. Duncan, G. Kalton and M.P. Singh (eds) *Panel Surveys*, pp. 226–41. New York: John Wiley.

——(1991) 'The science of data sharing: documentation' in J.E. Sieber (ed.) *Sharing Social Science Data: Advantages and Challenges*, pp. 91–115. London: Sage.

Deaton, A. (1985) 'Panel data from time series of cross-sections', *Journal of Econometrics* 30, 109–26.

Deecker, G., Murray, T.S. and Ellison, J. (1993) 'On providing client support for machine readable data files' in *Statistical Meta Information Systems: Proceedings of the Conference*, pp. 91–102. Luxembourg: Statistical Office of the European Communities.

Deleeck, H., Van Den Bosch, K. and de Lathouwer L. (eds) (1993) *Indicators of poverty and the Adequacy of Social Security in the EC*. Aldershot: Avebury.

Department of Social Security (1995) *Households Below Average Income 1975–94*. London: HMSO.

——(1996) *Households Below Average Income 1979–1993/4*. London: The Stationery Office.

Deville, J.-C. and Särndal, C.-E. (1992) 'Calibration estimators in survey sampling', *Journal of the American Statistical Association* 87, 376–82.

Dex, S. (1985) *The Sexual Division of Work*. Brighton: Wheatsheaf.

Diamond, I. and McDonald, J.W (1992) 'Analysis of current status data' in J. Trussell, R. Hankinson and J. Tilton (eds) *Demographic Applications of Event History Analysis*, pp. 231–52. Oxford: Clarendon Press.

Dickens, R. (1996) *Evolution of Individual Male Earnings in Great Britain: 1975–94*. London: London School of Economics, Centre for Economic Performance. Discussion paper 306.

Dirven, H. and Berghman J. (1991) *Poverty, Insecurity of Subsistence and Relative Deprivation in The Netherlands*. Tilburg: IVA/Department of Social Security Studies, Institute for Social Research, Tilburg University.

——(1992) 'The evolution of income poverty in The Netherlands: results from the Dutch socio-economic panel survey.' Paper presented at the International Sociological Association Third Social Science Methodology Conference, Trento, Italy.

Documentation Standards Working Group (1996) *Draft Guidelines for the Documentation of Research Data*. Colchester: ISER, University of Essex.

Douglas, J.W.B. (1975) 'Early hospital admissions and later disturbances of behaviour and learning', *Developmental Medicine and Child Neurology* 17, 456–80.

Drewett, J.R., Taylor, M. and Tanenbaum E. (1989) 'Creating a standardised and integrated knowledge-based expert system for the documentation of statistical series', *Eurostat News* (special edition).

Duncan, G.J. (1984) *Years of Fortunes of American Workers and Families*. Ann Arbor: Institute for Social Research, University of Michigan.

——(1988) 'The volatility of family income over the life course' in P. Baltes, D.L. Featherman and R.M. Lerner (eds) *Life-span Development and Behaviour*, pp. 317–57. Hillsdale, NJ: Lawrence Erlbaum Associates.

——(1989) *Panel Studies of Poverty: Prospects and Problems*. Ann Arbor: Institute for Social Research, University of Michigan.

——(1992) 'Household panel studies: prospects and problems'. In *Proceedings of the International Sociological Association Third International Conference on Social Science Methodology, Trento, Italy*. Ann Arbor: Institute for Survey Research, University of Michigan.

Duncan, G.J. and Hill, M.S. (1985) 'Conceptions of longitudinal households: fertile or futile?', *Journal of Economic and Social Measurement* 13, 361–75.

Duncan, G.J. and Holmlund, B. (1983). 'Was Adam Smith right, after all? Another test of the theory of compensating wage differentials', *Journal of Labor Economics* 1, 366–79.

Duncan, G.J. and Kalton, G. (1987) 'Issues of design and analysis of surveys across time', *International Statistical Review* 55, 97–117.

Duncan, G.J. and Mathiowetz, N.A. (1985) 'A validation study of economic survey data'. Mimeograph. Ann Arbor: Survey Research Center, Institute for Social Research.

Duncan, G.J. and Rodgers, W.L. (1988) 'Longitudinal aspects of childhood poverty', *Journal of Marriage and the Family* 50, 1007–21.

Duncan, G.J., Coe, R.D. and Hill, M.S. (1984) 'The dynamics of poverty' in G.J. Duncan (ed.) *Years of Poverty, Years of Plenty*, pp. 33–70. Ann Arbor: Institute for Social Research, University of Michigan.

Duncan, G.J., Juster, F.T. and Morgan J.N. (1984) 'The role of panel studies in a world of scarce research resources' in S. Sudman and M.A. Spaeth (eds) *The Collection and Analysis of Economic and Consumer Behavior Data*, pp. 301–28. Champaign, IL: Bureau of Economic and Business Research.

Duncan, G.J., Gustafsson, B., Hauser, R., Schmaus, G., Jenkins, S.P., Messinger, H., Muffels, R., Nolan, B., Ray, J.-C. and Voges, W. (1991) *Poverty and Social Assistance Dynamics in the United States, Canada and Europe*. Ann Arbor: Institute for Social Research, University of Michigan.

Duncan, G.J., Gustafsson, B., Hauser, R., Schmaus, G., Laren, D., Messinger, H., Muffels, R., Nolan, B. and Ray J.-C. (1993a) 'Poverty dynamics in eight countries', *Journal of Population Economics* 6, 3, 215–34.

Duncan, G.J., Smeeding, T. and Rodgers, W.L. (1993b) 'W(h)ither the middle class' in D. Papadimitriou and E. Wolfe (eds) *Poverty and Prosperity in the USA in the Late Twentieth Century*, pp. 240–71. London: Macmillan.

Eckland, B.K. (1968) 'Retrieving mobile cases in longitudinal surveys', *Public Opinion Quarterly* 32, 51–64.

Edwards, W.S., Sperry, S. and Edwards, B. (1993) 'Using CAPI in a longitudinal survey: a report from the medicare current beneficiary survey' in *Proceedings: Symposium 92, Design and Analysis of Longitudinal Surveys*, pp. 21–30. Ottawa: Statistics Canada.

Elder, G.H. (ed.) (1985a) *Life Course Dynamics: Trajectories and Transitions 1968–1980*. Ithaca: Cornell University Press.

——(1985b) 'Preface' in G.H. Elder (ed.) *Life Course Dynamics: Trajectories and Transitions 1968–80*, pp. 15–20. Ithaca: Cornell University Press.

——(1985c) 'Perspectives on the life course' in G.H. Elder (ed.) *Life Course Dynamics: Trajectories and Transitions 1968–80*, pp. 23–49. Ithaca: Cornell University Press.

Elliot, D. (1991) *Weighting for Nonresponse: a Survey Researcher's Guide*. London: Office of Population Censuses and Surveys.

Ellwood, D.T. (1986) *Targeting 'Would-be' Long Term Recipients of AFDC*. Princeton: Mathematica Policy Research.

——(1987) *Poverty Through the Eyes of Children*. Cambridge, MA: Harvard University, John F. Kennedy School of Government.

——(1988) *Poor Support*. New York: Basic Books.

Ellwood, D.T. and Kane, J. (1989) *The American Way of Ageing: an Event History Analysis*. Cambridge, MA: Harvard University, John F. Kennedy School of Government.

Elster, J. (1983) *Sour Grapes*. Cambridge: Cambridge University Press.

Erikson, R. and Goldthorpe, J.H. (1992) *The Constant Flux*. Oxford: Clarendon Press.

Ermisch, J. (1991) *Lone Parenthood: an Economic Analysis*. Cambridge: Cambridge University Press.

——(1995a) *Pre-marital Cohabitation, Childbearing and the Creation of One Parent Families*. Colchester: ESRC Research Centre on Micro-social Change, University of Essex. Working paper 95-17.

——(1995b) *Household Formation and Housing Tenure Decisions of Young People*. Colchester: ESRC Research Centre on Micro-social Change, University of Essex. Occasional paper 95-1.

——(1996) *Analysis of Leaving the Parental Home and Returning to it Using Panel Data*. Colchester: ESRC Research Centre on Micro-social Change, University of Essex. Working paper 96-1.

Ermisch, J. and Di Salvo, P. (1995) *An Economic Analysis of the Leaving Home Decision: Theory and a Dynamic Econometric Model*. Colchester: ESRC Research Centre on Micro-social Change University of Essex. Working paper 95-11.

——(1996) 'Surprises and housing tenure decisions', *Journal of Housing Economics* 5, 247–73.

Ernst, L.R. (1989) 'Weighting issues for longitudinal household and family estimates' in D. Kasprzyk, G.J. Duncan, G. Kalton and M.P. Singh (eds) *Panel Surveys*, pp. 139–59. New York: John Wiley.

European Commission (1994) *Statistical Information Systems in a Market Economy*. Luxembourg: Office for Official Publications of the European Communities.

Farber, H.S. (1994) 'The role of the panel study of income dynamics in the analysis of labor market dynamics'. Paper prepared for PSID Board of Overseers Meeting. Ann Arbor: Institute for Survey Research, University of Michigan.

Farrington, D., Gallagher, B., Morley, L., St. Ledger, R. and West, D. (1990) 'Minimising attrition in longitudinal research: methods of tracing and securing cooperation in a 24-year follow-up study' in D. Magnusson and L. Bergman (eds) *Data Quality in Longitudinal Research*. Cambridge: Cambridge University Press.

Ferber, R. (1964) 'Does a panel operation increase the reliability of survey data: the case of consumer savings' *Proceedings of the Section on Social Statistics: Journal of the American Statistical Association*, pp. 210–16.

Finch, C. (1981) 'General Household Survey letter experiments', *Survey Methodology Bulletin* 13, 30–37.

Ford, B. (1983) 'An overview of hot-deck procedures' in Panel on Incomplete Data (eds) *Incomplete Data in Sample Surveys*. Vol. 2. *Theory and Bibliographies*. New York: Academic Press.

Freedman, D., Thornton, A. and Camburn, D. (1980) 'Maintaining response rates in longitudinal studies', *Sociological Methods and Research* 9, 87–9.

Freeman, R. (1984) 'Longitudinal analysis of the effects of trade unions', *Journal of Labor Economics* 2, 1–26.

Fuller, W.A. (1987) *Measurement Error Models*. New York: John Wiley.

——(1989) 'Estimation of cross-sectional and change parameters' in D. Kasprzyk, G.J. Duncan, G. Kalton and M.P. Singh (eds) *Panel Surveys*, pp. 480–5. New York: John Wiley.

——(1990) 'Analysis of repeated surveys', *Survey Methodology* 16, 167–80.

Fuller, W.A., Adam, A. and Yansaneh, I.S. (1993) 'Estimators for longitudinal surveys with application to the US current population survey' in *Proceedings: Symposium 92, Design and Analysis of Longitudinal Surveys*, pp. 309–24. Ottawa: Statistics Canada.

Fuller, W.A., McLoughlin, M.M. and Baker, H.D. (1994) 'Regression weighting in the presence of nonresponse with application to the 1987–88 nationwide food consumption survey', *Survey Methodology* 20, 75–85.

Galler, H.P. and Poetter, H.-U. (1987) 'Unobserved heterogeneity in models of unemployment duration', *Materialen aus der Bildungsforschung des MPI*, 628–50.

Gallie, D. (ed.) (1989) *Employment in Britain*. Oxford: Blackwell.

Gerlach, K. and Schasse, U. (1990) 'On the job training differences by sex and firm size', *Zeitschrift fuer Wirtschafts- und Sozialwissenschaften*, 110, 2, 261–72.

Gershuny, J. and Buck, N. (2001) *Understanding Panel Data*. London: Sage.

Gershuny, J., Rose, D., Scott, J. and Buck, N. (eds) (1994) 'Introducing household panels' in N. Buck, J. Gershuny, D. Rose and J. Scott (eds) *Changing Households: the British Household Panel Survey 1990–1992*, pp. 10–26. Colchester: ESRC Research Centre on Micro-social Change, University of Essex.

Ghangurde, P.D. (1982) 'Rotation group bias in the LFS estimates', *Survey Methodology* 8, 86–101.

Goedhart, T., Halberstadt, V., Kapteyn, A. and Van Praag, B.M.S. (1977) 'The poverty line: concept and measurement', *Journal of Human Resources* 12, 503–20.

Goldstein, H. (1979) *The Design and Analysis of Longitudinal Studies*. London: Academic Press.

Goldthorpe, J.H. (1964) 'Social stratification in industrial society' in P. Halmos (ed.) *The Development of Industrial Society. The Sociological Review Monograph 8*, pp. 97–122.

——(1988) 'Intellectuals and the working class in modern Britain' in D. Rose (ed.) *Social Stratification and Economic Change*, pp. 39–56. London: Hutchinson.

Gordon, I. R. and Molho, I. (1995) 'Duration dependence in migration behaviour: cumulative inertia versus stochastic change' *Environment and Planning A* 27, 1961–75.

Gottschalk, P. and Ruggles, P. (1994) 'Using the panel study of income dynamics to study poverty and welfare dynamics'. Paper prepared for PSID Board of Overseers Meeting. Ann Arbor: Institute for Survey Research, University of Michigan.

Green, F. (ed.) (1989) *The Restructuring of the UK Economy*. London: Harvester Wheatsheaf.

Griliches, Z. and Hausman, J.A. (1986) 'Errors in variables in panel data' *Journal of Econometrics* 31, 93–118.

Groves, R.M. (1991) *Survey Errors and Survey Costs*. New York: Wiley.

Guy, L.A. (1993) 'The need for revised data documentation standards: new solutions for old problems', *IASSIST Quarterly* 17, 3/4, 42–8.

——(1999) 'Planet SOSIG: asking questions – the CASS survey question bank', *Ariadne* 22. URL: http://www.ariadne.ac.uk/issue22/planet-sosig/intro.html.

Hagenaars, J.A. (1990) *Categorical Longitudinal Data: Log Linear, Panel, Trend and Cohort Analysis*. Newbury Park, CA: Sage.

Hakim, C. (1995) 'Five feminist myths about women's employment', *British Journal of Sociology* 46, 429–55.

Halsey, A.H. (ed.) (1988) *British Social Trends Since 1900*. London: Macmillan.

Hamerle, A. and Ronning, G. (1995) 'Panel analysis for qualitative variables' in G. Arminger, C.C. Clogg and M.E. Sobel (eds) *Handbook of Statistical Modeling for the Social and Behavioral Sciences*, pp. 401–51. New York: Plenum Press.

Hamnett, C., McDowell, L. and Sarre, P. (eds) (1989) *The Changing Social Structure*. London: Sage.

Hand, D.J. (1993) 'Data, metadata and information' in *Statistical Meta Information Systems: Proceedings of the Conference*. Luxembourg: Statistical Office of the European Communities.

Haskey, J. (1995) 'Trends in marriage and cohabitation: the decline in marriage and the changing pattern of living in partnerships', *Population Trends* 80, 5–15.

Hausman, J.A. and Wise, D.A. (1977) 'Social experimentation, truncated distributions and efficient estimation', *Econometrica* 45, 319–39.

——(1979) 'Attrition bias in experimental and panel data: the Gary Income Maintenance Experiment', *Econometrica* 47, 455–73.

Heckman, J.J. and MaCurdy, T. (1980) 'A life cycle model of female labor supply', *Review of Economic Studies* 47, 47–74.

Heckman, J.J. and Robb, R. (1985) 'Alternative methods for evaluating the impact of interventions: an overview', *Journal of Econometrics* 30, 239–67.

Heckman, J.J. and Singer, B. (1982) 'The identification problem in econometric models for duration data' in W. Hilderbrand (ed.) *Advances in Econometrics: Proceedings of the World Meeting of the Econometric Society.* Cambridge: Cambridge University Press.

——(1984) 'Economic duration analysis', *Journal of Econometrics* 24, 63–132.

——(1985) *Longitudinal Analysis of Labour Market Data.* Cambridge: Cambridge University Press.

Herzog, T. and Rubin, D. (1983) 'Using multiple imputations to handle nonresponse in sample surveys' in Panel on Incomplete Data (eds) *Incomplete Data in Sample Surveys.* Vol. 2. *Theory and Bibliographies.* New York: Academic Press.

Hill, D. (1987) 'Response errors around the seam: analysis of change in a panel with overlapping reference periods' in *Proceedings of the Section on Survey Research Methods: Journal of the American Statistical Association*, pp. 210–15.

Hill, M. (1983) 'Trends in the economic situation of US families and children: 1970–80' in R. Nelson and F. Skidmore (eds) *American Families and the Economy: the High costs of Living*, pp. 9–58. Washington, DC: National Academy Press.

——(1985) 'The changing nature of poverty', *The Annals of the American Academy of Political and Social Science* 479, 31–47.

——(1992) *The Panel Study of Income Dynamics: a User's Guide.* Newbury Park, CA: Sage.

Hill, M. and Jenkins, S. (1999) *Poverty Among British Children: Chronic or Transitory?* Colchester: Institute for Social and Economic Research. Working paper 99-23.

Hill, M., Servais, M. and Solenberger, P. (1992) *Tangled Webs of Family Relationships: Untangling Them with Survey Data.* Ann Arbor: University of Michigan. Discussion paper.

Hinkins, S., Jones, H. and Scheuren, F. (1988) 'Design modifications for the SOI corporate sample: balancing multiple objectives' in *Proceedings of the Section on Survey Research Methods: Journal of the American Statistical Association*, pp. 216–21.

Hobcraft, J., Menken, J. and Preston, S. (1982) 'Age, period and cohort analysis in demography: a review', *Population Index* 41, 4–43.

Hofferth, S. (1985) 'Updating children's life course', *Journal of Marriage and the Family* 47, 93–113.

Hoffman, S.D. and Duncan, G.J. (1995) 'The effects of incomes, wages and AFDC benefits on marital disruption', *The Journal of Human Resources* 30, 19–41.

Holt, D. (1989) 'Panel conditioning: discussion' in D. Kasprzyk, G.J. Duncan, G. Kalton and M.P. Singh (eds) *Panel Surveys*. New York: Wiley.

Holt, D., McDonald, J.W. and Skinner, C.J. (1991) 'The effect of measurement error on event history analysis' in P.P. Biemer, R.M. Groves, L.E. Lyberg, N.A. Mathiowetz and S. Sudman (eds) *Measurement Errors in Surveys*, pp. 665–85. New York: John Wiley.

Horrigan, M.W. (1987) 'Time spent unemployed: a new look at data from the CPS', *Monthly Labour Review* 110, 7, 3–15.

Horvath, F.W. (1982) 'Forgotten unemployment: recall bias in retrospective data', *Monthly Labour Review* 105, 3, 40–3.

Hsiao, C. (1985) 'Benefits and limitations of panel data', *Econometric Reviews* 4, 121–74.

——(1986) *Analysis of Panel Data*. Cambridge: Cambridge University Press.

——(1995) 'Panel analysis for metric data' in G. Arminger, C.C. Clogg and M.E. Sobel (eds) *Handbook of Statistical Modeling for the Social and Behavioral Sciences*, pp. 361–400. New York: Plenum Press.

Hsiao, C. and Huang, H. (1984) 'Obtaining cross-sectional estimates from a longitudinal survey: experiences of the income survey development program' in *Proceedings of the Section on Survey Research Methods: Journal of the American Statistical Association*, pp. 670–75.

Huang, H. (1984) 'Obtaining cross-sectional estimates from a longitudinal survey: experiences of the Income Survey Development Program' in *Proceedings of the Section on Survey Research Methods: American Statistical Association Conference*.

Huebler, O. (1989) 'Individual overtime functions with double correction for selectivity bias', *Economics Letters* 9, 87–90.

Huebler, O. and Gerlach, K. (1990) 'Sectoral wage patterns, individual earnings and the efficiency wage hypothesis' in K. Heinz (ed.) *Economics of Wage Determination: Studies in Contemporary Economics*, pp. 105–24. New York: Springer-Verlag.

Huff Stevens, A. (1994) 'Persistence in poverty and welfare: the dynamics of poverty spells: updating Bane and Ellwood', *American Economic Review: Papers and Proceedings* 84, 34–7.

——(1995) *Climbing Out of Poverty, Falling Back in: Measuring the Persistence of Poverty over Multiple Spells*. Cambridge, MA: National Bureau of Economic Research. Working paper 5390.

Huggins, V. (1987) 'Evaluation of missing wave data from the survey of income and program participation (SIPP)' in *Proceedings of the Section on Survey Research Methods: Journal of the American Statistical Association*, pp. 205–9.

Huggins, V. and Fischer, D.P. (1994). 'The redesign of the survey of income and program participation' in *Proceedings of the Section on Survey Research Methods: Journal of the American Statistical Association*, pp. 668–73.

Hughes, G.A. and McCormick, B. (1981) 'Do council housing policies reduce migration between regions?', *Economic Journal* 91, 919–37.

——(1985) 'Migration intentions in the UK. Which households want to migrate and which succeed?', *Economic Journal* 95 (supplement), 113–23.

Hujer, R. and Schneider, H. (1989) 'The analysis of labour market mobility using panel data', *European Economic Review* 33, 530–6.

Humphreys, K. and Skinner, C.J. (1994) 'Review of PANMARK', *Applied Statistics* 43, 415–7.

Hutton, S. and Walker, R. (1988) *Quasi-cohort Analysis of the Changing Financial Circumstances of Young People.* ESRC Research Proposal. York: Social Policy Research Unit.

Jabine, T.B. (1990) *SIPP Quality Profile.* Washington, DC: US Bureau of the Census.

Jabine, T.B., Straf, M.L., Tanur, J.M. and Tourangean, R. (eds) (1984) *Cognitive Aspects of Survey Methodology.* Washington, DC: National Academy Press.

Jabine, T.B., King, K.E. and Petroni, R.J. (1990) *Survey of Income and Program Participation: Quality Profile.* Washington, DC: US Bureau of the Census.

Jakubson, G. H. (1988) 'The sensitivity of labor supply parameter estimates to unobserved individual effects: fixed and random effects estimates in a nonlinear model using panel data', *Journal of Labor Economics* 6, 3, 302–29.

Janson, C.-G. (1990) 'Retrospective data, undesirable behaviour and the longitudinal perspective' in D. Magnusson and L. Bergman (eds) *Data Quality in Longitudinal Research*, pp. 100–21. Cambridge: Cambridge University Press.

Jarvis, S. and Jenkins, S.P. (1995) *Do the Poor Stay Poor? New Evidence About Income Dynamics from the British Household Panel Survey.* Colchester: ESRC Research Centre on Micro-social Change, University of Essex. Occasional paper 95-2.

——(1996) *Changing Places: Income Mobility and Poverty Dynamics in Britain.* Colchester: ESRC Research Centre on Micro-social Change, University of Essex. Working paper 96-19.

——(1999) 'Marital splits and income changes: evidence from one British household panel survey', *Population Studier* 53, 2, 237–54.

Jean, A.C. and McArthur, E.K. (1987) 'Tracking persons over time' in *SIPP Working Paper Series*, No. 8701. Washington, DC: US Bureau of the Census.

Jenkins, S.P. (1995) 'Easy estimation methods for discrete-time duration models', *Oxford Bulletin of Economics and Statistics* 57, 129–38.

Johnson, J.H., Salt, J. and Wood P. (1974) *Housing and the Migration of Labour in England and Wales.* Farnborough: Saxon House.

Jöreskog, K.G. and Sörbom, D. (1979) *Advances in Factor Analysis and Structural Equation Models.* Cambridge, MA: Abt Associates.

Joshi, H. (ed.) (1989) *The Changing Population of Britain.* Oxford: Blackwell.

Journal of Official Statistics (1999) *Special Issue on Survey Non-response* 15, 2.

Journal of Social Policy (1987) *Special Issue on Poverty* 16.

Kalbfleisch, J.D. and Prentice, R.L. (1980) *The Statistical Analysis of Failure Time Data.* New York: John Wiley.

Kalton, G. (1983) *Compensating for Missing Survey Data.* Ann Arbor: Institute for Social Research, University of Michigan.

——(1986) 'Handling wave nonresponse in panel surveys', *Journal of Official Statistics* 2, 303–14.

——(1989) 'Modeling considerations: discussion from a survey sampling perspective' in D. Kasprzyk, G.J. Duncan, G. Kalton and M.P. Singh (eds) *Panel Surveys*. New York: Wiley.

Kalton, G. and Brick, J.M. (1995) 'Weighting schemes for household panel surveys', *Survey Methodology* 21, 33–44.

Kalton, G. and Kasprzyk, D. (1986) 'The treatment of missing survey data', *Survey Methodology* 12, 1–16.

Kalton, G. and Lepkowski, J.M. (1985) 'Following rules in SIPP', *Journal of Economic and Social Measurement* 13, 319–29.

Kalton, G. and Miller, M.E. (1991) 'The seam effect with social security income in the survey of income and program participation', *Journal of Official Statistics* 7, 235–45.

Kalton, G., Lepkowski, J.M. and Lin, T. (1985) 'Compensating for wave nonresponse in the 1979 ISDP research panel' in *Proceedings of the Section on Survey Research Methods: Journal of the American Statistical Association* 372–7.

Kalton, G., McMillen, D. and Kasprzyk, D. (1986) 'Nonsampling error issues in the Survey of Income and Program Participation' in *SIPP Working Paper Series*, No. 8602. Washington, DC: US Bureau of the Census.

Kalton, G., Kasprzyk, D. and McMillen, D.B. (1989) 'Nonsampling errors in panel surveys' in D. Kasprzyk, G.J. Duncan, G. Kalton and M.P. Singh (eds) *Panel Surveys*, pp. 249–70. New York: John Wiley.

Kapteyn, A. and Melenberg, B. (1990) *Technische Bijlage bij Inkomens en Bestedingen van Ouderen*. Tilburg: Economic Institute, Tilburg University.

Kapteyn, A., Kooreman, P. and Willemse, R. (1988) 'Some methodological issues in the implementation of subjective poverty definitions', *Journal of Human Resources* 23, 222–42.

Kasprzyk, D. (1988) *The Survey of Income and Program Participation: an Overview and Discussion of Research Issues*. Washington, DC: US Bureau of the Census. Working paper 8830.

Kasprzyk, D., Duncan, G.J. Kalton, G. and Singh, M.P. (eds) (1989) *Panel Surveys*. New York: John Wiley.

Kass, G.V. (1980) 'An exploratory technique for investigating large quantities of categorical data', *Applied Statistics* 29, 119–27.

Kelly, M. (1999) 'What users want from a tool for analysing and documenting electronic questionnaires: the user requirements for the TADEQ project' in R. Banks, C. Christie, J. Currall, J. Francis, P. Harris, B. Lee, J. Martin, C. Payne and A. Westlake (eds) *Leading Survey and Statistical Computing into the New Millennium: Proceedings of the Third ASC International Conference*, pp. 419–432. Chesham: Association for Survey Computing.

Kemp, G.C.R. (1991) *The Use of Panel Data in Econometric Analysis: a Survey*. Colchester: ESRC Research Centre on Micro-social Change, University of Essex. Working paper 4.

Kerr, C.C., Dunlop, J.T., Harbison, F.H. and Myers, C.A. (1960) *Industrialism and Industrial Man*. Cambridge, MA: Harvard University Press.

Kessler, R.C. and Greenberg, D.F. (1981) *Linear Panel Analysis: Models of Quantitative Change*. New York: Academic Press.

Keyfitz, N. (1951) 'Sampling with probabilities proportional to size: adjustment for changes in the probabilities', *Journal of the American Statistical Association* 46, 183–201.

Kiernan, K.E. (1992) 'The impact of family disruption in childhood on transitions made in young adult life', *Population Studies* 46, 2, 213–34.

Kiernan, K.E. and Wicks, M. (1990) *Family Change and Future Policy*. London: Family Policy Studies Centre and Joseph Rowntree Memorial Trust.

Kish, L. (1965) *Survey Sampling*. New York: John Wiley.

——(1992). 'Weighting for unequal P_i', *Journal of Official Statistics* 8, 183–200.

Kish, L. and Scott, A. (1971) 'Retaining units after changing strata and probabilities', *Journal of the American Statistical Association* 66, 461–70.

Kshiti, M.S. (1961) *Hinduism*. Harmondsworth: Penguin.

Kuha, J. and Skinner, C.J. (1997) 'Categorical data analysis and mis-classification' in L. Lyberg, P. Biemer, M. Collins, E. de Leeuw, C. Dippo, N. Schwarz and D. Trewin (eds) *Survey Measurement and Process Quality*, pp. 633–70. New York: John Wiley.

Labouvie, E. and Nesselroade, J. (1985) 'Age, period and cohort analysis and the study of individual development and social change' in J. Nesselroade and A. Von Eye (eds) *Individual Development and Social Change: Explanatory Analysis*, pp. 189–212. Orlando, FL: Academic Press.

Lancaster, A. (1979) 'Econometric methods for the duration of unemployment', *Econometrica* 47, 939–56.

Langeheine, R. (1988) 'Manifest and latent Markov chain models for categorical panel data', *Journal of Education Statistics* 13, 299–312.

Laurie, H., Smith, R. and Scott, L. (1999) 'Strategies for reducing non-response in a longitudinal panel survey', *Journal of Official Statistics* 15, 2, 269–82.

Lavallée, P. (1995) 'Cross-sectional weighting of longitudinal surveys of individuals and households using the weight share method', *Survey Methodology* 21, 25–32.

Lavallée, P. and Hunter, L. (1993) 'Weighting for the survey of labour and income dynamics' in *Proceedings: Symposium 92, Design and analysis of longitudinal surveys*, pp. 65–75. Ottawa: Statistics Canada.

Lazarsfeld, P.F. (1948) 'The use of panels in social research', *Proceedings of the American Philosophical Society* 42, 405–10.

Lazarsfeld, P.F. and Fiske, M. (1938) 'The panel as a new tool for measuring public opinion', *Public Opinion Quarterly* 2, 596–612.

Lemaitre, G. (1988) 'A look at response errors in the labour force survey', *Canadian Journal of Statistics* 16, 127–41.

Lepkowski, J.M. (1989) 'Treatment of wave nonresponse in panel surveys' in D. Kasprzyk, G.J. Duncan, G. Kalton and M.P. Singh (eds) *Panel Surveys*, pp. 348–74. New York: John Wiley.

Lepkowski, J.M., Kalton, G. and Kasprzyk, D. (1989) 'Weighting adjustments for partial nonresponse in the 1984 SIPP Panel' in *Proceedings of the Section on Survey Research Methods: Journal of the American Statistical Association*, pp. 296–301.

Lepkowski, J.M., Miller, D.P., Kalton, G. and Singh, R. (1993) 'Imputation for wave nonresponse in the SIPP' in *Proceedings: Symposium 92, Design and Analysis of Longitudinal Surveys*, pp. 99–109. Ottawa: Statistics Canada.

Lessler, J.T. and Kalsbeek, W. (1992) *Nonsampling Errors in Surveys*. New York: John Wiley.

Lievesley, D. and Waterton, J. (1985) 'Measuring individual attitude changes' in R. Jowell and S. Witherspoon (eds) *British Social Attitudes: The 1985 Report*. Aldershot: Gower.

Lillard, L.A. (1989) 'Sample dynamics: some behavioral issues' in D. Kasprzyk, G.J. Duncan, G. Kalton and M.P. Singh (eds) *Panel Surveys*, pp. 497–511. New York: John Wiley.

Lillard, L.A. and Waite, L.J. (1993) 'A joint model of marital childbearing and marital disruption', *Demography* 30, 653–82.

Lillard, L.A. and Willis, R. (1978) 'Dynamic aspects of earnings mobility', *Econometrica* 46, 985–1012.

Lillard, L.A., Brien, M.A. and Waite, L.J. (1995) 'Premarital cohabitation and subsequent marital dissolution', *Demography* 32, 437–58.

Little, R.J.A. (1986) 'Survey nonresponse adjustments for estimates of means', *International Statistical Review* 54, 139–57.

——(1988) 'Missing data adjustments in large surveys', *Journal of Business and Economic Statistics* 6, 287–96.

Little, R.J.A. and Su, H.-L. (1989) 'Item nonresponse in panel surveys' in D. Kasprzyk, G.J. Duncan, G. Kalton and M.P. Singh (eds) *Panel Surveys*. New York: Wiley.

Loftus, E.F., Smith, K.D., Klinger, M.R. and Fiedler, J. (1992) 'Memory and mismemory for health events' in J. Tanur (ed.) *Questions about Questions: Inquiries into the Cognitive Bases of Surveys*, pp. 102–36. New York: Russell Sage.

Lyberg, L., Biemer, P., Collins, M., de Leeuw, E., Dippo, C., Schwarz, N. and Trewin, D. (eds) (1997) *Survey Measurement and Process Quality*. New York: John Wiley.

McAllister, R.J., Goe, S. and Butler, E.W. (1973) 'Tracking respondents in longitudinal surveys: some preliminary considerations', *Public Opinion Quarterly* 37, 413–16.

McFadden, D. (1984) 'Econometric analysis of qualitative response models' in Z. Griliches and M.D. Intriligator (eds) *Handbook of Econometrics*, vol. II, pp. 1395–457.

McLaughlin, E., Millar, J. and Cooke, K. (1989) *Work and Welfare Benefits*. Aldershot: Gower.

McMillen, D.B. and Herriot, R. (1985) 'Towards a longitudinal definition of households', *Journal of Economic and Social Measurement* 13, 349–60.

MaCurdy, T. (1981) 'An empirical model of labor supply in a life cycle setting', *Journal of Political Economy* 89, 1059–85.

Maddala, G.S. (1983) *Limited Dependent and Qualitative Variables in Econometrics*. Cambridge: Cambridge University Press. Econometric Society Monograph 3.

Magnusson, D. and Bergman, L.R. (eds) (1990) *Data Quality in Longitudinal Research*. New York: Cambridge University Press.

Manners, T and Deacon, K. (1997) 'An Integrated Household Survey in the UK' in *Actes de la 4e Conférence Internationale des Utilisateurs de Blaise*. Paris: INSEE. URL: http: //www.blaiseusers.org/bucpdfs/manners.pdf.

Mare, R.D. (1994) 'The uses of the panel study of income dynamics for the study of intergenerational mobility'. Paper prepared for PSID Board of Overseers Meeting. Ann Arbor: Institute for Survey Research, University of Michigan.

Markus, G.B. (1979) *Analysing Panel Data*. Beverly Hills, CA: Sage.

Marshall, G., Rose, D., Newby, H. and Vogler, C. (1989). *Social Class in Modern Britain*. London: Unwin Hyman.

Martin, J. (1996) *Quality in Social Research*. Plenary lecture given at the Fourth International Sociological Association Social Science Methods Conference, University of Essex, Colchester. London: ONS Social Survey Division

Mathiowetz, N.A. (1985) 'The problem of omissions and telescoping error: new evidence from a study of unemployment' in *Proceedings of the Section on Survey Research Methods: Journal of the American Statistical Association*, pp. 482–7.

Mathiowetz, N.A. and Duncan, G.J. (1988) 'Out of work, out of mind: response errors in retrospective reports of unemployment', *Journal of Business and Economic Statistics* 6, 221–9.

Mayer, K.-U. and Huinink, J. (1990) 'Age, period and cohort in the study of life course: a comparison of classical A-P-C analysis with event history analysis or Farewell to Lexis?' in D. Magnusson and L. Bergman (eds) *Data Quality in Longitudinal Research*, pp. 211–32. Cambridge: Cambridge University Press.

Mayer, K.-U. and Tuma, N. (eds) (1987) *Applications of Event History Analysis in Life Course Research*. Berlin: Max Planck Institut fur Bildungsforschung.

Means, B. and Loftus, E.F. (1991) 'When personal history repeats itself: decomposing memories for recurring events', *Applied Cognitive Psychology* 5, 4, 297–318.

Means, B., Swan, G.E., Jobe, J.B. and Esposito, J.L. (1991) 'An alternative approach to obtaining personal history data' in P. Biemer, R.M. Groves, L. Lyberg, N. Mathiowetz and S. Sudman (eds) *Measurement Error in Surveys*, pp. 167–84. New York: John Wiley.

Mednick, S.A., Harwary, M. and Finello, K.M. (1984) *Handbook of Longitudinal Research*. New York: Praeger.

Merkle, L. and Zimmermann, K. (1992) 'Savings, remittances and return migrations', *Economic Letters* 38, 77–81.

Michaud, S. and Hunter, L. (1993) 'Strategy for minimising the impact of nonresponse for the survey of labour and income dynamics' in *Proceedings:*

Symposium 92, Design and analysis of longitudinal surveys, pp. 89–98. Ottawa: Statistics Canada.

Mills, C.W. (1959) *The Sociological Imagination*. Oxford: Oxford University Press.

Mincer, J. and Ofek, H. (1982) 'Interrupted work careers', *Journal of Human Resources* 17, 3–24.

Mitchell, D. and Cooke, K. (1988) 'The costs of childrearing' in R. Walker and G. Parker (eds) *Money Matters*, pp. 27–45. Sage: London.

Mooney, H.W. (1962) *Methodology in Two Californian Health Surveys*. Washington, DC: US Department of Health, Education and Welfare. Public Health Monograph 70.

Morgenstern, R.D. and Barrett, N.S. (1974) 'The retrospective bias in unemployment reporting by sex, race and age', *Journal of the American Statistical Association* 69, 355–7.

Moss, L. and Goldstein, H. (1979) *The Recall Method in Social Surveys*. London: University of London, Institute of Education.

Mroz, T.A. (1987) 'The sensitivity of an empirical model of married women's hours of work to economic and statistical assumptions', *Econometrica* 4, 765–99.

Mueller, K., Wagner, G., Hauser, R. and Frick, J. (1992) *Income transition in East Germany – Measurement by Means of Objective and Subjective Indicators*. Colchester: University of Essex. Working paper 30 of the European Science Foundation Scientific Network of Household Panel Studies.

Muffels, R. (1993) 'Welfare economic effects of social security: essays on poverty, social security and labour market: evidence from panel data' in *Reeks Sociale Zekerheidswetenschap Rapporten*, vol. 21, p. 245. Tilburg: Tilburg University

Muffels, R., Kapteyn, A., de Vries, A. and Berghman, J. (1990) *Poverty in The Netherlands: Report on the Dutch Contribution to an International Comparative Study on Poverty and the Financial Efficacy of the Social Security System*. The Hague: VUGA.

Muffels, R., Berghman, J. and Dirven, H. (1992) 'A multimethod approach to monitor the evolution of poverty', *Journal of European Social Policy* 2, 3, 193–213.

Murphy, M. (1985) 'Demographic and socio-economic influences on recent British marital breakdown patterns', *Population Studies* 39, 441–60.

——(1990) 'Minimising attrition in longitudinal studies: means or ends?' in D. Magnusson and L. Bergman (eds) *Data Quality in Longitudinal Research*. Cambridge: Cambridge University Press.

Murray, T.S., Michaud, S., Egan, M. and Lemaitre, G. (1991) 'Invisible seams? the experience with the Canadian labour market activity survey' in *Proceedings of the 1991 Bureau of the Census Annual Research Conference*, pp. 715–30. Washington, DC: US Department of Commerce.

NCBS (1991) *The Socio-economic Panel Survey, Content, Design and Organisation*. Voorburg Heerlen: Netherlands Central Bureau of Statistics (NCBS), Income and Consumption Branch.

Nelson, D., McMillen, D and Kasprzyk, D. (1985) *An Overview of the SIPP, Update 1*. Washington, DC: US Bureau of the Census. Working paper 8401.

Nesselroade, J. and Baltes, P. (eds) (1979) *Longitudinal Research in the Study of Behavior and Development*. New York: Academic Press.

Nesselroade, J. and Von Eye, A. (eds) (1985) *Individual Development and Social Change: Explanatory Analysis*. Orlando, FL: Academic Press.

Neter, J. and Waksberg, J. (1964) 'A study of response errors in expenditure data from household interviews', *Journal of the American Statistical Association* 59, 18–55.

Nicholson, J.L. (1979) 'The assessment of poverty and the information we need' in *Social Security Research: the Definition and Measurement of Poverty*. London: HMSO.

Oh, H.L. and Scheuren, F. (1983) 'Weighting adjustments for unit nonresponse' in W.G. Madow, I. Olkin and D. Rubin (eds) *Incomplete Data in Sample Surveys*. Vol. 2. *Theory and Bibliographies*, pp. 143–84. New York: Academic Press.

O'Higgins, M. and Jenkins, S.P. (1989) *Poverty in Europe: Estimates for the Numbers in Poverty in 1975, 1980, 1985*. European Programme to Combat Poverty, Animation and Dissemination Service, Evaluation Unit. Bath: Centre for Analysis of Social Policy, University of Bath.

O'Higgins, M., Bradshaw, J. and Walker, R. (1988) 'Income distribution over the life cycle' in R. Walker and G. Parker (eds) *Money Matters*, pp. 227–53. London: Sage.

Ornstein, M. (1998) 'Survey sampling', *Current Sociology* 46, 4, 75–87.

O'Muircheartaigh, C. (1989) 'Sources of nonsampling error: discussion' in D. Kasprzyk, G.J. Duncan, G. Kalton and M.P. Singh (eds) *Panel Surveys*. New York: Wiley.

Pahl, R.E. (1984) *Divisions of Labour*. Oxford: Blackwell.

Panel on Incomplete Data (1983) *Incomplete Data in Sample Surveys* (3 vols). New York: Academic Press.

Pennell, S.G. and Lepkowski, J.M. (1992) 'Panel conditioning effects in the survey of income and program participation' in *Proceedings of the Section on Survey Research Methods: Journal of the American Statistical Association*, pp. 566–71.

Peters, E.H. (1988) 'Retrospective versus panel data in analysing life cycle events', *Journal of Human Resources* 23, 488–513.

Petersen, T. (1993) 'Recent advances in longitudinal methodology', *Annual Review of Sociology* 19, 425–54.

——(1995) 'Analysis of event histories' in G. Arminger, C.C. Clogg and M.E. Sobel (eds) *Handbook of Statistical Modeling for the Social and Behavioral Sciences*, pp. 453–517. New York: Plenum Press.

Platek, R. and Gray, G. (1983) 'Imputation methodology' in Panel on Incomplete Data (eds) *Incomplete Data in Sample Surveys*. Vol. 2. *Theory and Bibliographies*. New York: Academic Press.

Plewis, I. (1985) *Analysing Change: Measurement and Explanation using Longitudinal Data*. Chichester: John Wiley.

Poterba, J.M. and Summers, J.H. (1984) 'Response variation in the CPS: caveats for the unemployment analyst', *Monthly Labour Review* 107, 3, 37–43.

——(1986) 'Reporting errors and labour market dynamics', *Econometrica* 54, 1319–38.

Purdon, S., Campanelli, P. and Sturgis, P. (1999) 'Interviewers' calling strategies on face-to-face interview surveys', *Journal of Official Statistics* 15, 2, 199–216.

Rao, P. (1983) 'Callbacks, follow-ups, and repeated telephone calls' in Panel on Incomplete Data (eds) *Incomplete Data in Sample Surveys*. Vol. 2. *Theory and Bibliographies*. New York: Academic Press.

Rawls, J.A. (1973) *A Theory of Justice*. Oxford: Oxford University Press.

Redmond, G. (1997) *Imputing Council Tax Bands for Households in the British Household Panel Study*. Colchester: ESRC Research Centre on Micro-social Change, University of Essex. Working paper 97-10.

Rendtell, U. (1990) 'Teilnahmebereitschaft in panelstudien: zwischen beeinflussung, vertrauen und sozialer selektion', *Kolner Sozialpsychologie* 42, 280–99.

Richards, T., White, M.J. and Tsui, A.O. (1987) 'Changing living arrangements: a hazard model of transitions among household types', *Demography* 24, 77–97

Rizzo, L., Kalton, G. and Brick, J.M. (1996) 'A comparison of some weighting adjustment methods for panel nonresponse', *Survey Methodology* 22, 43–53.

Robbin, A. and Frost-Kumpf, L. (1992) *Learning About, Diagnosing, And Communicating Error in Longitudinal Panel Surveys*. Colchester: University of Essex. Working paper 44 of the European Science Foundation Scientific Network on Household Panel Studies.

Rockwell, R.C. (1993) 'Codebooks in the world of networked data library services', *IASSIST Quarterly* 17, 1, and 2, 8–12.

Rodgers, W.L. (1989). 'Comparisons of alternative approaches to the estimation of simple causal models from panel data' in D. Kasprzyk, G.J. Duncan, G. Kalton and M.P. Singh (eds) *Panel Surveys*, pp. 432–56. New York: John Wiley.

Rodgers, W.L. and Herzog, A.R. (1989) 'Covariances of measurement errors in survey responses', *Journal of Official Statistics* 3, 4, 403–418.

Rose, D. (ed.) (1988) *Social Stratification and Economic Change*. London: Hutchinson.

Rose, D. and Sullivan, O. (1996) *Introducing Data Analysis for Social Scientists*. Milton Keynes: Open University Press.

Rose, D., Vogler, C., Marshall, G. and Newby, H. (1984) 'Economic restructuring: the British experience', *Annals of the American Academy of Political and Social Science* 475, 137–57.

Rose, D., Buck, N. and Corti, L. (1991) 'Design issues in the British household panel study', *Bulletin de Methodologie Sociologique* 32, 14–43.

Rose, D., Buck, N. and Johnston, R. (1994) 'The British household panel study: a valuable new resource for geographical research', *Area* 26, 4, 368–76.

Rosenzweig, M.R. and Wolpin, K.I. (1993) 'Intergenerational support and the life cycle incomes of young men and their parents: human capital investments, coresidence and intergenerational transfers', *Journal of Labor Economics* 11, 84–112.

——(1994) 'Parental and public transfers to young women and their children', *American Economic Review* 84, 1195–212.

Rowntree, B.S. (1901) *Poverty: a Study of Town Life*. London: Macmillan.

Rubin, D. (1983) 'Conceptual issues in the presence of nonresponse' in Panel on Incomplete Data (eds) *Incomplete Data in Sample Surveys. Vol. 2. Theory and Bibliographies*. New York: Academic Press.

Ruggles, P. (1990) *Drawing the Line*. Washington, DC: Urban Institute Press.

Ruggles, P. and Williams, R. (1989) 'Longitudinal measures of poverty: accounting for income and assets over time', *Review of Income and Wealth* 3, 225–43.

Sande, I.G. (1982) 'Imputation in surveys: coping with reality', *American Statistician* 36, 145–52.

Savage, M.J., Barlow, J., Dickens, P. and Fielding, A. (1992) *Property, Bureaucracy and Culture: Middle Class Formation in Contemporary Britain*. London: Routledge.

Sawhill, I.V. (1988) 'Poverty in the US: why is it so persistent?', *Journal of Economic Literature* 26, 1073–119.

Schaber, G. (1990) 'Panel studies of households' in *ESF Communications No. 23: Supplement on ESF Scientific Networks* 42–3. Strasbourg: European Science Foundation.

Schaber, G., Schmauss, G. and Wagner, G. (1992) *The PACO Project*. Colchester: University of Essex. Working paper 29 of the European Science Foundation Scientific Network of Household Panel Studies.

Scheuren, F. (1989) 'Nonresponse adjustments: discussion' in D. Kasprzyk, G.J. Duncan, G. Kalton and M.P. Singh (eds) *Panel Surveys*. New York: Wiley.

Schulsinger, F., Mednick, S.A. and Knop, J. (eds) (1981) *Longitudinal Research*. Boston: Martinus Nijhoff.

Scott, J. (1995) 'Using household panels to study micro-social change', *Innovation: The European Journal of Social Sciences* 8, 61–74.

Sen, K. (1961) *Hinduism*. London: Penguin.

Shaw, A., Walker, R, Ashworth, K., Jenkins, S.P. and Middleton, S. (1996) *Moving Off Income Support: Barriers and Bridges*. London: Department of Social Security. Research Report 53.

Short, K.S. and Woodrow, K.A. (1985) 'An exploration of the applicability of hazard models in analysing the survey of income and programme participation: labour force transitions' in *Proceedings of the Section on Social Statistics: Journal of the American Statistical Association*, pp. 345–50.

Sieber, J.E (ed.) (1991) *Sharing Social Science Data: Advantages and Challenges*. London: Sage.

Silberstein, A.R. and Jacobs, C.A. (1989) 'Symptoms of repeated interview effects in the consumer expenditure interview survey' in D. Kasprzyk, G.J. Duncan, G. Kalton and M.P. Singh (eds) *Panel Surveys*, pp. 289–303. New York: John Wiley.

Singh, A.C. and Rao, J.N.K. (1995) 'On the adjustment of gross flow estimates for classification error with application to data from the Canadian labour force survey', *Journal of the American Statistical Association* 90, 478–88.

Singh, M.P. (1993) 'Methodological experiments in the survey of income and program participation' in *Proceedings: Symposium 92, Design and analysis of longitudinal surveys*, pp. 157–66. Ottawa: Statistics Canada.

Singh, M.P., Huggins, V. and Kasprzyk, D. (1990) *Handling Single Wave Nonresponse in Panel Surveys*. Washington, DC: US Bureau of the Census. Working paper 9009.

Skinner, C.J. (1993) 'Logistic modelling of longitudinal survey data with measurement error' in *Proceedings: Symposium 92, Design and analysis of longitudinal surveys*, pp. 269–76. Ottawa: Statistics Canada.

Skinner, C.J. and Humphreys, K. (1999) 'Weibull regression for lifetimes measured with error', *Lifetime Data Analysis* 5, 23–37.

Skinner, C.J. and Torelli, N. (1993) 'Measurement error and the estimation of gross flows from longitudinal economic data', *Statistica* 53, 391–405.

Smeeding, T. and Burkhauser, R. (1999) 'Panel data and public policy: national and cross national perspectives'. Paper given at the Institute for Social and Economic Research Tenth Anniversary Conference, University of Essex, Colchester, 26–28 May. Syracuse, NY: Syracuse University.

Smeeding, T. and Rainwater, L. (1992) *Cross-national Trends in Income Poverty and Dependency: the Evidence for Young Adults in the Eighties*. Syracuse, NY: Syracuse University.

Smith, D.J. (ed.) (1992) *Understanding the Underclass*. London: Policy Studies Institute.

Snijkers, G., Hox, J. and de Leeuw, E. (1999) 'Interviewers' tactics for fighting survey nonresponse', *Journal of Official Statistics* 15, 2, 185–98.

Social Science Research Council (UK) (1975) *Longitudinal Studies: Report of a Social Science Research Council Working Party*. London: Social Science Research Council.

Solesbury, W. (1991) *Dissemination and Accountability*. Lecture to Directors of Research Centres in the Social Sciences (DORCISS), Edinburgh, UK. Swindon: ESRC

Solon, G. (1989) 'The value of panel data in economic research' in D. Kasprzyk, G.J. Duncan, G. Kalton and M.P. Singh (eds) *Panel Surveys*, pp. 486–96. New York: John Wiley.

——(1992) 'Intergenerational income mobility in the United States', *The American Economic Review* 82, 393–408.

Solon, G., Corcoran, M., Gordon, R. and Laren, D. (1991) 'A longitudinal analysis of sibling correlations in economic status', *The Journal of Human Resources* 26, 509–34.

Sonquist, J.A., Baker, E.L. and Morgan, J.N. (1973) *Searching for Structure*. Ann Arbor: Institute for Social Research, University of Michigan.

Statistical Office of the European Communities (1993) *Proceedings of the Conference on Statistical Meta Information Systems*. Luxembourg: Statistical Office of the European Communities.

Subcommittee on Federal Longitudinal Surveys (1986) *Federal Longitudinal Surveys*. Washington, DC: Office of Management and Budget. Statistical Policy Working paper 13.

Sudman, S and Bradburn, N.M. (1974) *Response Effects in Surveys*. Chicago: Aldine.

——(1983) *Asking Questions*. San Francisco: Jossey-Bass.

Sudman, S. and Ferber, R. (1979) *Consumer Panels*. Chicago: American Marketing Association.

Sundgren B. (1993) 'Modelling meta-information systems' in *Proceedings of the Conference on Statistical Meta Information Systems*. Luxembourg: Statistical Office of the European Communities.

Sundgren B., Gillman, D. Appel, W.V. and LaPlant, W.P. (1996) 'Towards a unified data and metadata system at the Census bureau' in *Proceedings of the 1996 Bureau of the Census Annual Research Conference*. Washington, DC: US Department of Commerce. URL: http: //www.census.gov/prod/2/gen/96arc/arc96.html/viiigil.pdf.

Sunter, A.B. (1986) 'Implicit longitudinal files: a useful technique', *Journal of Official Statistics* 2, 161–8.

Survey Research Center (1993) *The Panel Study of Income Dynamics Relationship File*. Ann Arbor: Institute for Social Research, University of Michigan.

Tanenbaum, E. (1982) 'The design of a current awareness facility for British social and economic statistics', *International Social Science Journal* 34, 723–36.

Tanenbaum, E. and Taylor, A. (1991) 'Developing social science data archives', *International Social Science Journal*, February.

Taylor, A. (1994) 'Sample characteristics, attrition and weighting' in N. Buck, J. Gershuny, D. Rose, J. Scott (eds) *Changing Households: the British Household Panel Survey 1990–1992*, pp. 291–311. Colchester: ESRC Research Centre on Micro-social Change, University of Essex.

Taylor, M.F., Prentice, E.C.A. and Brice, J. (1992) *British Household Panel Study Wave One: Outline of the BHPS Documentation System*. Colchester: ESRC Research Centre on Micro-social Change, University of Essex. Technical paper 5.

Taylor, M., Keen, M., Buck, N. and Corti, L. (1994) 'Income, welfare and consumption' in N. Buck, J. Gershuny, D. Rose and J. Scott (eds) *Changing Households: the British Household Panel Survey 1990–92*. Colchester: ESRC Research Centre on Micro-social Change, University of Essex.

Taylor, M.F., Brice, J., Buck, N. and Prentice, E.C.A. (eds) (1999) *British Household Panel Study User Manual* (2 vols). Colchester: University of Essex.

Thomas, R. (1980) 'Non-response on household surveys', *Survey Methodology Bulletin* 10, 3–17.

Thornton, A., Freedman, A. and Camburn, D. (1979) 'Maintaining response rates in longitudinal studies', *Sociological Methods and Research*, 9, 87–8.

——(1982) 'Obtaining respondent co-operation in family panel studies', *Sociological Methods and Research* 11, 35–51.

Traugott, M.W. and Katosh, J.P. (1979) 'Response validity in surveys of voting behavior', *Public Opinion Quarterly* 43, 3, 359–77.

Tremblay, A. (1994) 'Longitudinal imputation of SIPP food stamp benefits' in *Proceedings of the Section on Survey Research Methods: Journal of the American Statistical Association*, pp. 809–14.

Trivellato, U. and Torelli, N. (1989) 'Longitudinal analysis of unemployment duration from a household survey with rotating sample: a case study with Italian labour force data' in *Proceedings of the 1989 Bureau of the Census Annual Research Conference*, pp. 408–27. Washington, DC: US Department of Commerce.

Tuma, N.B. and Hannan, M.T. (1984) *Social Dynamics: Models and Methods*. Orlando, FL: Academic Press.

Uncles, M.D. (ed.) (1988). *Longitudinal Data Analysis: Methods and Applications*. London: Pion Limited.

United Nations Economic Commission for Europe (UNECE) Statistical Division (1999) *Conference of European Statisticians, UNECE Work Session on Statistical Metadata*, Geneva, Switzerland 22–24 September 1999. Geneva: UNECE.

US Bureau of the Census (1978) *The Current Population Survey: Design and Methodology*. Washington, DC: US Bureau of the Census. Technical paper 40.

——(1989) 'Money income and poverty status in the United States: 1988', *Current Population Reports*, Series P-60, 166.

——(1999) *SIPP Quality Profile 1998*, 3rd edition. Washington, DC: US Bureau of the Census. SIPP Working Paper Number 230.

US Bureau of Labor Statistics and US Census Bureau (2000) *Current Population Survey. Design Methodology*. Washington, DC: US Bureau of Labor Statistics. Technical Paper 63.

van der Pol, F.J.R. (1988) *Design Issues in Panel Studies*. Amsterdam: Sociometric Research Foundation.

——(1989) *Issues of Design and Analysis of Panels*. Amsterdam: Sociometric Research Foundation.

——(1993) 'Weighting panel survey data'. Paper presented at the Symposium on Analysis of Longitudinal Data, Tampere, Finland.

van der Pol, F.J.R. and Langeheine, R. (1989) 'Mixed Markov models, mover–stayer models and the EM algorithm with an application to labour market data from the Netherlands Socio-economic Panel' in R. Coppi and S. Bolasco (eds) *Multiway Data Analysis*, pp. 485–95. Amsterdam: North Holland.

——(1997) 'Separating change and error in panel data with an application to labor market data' in L. Lyberg, P. Biemer, M. Collins, E. de Leeuw, C. Dippo, N. Schwarz and D. Trewin (eds) *Survey Measurement and Process Quality*. New York: John Wiley.

van der Pol, F.J.R., Langeheine, R. and de Jong, W. (1991) *PANMARK User Manual: Panel Analysis Using Markov Chains, version Q2*. Amsterdam: The Netherlands Central Bureau of Statistics.

Veroff, J., Hatchett, S. and Douvan, E. (1992) 'Consequences of participating in a longitudinal study of marriage', *Public Opinion Quarterly* 56, 315–27.

Wagner, G.G., Schupp, J. and Rendtell, J.U. (1991) *The Socioeconomic Panel (SOEP) for Germany, Methods of Production and Managements of Longitudinal Data*. Berlin: Deutschen Institut fuer Wirtschaftsforschung. Discussion paper 31A.

Walker, R. and Huby, M. (1989) 'Social security spending in the United Kingdom: bridging the north–south divide', *Environment and Planning C: Government and Policy* 7, 321–40.

Walker, R. and Lawton, D. (1988) 'Social assistance and territorial justice: the example of single payments', *Journal of Social Policy* 17, 4, 437–76.

Walker, R., Ashworth, K. and Vincent, J. (1991) *Social Security Objectives: Taking Account of Time*. Loughborough: Loughborough University of Technology, Centre for Research in Social Policy. Working paper 136.

Wall, W.D. and Williams, H. (1970) *Longitudinal Studies and the Social Sciences*. London: Heinemann Educational Books.

Wansbeek, T.J. and Koning, R.H. (1991) 'Measurement error and panel data', *Statistica Neerlandica* 45, 85–92.

Waterton, J. and Lievesley, D. (1989) 'Evidence of conditioning effects in the British social attitudes panel survey' in D. Kasprzyk, G.J. Duncan, G. Kalton and M.P. Singh (eds) *Panel Surveys,* pp. 319–39. New York: John Wiley.

Webb, S. (1995) *Poverty Dynamics in Great Britain: Preliminary Analysis from the British Household Panel Survey*. London: Institute for Fiscal Studies. Commentary 48.

Weibel, S., Godby, J. and Miller, E. (1995) *OCLC/NCSA Metadata Workshop Report*. URL: http: //www.oclc.org: 5046/oclc/research/conferences/metadata/dublin_core_report.html.

Wells, J. (1989) 'Uneven development and de-industrialisation in the UK since 1979' in F. Green (ed.) *The Restructuring of the UK Economy*, pp. 25–64. London: Harvester Wheatsheaf.

Williams, R. (1973) *The Country and the City*. London: Chatto and Windus.

Willis, R.J. and Michael, R.T. (1994) 'Innovation in family formation: evidence on cohabitation in the US' in J. Ermisch and N. Ogawa (eds) *The Family, the Market, and the State in Ageing Societies*, pp. 9–45. Oxford: Oxford University Press.

Wilson, W.J. (1991) 'Studying inner-city social dislocations: the challenge of public agenda research', *American Sociological Review* 56, 1–14.

Winklemann, R. and Zimmermann, K.F. (1991) *Count Data Models for Demographic Data*. Munich: Wirtsschaftwissen-schaftliche Beitraege. Discussion paper 91/26.

Wu, Z. and Balakrishnan, T.R. (1995) 'Dissolution of premarital cohabitation in Canada', *Demography* 32, 521–32.

Yamaguchi, K. (1991) *Event History Analysis*. Newbury Park, CA: Sage.

Young, M. and Wilmott, P. (1975) *The Symmetrical Family*. London: Penguin.

Index

302   *Index*